C0-BEF-245

PLAY and AGGRESSION

DONALD SYMONS

PLAY and AGGRESSION

A STUDY OF RHESUS MONKEYS

Columbia University Press

New York

1978

Donald Symons is Assistant Professor of Anthropology,
University of California, Santa Barbara

Library of Congress Cataloging in Publication Data
Symons, Donald, 1942–
Play and aggression.
Bibliography: p.
Includes index.
1. Rhesus monkey—Behavior. 2. Play behavior in animals.
3. Aggressive behavior in animals. I. Title.
QL737.P93S92 156′.23 77-24638
ISBN 0-231-04334-1

Columbia University Press
New York Guildford, Surrey

Printed in the United States of America

To Marie and Lester Symons

Acknowledgments

This book exists because throughout its evolutionary history I received many kinds of assistance from many people. I thank Carlos Nagel for suggesting La Cueva as a study site and Ronald Myers for permission to work there. Victor Bracero, Israel Cordero, Jacinto Rosado, and Negro Flores were extremely helpful in dealing with the logistical problems of fieldwork, and I thank them for their assistance and their many kindnesses. I am grateful to Alice Davis for her communications during the fieldwork and for many years of help and encouragement. The fieldwork was in part supported by Public Health Service Grant 08623.

I am greatly indebted to my former students, Kevin Bagley, Leslie Herleickson, Kathy Johnson, Maggie La Pley, Rachel Morris, Julie Newendorp, Steve Nordeen, Patricia Sanderson, and Hank Speight, whose assistance in data analysis made this work possible.

Steve Craig, William Hudson, and Albert Spaulding advised about quantitative and statistical matters; they should not, of course, be held responsible for any remaining deficiencies.

I thank Elvin Hatch and Charlotte Symons for translating important papers in the play literature. Robert Gottsdanker introduced me to the literature on skill development and Priscilla Robertson convinced me that the Battle of Waterloo was not won in the playing fields of Eton. I am grateful to John Melville Bishop and Paul Heuston for their considerable skill in making prints from my often marginal negatives. Photos 3.5, 3.12, 3.14, 3.18, 3.19, 3.25, 3.26, 3.27 and 3.32 were made by John Melville Bishop, and Je Goolsby made the line drawings which appear in chapter 3. I owe more than words can (or, fortunately, need to) express to Charlotte Symons who edited all the drafts of this work and who, by insisting that I say what I mean, helped me to discover precisely what it was that I did mean.

I thank those scholars who read and commented on all or part of one or several drafts of this work: Owen Aldis, John Baldwin, George Barlow, Marc Bekoff, Paul Bohannan, D. E. Brown, Douglas K.

Candland, Phyllis Dolhinow, Charles Erasmus, Elvin Hatch, Phillip Walker and Sherwood Washburn. I would like especially to thank John Baldwin for a very close, thoughtful, and critical reading of the entire manuscript. The work profited from the advice of each of these people, but since in no case did I follow every suggestion, I alone am responsible for its deficiencies. I am grateful to Irwin Bernstein, Susan Duvall, and Donald Lindburg for allowing me to cite unpublished data or observations. I thank Elizabeth Brown, Nancy Fraser, Mary Shannon, and Jeanette Woodward for typing the manuscript.

Finally, I thank Sherwood Washburn for encouraging my interest in the behavior of nonhuman primates and for years of patience, support, and wisdom.

Contents

"Thirteen minutes and a half ago," [the Other Professor] went on, looking first at Bruno and then at his watch as he spoke, "you said 'this Cat's very kind to the Mouses.' It must be a singular animal!"

"So it *are,*" said Bruno, after carefully examining the Cat, to make sure how many there were of it.

"But how do you know it's kind to the Mouses—or, more correctly speaking, the *Mice?*"

" 'Cause it *plays* with the Mouses," said Bruno; "for to amuse them, oo know."

"But that is just what I *don't* know," the Other Professor rejoined. "My belief is, it plays with them to *kill* them!"

"Oh, that's quite a *accident!*"

Lewis Carroll, *Silvie and Bruno Concluded*

Chapter one

Introduction: The Concept of Function

What the adaptive or functional significance of behavior patterns is, and how evolutionary processes produce behavioral adaptations, are fundamental biological problems. The nature of such "ultimate" causes can be difficult to determine in the behavior of adult animals, and in the study of immature animals the difficulties are even more numerous and complex. This is especially true of the behavior patterns usually designated "play." What constitutes "play," what its adaptive significance is, and indeed whether it is a valid category of behavior at all, are sources of considerable controversy.

Some behavior patterns, such as eating, drinking, sleeping, and fleeing from predators (shared by mature and immature animals), as well as patterns such as suckling or clinging to the mother (confined to immature animals), have clear immediate benefit and obvious adaptive significance. Behavior patterns with clear immediate benefits are seldom referred to as "play." In a few animal species, mostly mammals, immature animals exhibit behavior patterns with no apparent immediate benefit or clear-cut adaptive significance. Some of these patterns of behavior, especially those which resemble but are not identical to patterns of fighting, fleeing, chasing, and predation, are referred to as "play" by almost all observers. Many observers also refer to patterns such as incomplete sexual behavior and infant caretaking as "play," whereas others maintain that these patterns can not be so classified.

But the matter is even more difficult. Some students of the ontogenetic development of behavior maintain that "play" is neither a valid category nor a useful descriptive device. For example, Lazar and

Beckhorn (1974) suggest that the behavior patterns of immature animals are precursors of adult behavior patterns, and that those patterns commonly labeled "play" are components of the developmental process which includes all the behavior patterns exhibited by immature animals. They maintain that the developmental process, rather than "play," an arbitrary component, is the proper unit of study. Ghiselin (1974), on the other hand, considers "play" to be a nonarbitrary category of behavior with no developmental adaptive significance at all. Ghiselin believes play serves immediate, nondevelopmental, functions because by playing, immature animals are protected from genuinely competitive interactions. A full consideration of these disparate views will be deferred until chapter 7.

A convenient strategy with which to approach questions about the structure and function of the behavior patterns of immature animals that do not provide obvious immediate benefits is to accept provisionally the category "play" for behavior patterns that: (1) are similar to agonistic patterns of fighting, chasing, and fleeing; (2) are inhibited compared with these agonistic behaviors; and (3) are not associated with stereotyped agonistic signals of threat and submission.[1] This "aggressive play" is the most commonly reported kind of social play among mammals (Aldis 1975) including nonhuman primates.[2]

Behavioral potentials evolve through natural selection, and play, a form of activity which is widespread among young mammals, can be expected to serve important adaptive functions, contributing in specific ways to reproductive success. If play were not functional, animals that played would be at a selective disadvantage compared to nonplaying animals that husbanded their resources, used their time more profit-

1. In chapter 7 the question "what is play?" is discussed in detail. I accept the category "predatory play" for the same reasons I accept "aggressive play," but predation is not emphasized here since rhesus monkeys are nonpredators, and this book deals primarily with aggressive play.

2. Play is described in *Lemur catta* as chasing, wrestling, and mock biting (Jolly 1966a); in howling monkeys (*Alouatta palliata*) as chasing and wrestling (Richard 1970); in Nilgiri langurs (*Presbytis johnii*) as running, climbing, hanging, chasing, and wrestling (Poirier 1970); in spectacled langurs (*P. obscurus*) as grasping, wrestling, and mouthing (Horwich 1974); in hamadryas baboons (*Papio hamadryas*) as chasing and wrestling (Kummer 1968); in vervet monkeys (*Cercopithecus aethiops*) as wrestling, grabbing at, grappling with one another's arms, mouthing, gamboling, and chasing (Struhsaker 1967a); in gorillas (*Gorilla gorilla*) as chasing, striking, and wrestling (Carpenter 1964); and in chimpanzees (*Pan troglodytes*) as chasing, wrestling, sparring, playbiting, thumping, kicking, butting with the head, tickling, and poking (Lawick-Goodall 1968).

ably, and avoided the inevitable risks of injury and exposure to predators. Hinde (1975:7) writes: "Only characters which confer a positive biological advantage can survive for long against the forces of mutation and selection."[3] Yet the functions of play are not clear.

Experiments by Harlow and his associates (reviewed by Mitchell 1970) have demonstrated severe behavioral deficits in rhesus monkeys (*Macaca mulatta*) raised without peer contact. Such behavioral deficits are frequently attributed to the lack of social play, and the experiments are cited as evidence that play serves a variety of functions (e.g., see Poirier and Smith 1974). These experiments are inadequate to demonstrate adaptive function in two respects: first, monkeys were deprived not merely of play but of all peer contact, so it is not possible to assess the specific contribution of play to normal development (Marler and Hamilton 1966, Hinde 1966, Dolhinow and Bishop 1970, Bekoff 1976b);[4] second, even if it could be shown that play deprivation produces specific behavioral deficits, it does not necessarily follow that the adaptive function of play is to produce the normal behavior. This point is pursued below.

Function in Evolutionary Biology

Some events that precede an item of behavior are referred to as its proximate causes and some events that follow it are referred to as its consequents; some of the beneficial consequents are referred to as its functions (Hinde 1975). Williams (1966) points out that the principles and procedures for answering the question "what is function?" are not highly developed; that is, there are no generally agreed upon criteria for identifying the adaptive significance of characteristics of plants and animals. Williams argues that development of the special concepts and procedures required to study the principles of adaptation has been impeded by unnecessary additions and qualifications to the

3. Hinde lists three possible explanations for the existence of a character that appears not to be biologically advantageous: (1) it may be the byproduct of an adaptive character; (2) its normal use may be functional, but it may appear occasionally in nonfunctional contexts; (3) it may be a relict of a formerly adaptive character in the process of being lost.

4. By manipulating feeding patterns in captive primate groups, Baldwin and Baldwin (1976) and Oakley and Reynolds (1976) altered the frequencies of social play. Such techniques may eventually allow experimental determination of the effects of play.

theory of natural selection, such as group selection, and he advocates the following parsimonious doctrine: ". . . adaptation is a special and onerous concept that should be used only where it is really necessary. When it must be recognized, it should be attributed to no higher a level of organization than is demanded by the evidence (Williams 1966:4–5)."

The central, and crucial, point in Williams's approach to the study of adaptation is that function must be distinguished from effect. Williams argues that, of all the effects produced by a biological mechanism, at least one may correctly be called its function, or goal, or purpose. A function can be distinguished from an incidental effect inasmuch as it is produced with sufficient precision, economy, and efficiency to rule out chance as an adequate explanation of its existence. In other words, evidence that a structure or behavior pattern evolved through the process of natural selection to serve a particular purpose or function is to be found in the design of that structure or behavior pattern. For example, the detailed structure of the vertebrate eye provides overwhelming evidence of functional design for effective vision, and indicates continued selection for this purpose throughout the evolutionary history of vertebrates. But all beneficial effects are not functions. Williams (p. 12) writes:

> A frequent practice is to recognize adaptation in any recognizable benefit arising from the activities of an organism. I believe that this is an insufficient basis for postulating adaptation and that it has led to some serious errors. A benefit can be the result of chance instead of design. *The decision as to the purpose of a mechanism must be based on an examination of the machinery and an argument as to the appropriateness of the means to the end. It cannot be based on value judgments of actual or probable consequences* [emphasis added].[5]

As a presumably noncontroversial illustration of his distinction between effect and function, Williams imagines a fox that makes its way laboriously through heavy midwinter snow to a hen house, steals a hen, and departs. On subsequent visits to the hen house the fox follows the path it has already tramped down through the snow, thereby conserving energy and reducing hen-stealing time. Williams

5. Hinde (1975) draws a similar distinction between function in the "weak" sense of a beneficial consequence and the "strong" sense of a beneficial consequence that is maintained in the population by natural selection.

argues that, despite the benefits and possible increase in fitness accruing to the fox as a result of its having tramped down the snow with its feet, nothing in the structure of fox feet or legs suggests that they are designed for snow packing or removal. The structural features of fox feet and legs can be explained adequately as adaptations for running and walking. No anatomical evidence exists that natural selection favored foxes whose feet were more efficient at snow-packing over foxes whose feet were less efficient at snow-packing. Walking and running, then, are properly called the functions of fox limbs, while snow-packing is simply a fortuitous effect. The capacity of fox brains to detect and make use of the easiest path is, however, an adaptation.

While a biological mechanism may serve more than one function at the same time (Beer 1975, Eberhard 1975), the distinction Williams draws is not between major and minor functions; if an effect is not evidenced to some degree in design, it cannot properly be called a function. But a functional explanation is a hypothesis, and as such it is subject to revision in the light of additional evidence. More exacting anatomical work on fox feet, for example, could reveal details not easily explained as adaptations to walking and running, but more appropriately interpreted as snow-packing specializations.

Not all biologists believe, as Williams does, that parsimony is an appropriate principle to guide the study of evolutionary adaptation. Williams's view on adaptation have been challenged by Wilson (1975a, 1975b), who writes that, by advocating "the a priori rule of choosing the simplest possible explanation of a biological phenomenon" (1975b:30), Williams commits the Fallacy of Simplifying the Cause. Wilson (1975b:577) defines "adaptation" as "any structure, physiological process, or behavioral pattern that makes an organism more fit to survive and to reproduce in comparison with other members of the same species. Also, the evolutionary process leading to the formation of such a trait." Wilson (1975b) maintains that the goal of the study of biological phenomena is to explain mechanisms as correctly, not as simply, as possible. Toward that end he advocates the strategy of first enumerating all possible explanations for the existence of a biological mechanism, and then devising tests to eliminate some of them.

Although Wilson rejects parsimony as a guiding principle in evolutionary biology, he seems to imply that, in some circumstances, it can be a useful strategy. In his 1966 book, *Adaptation and Natural Selec-*

tion, Williams, largely on the basis of parsimony, rejected the notion of group selection, and Wilson apparently believes that this approach was useful and appropriate, since he writes (1975a:140): "At that time there was an urgent need to rebut V. C. Wynne-Edwards' *Animal Dispersion in Relation to Social Behaviour,* a task Williams performed with distinction." But since 1966, Wilson argues, rigorous models have been developed of how group selection might work, and to continue to reject group selection out of hand in 1975, as Williams does in his book *Sex and Evolution,* suggests a devotion to parsimony that is no longer appropriate but "apparently puritanical" (Wilson 1975a:140).

I bring up this point because, although I adhere to Williams's views on the study of adaptation, even readers who reject these views may wish to consider the possibility that the present state of play theory is in some respects comparable to the state of group selection theory in 1966; Occam's Razor (multiplicity ought not to be posited without necessity) may, even if it must eventually be abandoned, prove a useful tool for the present.

The Functions of Play

Hinde (1975:13) writes that "because hard evidence is so difficult to obtain, it has become respectable to speculate about the function of behaviour in a manner that would never be permissible in studies of [proximate] causation." Since play has rarely been described in sufficient detail to elucidate its design there has been little restraint on imputing its possible functions; in the absence of evidence, hypotheses abound. Following is a representative, but by no means exhaustive, list of functions that have been attributed to animal play:

Establish dominance rank (Carpenter 1934, Rosenblum 1961, Harlow and Harlow 1965, Hall 1965, Millar 1968, Harlow 1969, Dolhinow and Bishop 1970, Poirier 1970, 1972, Dolhinow 1971, Bekoff 1972, Gottier 1972, Jolly 1972, Poirier and Smith 1974);

Learn both dominant and subordinate roles (Jay 1965);

Learn to control behavior in a social environment by controlling the level of arousal (Chance and Jolly 1970);

Optimize levels of sensory stimulation (Millar 1968, Baldwin and Baldwin 1977);

Learn to mitigate or control aggression (Dolhinow and Bishop 1970, Suomi and Harlow 1971);

Test other animals' strengths and abilities (Fagen 1974);
Protect individuals by preventing competitive interactions (Ghiselin 1974);
Learn communication skills (Mason 1965, Dolhinow 1971, Jolly 1972, Poirier and Smith 1974, West 1974);
Develop and maintain friendly relations (West 1974);
Learn patterns of social cooperation (Poirier and Smith 1974);
Learn to interact in a social world and establish social relationships (Carpenter 1934, Jay 1965, Southwick et al. 1965, Millar 1968, Dolhinow 1971, Suomi and Harlow 1971, Poirier 1972, Poirier and Smith 1974);
Develop a fully integrated personality (Poirier 1972);
Learn the identity of the partner (Poirier and Smith 1974, Wilson and Kleiman 1974);
Learn which species one belongs to (Poirier 1972);
Obtain exercise (Brownlee 1954, Ewer 1968, Leyhausen 1973, West 1974);
Increase general motor skills (Southwick et al. 1965, Dolhinow and Bishop 1970, Poirier 1970, Dolhinow 1971);
Practice and perfect adult activities (Groos 1898, Hansen 1962, Washburn and Hamburg 1965b, Suomi and Harlow 1971, Symons 1973, Aldis 1975);
Produce novel behavior (Fedigan 1972, Miller 1973, Fagen 1974, Wilson 1975b).

Sherlock Holmes once remarked to Watson, "we are suffering from a plethora of surmise, conjecture, and hypothesis." While Wilson (1975b) advocates listing all possible explanations for the existence of a biological mechanism and then devising tests to eliminate some, in the case of play such a list threatens to become unwieldy, and many of the listed functions are possibly so vague as to be untestable (Müller-Schwarze 1971, Welker 1971).

Testing Functional Theories

Two schools of thought exist regarding the appropriate criteria to evaluate functional theories of play: the "experiment" school and the "design" school. Many play theorists fare badly at the hands of adherents of both.

Members of the experiment school maintain that the functions of play can be deduced only by specifically depriving animals of play and observing their subsequent behavioral, physiological, or physical deficits compared with nondeprived animals. Since such experiments have not been performed, members of this school hold that little evidence exists on the functions of play (Beach 1945, Müller-Schwarze 1971). Müller-Schwarze (1971:240), referring to the lack of play-deprivation experiments, writes: "The amount of time and paper spent on speculations on possible functions of motor play in immature animals is in inverse proportion to the amount of facts available on this question."

Members of the design school maintain that function can be deduced only from design. They argue that even were play-deprivation experiments to reveal that playing has certain beneficial effects, this evidence would not be sufficient to demonstrate function. In the absence of rigorous arguments that play has a recognizable design, it is possible for members of this school to reject all functional theories as unsupported. Thus, although the above list of possible functions of play makes it clear that the function most frequently and persistently attributed to play is learning of one sort or another, Ghiselin (1974:259) could write: "Any learning that goes on during play is quite incidental." He apparently means that although learning may be an effect of play, learning is not its adaptive function: "Even were play a necessary condition for normal development, as may well be the case, it does not follow that animals play for that reason" (Ghiselin 1974:260).

Recently published evidence of both the experimental and the design types fails to support many functional theories of play. Based on a naturally occurring experiment, Baldwin and Baldwin (1973, 1974, 1977) question the notion that social play is required for normal social development. The Baldwins studied two troops of squirrels monkeys (*Saimiri oerstedi*) in a natural forest at Barqueta in southwestern Panama. Food at Barqueta was scarce, and the monkeys spent 95 percent of their waking 14 hours per day foraging; all social interactions occurred much less frequently at this site than in the other environments in which the Baldwins observed squirrel monkeys. During 261 hours of close-range observation at Barqueta they did not observe a single instance of play. The Baldwins believe that if play occurred in any season at least some play would have occurred during the course of their field study; since play was not observed, they conclude that the monkeys at Barqueta never play. Nevertheless, the troops were cohesive, monkeys maintained close individual distances, agonistic behavior was observed infrequently, and a normal proportion of adult females carried young. Baldwin and Baldwin (1977) also point out that some species of nonhuman primate do not play, and yet lead a social existence and are reproductively successful. They conclude that at least among squirrel monkeys, social organizations and many normal social behaviors can develop in the absence of play.

I have argued (Symons 1974) that in the absence of experiment of any kind, functional theories can be evaluated by considering whether the behavioral events of play are designed to produce the specific consequences predicted by the theories. Thus, contrary to several theorists, it is most unlikely that rhesus monkeys learn, practice, or refine agonistic communicative skills during aggressive play, since agonistic signals do not occur during play, and the signals that do occur are limited to the play context (Symons 1974). Similarly, Aldis (1975) criticizes the view held by many theorists that a variety of social skills are learned during play, since the patterns of social communication upon which the learning of these skills depends occur only in non-play contexts. Meier and Devanney (1974) imply that play is not requisite to becoming a functioning group member since infants are responding as established members of their group by the time they begin to engage in vigorous play.

Aggressive Play among Rhesus Monkeys

The social behavior of rhesus monkeys has been sudied in captivity (Rosenblum 1961, Hansen 1962, 1966, Bernstein and Draper 1964, Hinde et al. 1964, Harlow and Harlow 1965, Hinde and Spencer-Booth 1967, Harlow 1969), in the Puerto Rican island colonies (Altmann 1962a, Koford 1963a, Sade 1966), and in India (Southwick et al. 1965, Neville 1968a, Lindburg 1971). Although each of these studies mentions social play, none focuses on it, and descriptions of play have been brief. Koford (1963a) writes: "Mounting, wrestling, biting and chasing are part of the play among infants and immatures." Sade (1966) describes rhesus play as "rather stereotyped" pawing, rolling, rearing, leaping, mouthing, and nibbling. Southwick et al. (1965) describe rhesus play as consisting of chasing, jumping, and wrestling. In the classic catalogue of rhesus behavior constructed by Altmann (1962a) "plays with" is listed as one element, although Altmann notes that play is not a single behavior pattern but involves many patterns in a modified form, and requires motion-picture analysis for detailed description. The studies at the Wisconsin primate laboratories quantify many aspects of immature rhesus behavior but use very broad descriptive categories for social play. Rosenblum (1961), for example, describes "rough-and-tumble" rhesus play as consisting of biting, mouthing, tumbling, wrestling, and interlocked rolling. Clearly, most rhesus play consists of patterns similar to those of serious aggression.

The most compelling evidence of the functions of a behavior pattern is to be found in description of sufficient accuracy to reveal design. In order to obtain such description, for six months during 1969–70 I observed and filmed aggressive play (playfighting and playchasing) in a group of free-ranging rhesus monkeys on La Cueva Island, near the village of La Parguera in southwestern Puerto Rico. Field observations and the analysis of motion picture film form a supplementary record which is the basis of this book.

Plan of the Book

In chapter 2 the study site, the conditions and methods of observation, and the techniques of data collection and analysis are described. In chapter 3 rhesus aggressive play, illustrated with line drawings and photographs, is described. Qualitative description demonstrates that, in that it is a structured and coherent activity, aggressive play has a design. In chapter 4 quantitative data of various parameters of aggressive play are presented. These data can be considered as a part of the description of design, enriching the qualitative description of chapter 3, and providing information about sex differences in play. In chapters 5 and 6 the findings on playchasing and playfighting respectively are summarized and interpreted in light of the descriptive literature on animal play. On the basis of design, it is suggested that the adaptive function of aggressive play is to practice, or rehearse, and thereby to perfect behaviors used in high-intensity intraspecific aggression and in predator avoidance. In chapter 7 objections to the hypothesis that specific skills are practiced in play are reviewed and analyzed critically. The nature and adaptive significance of skill is discussed, and the history of attempts to characterize and to define play is reviewed, including the suggestion that "play" is neither a valid concept nor a useful category of behavior. In chapter 8 the currently popular theory that the function of play is to produce novel behavior is discussed critically. The importance of observing behavior in the natural habitat to assess its adaptive significance is stressed. The functional significance of human play is discussed briefly and compared to that of nonhuman animal play. In chapter 9 the sex differences in rhesus aggressive play are viewed as a natural experiment on adaptive function which provide an independent, complementary method of assessing functional hypotheses based on design. The literature on the behavior of rhesus monkeys is reviewed; clear-cut male-female differences in reproductive strategies are elucidated and used to explain sex-differences in play. In chapter 10 it is argued that human warfare and animal fighting are not homologous, nor are the developmental processes upon which they are based. Chapter 11 contains a summary and conclusions based on the preceding argument.

Chapter two

Materials and Methods

The Study Site

La Cueva, an 80-acre island (fig. 2.1), off the southwestern coast of Puerto Rico about two miles west of the village of La Parguera was the study site. Approximately half of La Cueva is mangrove swamp and, as this part of Puerto Rico recieves only 15–35 inches of rain per year (mostly from August to November), the nonmangrove vegetation consists primarily of dry-loving grasses, shrubs, low trees, and cactus. Commercial monkey chow and water were provided at six feeding stations.

Approximately 200 monkeys constituting four social groups (A, C, E, and I) and a few solitary adult males lived on La Cueva. Most of the adults were brought directly from India in 1961 and 1962, but I Group was brought intact from another island colony, Cayo Santiago (Vandenbergh 1967). The groups ranged over the entire island, no group maintaining a territory, and were ranked in a dominance hierarchy that correlated directly with group size. A dominant group moving into an area occupied by a subordinate group always displaced the subordinate group (Vessey 1968).

There were no predators on La Cueva, and monkeys usually ignored the other animals (mostly rats, lizards, and crabs), with which they shared the island. Breeding was seasonal: Vandenbergh and Vessey (1968) report that mating activities extended from September to April, births from March to November. During the 1969–70 season, although male masturbation was observed in September, estrus and copulation were not observed until early October.

The La Cueva rhesus colony was in several respects an ideal subject

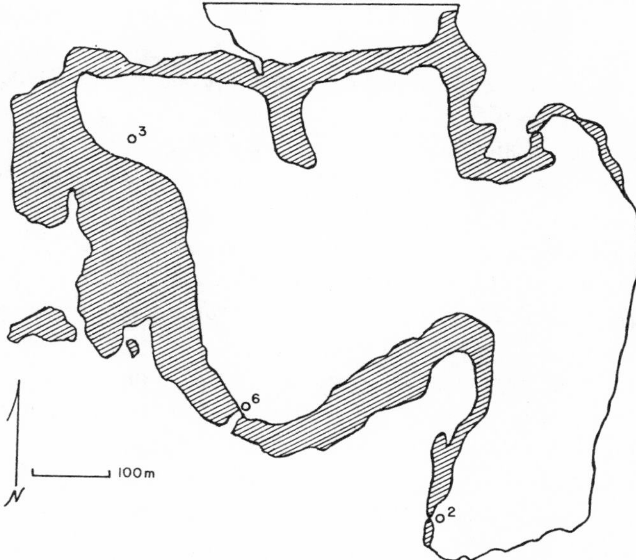

Figure 2.1 *La Cueva Island. Circles denote feeding stations nos. 2, 3 and 6, which are mentioned in the text. Shaded areas denote mangrove swamp.*

for a study of aggressive play. Monkeys were trapped periodically and tattooed for identification so that ages and genealogies were known and it was possible to learn very quickly to recognize individuals. Moreover, the monkeys were used to human observers, making habituation rapid and close observation possible. The heterogeneous environment contained trees, shrubs, grass, open ground, and enclosed bodies of water, providing a rich arena for play, a behavior that varies substantially with the terrain. The social environment also was rich, with monkeys of all ages and sexes available in social groups of approximately normal size for forest-living rhesus monkeys (Southwick et al. 1965, Lindburg 1971) so that play could be observed within and between all classes of monkey, including intergroup play. Finally, although 2.5 monkeys per acre is crowded compared with Indian forest-living rhesus, there was enough space and cover so that animals could avoid each other and flee from attack or play.

The Study Group

C Group, the largest and highest ranking group on the island, was selected for the present study for several reasons: (1) it contained the largest number of immature animals and hence provided the maximum amount of social play: (2) because it was the highest ranking group it never was displaced from an area by another group, and therefore observations were interrupted fewer times because of group movement than would have been the case with any other group; (3) C Group spent much of its time in areas favorable for observation and filming.

C Group was composed of approximately 76 monkeys (table 2.1), the number varying as males left, and extra-group males joined, the group during the mating season. Like other large rhesus groups, C Group consisted of two subgroups: the central subgroup comprised two adult males (140 and 161) and all adult females and their immature offspring. One three-year-old male (C4), the son of C Group's highest ranking female, belonged to the central subgroup; all other males three years old or older belonged to the peripheral male subgroup. The peripheral males were spatially separate from the central group, its members often were to be found together, and most of their social interactions were with each other.

C Group slept in mangrove trees at night and became active at daybreak. Sometime during the morning they usually moved off through the mangroves, although occasionally they remained in one location for the entire day and slept there again that night. The monkeys spent most of the day resting, grooming, and sleeping in the mangroves, making at least one trip to a feeding station during the day. They fed again around nightfall and almost invariably spent the night in the mangroves near the feeding station at which they last fed. Although at some time during the study I observed C Group on every portion of the island, it was usually to be found along the western border.

Methods of Observation

Observation was initiated August 12, 1969, but detailed field notes were not taken at that time. I spent the first two weeks becoming famil-

Table 2.1 Composition of C Group[a]

Infants		Yearlings		2-Year-Olds		3-Year-Olds	
M	F	M	F	M	F	M	F
127-69	A5-69	241-I7	127-68	47-H1	214-G1	127-C4	150-D5
57-69	263-69		181-I4	228-G2	138-G7	188-E5[b]	223-B7
289-69	150-69		150-L3	289-H4	270-F7	187-E4[b]	214-D9
280-69	270-69		113-L6	241-G6			47-C5
309-69	223-69		125-68				60-C0
241-69	221-69		223-J4				
292-69	125-69		138-L2				
181-69							
214-69							
D4-69							
138-69							

4-Year-Olds		5-Year-Olds		6+ Year-Olds	
M	F	M	F	M	F
188-C6[b]	60-309	34-287[b]	214-284	140	47
184-B2[b]	214-A8	BJ-FU[b]	125-280	161	57
241-B3[b]	47-A5		113-D4	CA[b]	127
			181-289	216-286[b]	138
					150
					211
					214
					228
					241
					125
					220
					221
					223
					181
					134
					57-292
					226-270
					138-263

[a] An animal's designation is to the right of the hyphen, its mother's designation to the left. Thus H1 is 47's 2-year-old son. Untattooed animals are designated by their mother's name plus their year of birth. Thus 127–68 is 127's untattooed yearling daughter, born in 1968. Some animals of more than six years of age were brought from India and their mothers are not known.

[b] Peripheral males

iar with La Cueva and the monkey population and learning to identify each noninfant C Group monkey. By August 27 I was familiar with the monkeys' daily schedules and movement patterns and I recognized individually all members of C Group, except infants, whether or not their tattoos were visible. Note-taking was then begun and it was continued until February 23, 1970. Field notes were recorded for 300 hours of observation.[1]

When C Group monkeys were on the inland side of the mangroves, observation was made from land; when they were on the ocean side, observation was made from a boat, although only rarely. C Group's typical movement pattern was from one feeding station to another, and frequently it was possible to anticipate the group's movement and arrive ahead of it. I approached the group slowly and conspicuously, attempting to be visible and unthreatening, and the monkeys usually ignored my approach. When I encountered monkeys engaged in aggressive play I observed them until play ended or they moved into dense cover.

Play occurred primarily in the early morning and late afternoon, often reaching a peak at dusk. Observation was begun at daybreak, when the monkeys began to come down from the trees in which they slept. Aggressive play was common at this time, especially just after the animals had fed. Often by 9:00 or 9:30 A.M. the monkeys began resting, grooming, and sleeping. Observation usually was ended when there was no longer play to observe, and begun again in the cooler, late afternoon, usually after 3:00 P.M., and continued until it became too dark to see activity clearly.

When afternoon observations had been made the previous day, it was almost always possible to find C Group easily the following morning since they spent the night where they were at dusk. Finding the group for afternoon observation, however, was not always so easy. First, I would circle the island by boat, and check each feeding station. If this was unsuccessful I searched the interior of the island, beginning with the most likely locations. Usually I found C Group within 15 or 20 minutes, but sometimes it took longer, and on a few occasions I was never able to find them.

Methods of Recording and Analyzing Data

Field notes were recorded on a small cartridge tape recorder which I carried in a backpack, the microphone clipped to my shirt, permitting

1. I returned to La Cueva with a professional photographer, John Bishop, for six weeks during the summer of 1975 to obtain 9600 feet of 16mm motion picture footage of rhesus aggressive play. Systematic field notes were not made, but subsequent analysis of the footage contributed to the detailed descriptions of playfighting in chapter 3.

uninterrupted observation. Although this technique is far more efficient than written notes, it was nevertheless possible to see and record only a small fraction of the monkeys' complex play activities. Observation was made easier by a pair of 7 x 35 Bausch and Lomb binoculars, and the duration of playfights was determined with a stopwatch. After each period of observation the tape-recorded notes were transcribed by typewriter. They were subsequently photocopied, pasted on McBee keysort cards, and the cards were coded and punched for various aspects of aggressive play.

With time my ability to see and to record the details of aggressive play increased: during the first weeks I often recorded only the existence of play between specific individuals, but gradually I was able to record such features as the initiation of play, play soliciting, and many details of play itself.

Black and white photographs, as well as some color slides, were made with two 35 mm Leica M-3 cameras with 50 mm and 90 mm lenses. Motion pictures were made with a Canon super-8 Auto-Zoom model 1218 (88-c) with an electric zoom lens f/1.8, 7.5–90 mm. Almost all motion pictures of playfighting were made at high speed (54fps). When I was photographing I did not take field notes, but if some especially interesting events occurred I summarized my observations later. (These summaries are not included in the quantified data.) Motion pictures were analyzed with a Kodak Ektagraphic MFS-8 projector and a Kodak Instamatic M-70 projector. The former allows automatic viewing at 6, 18, and 54 fps, and also permits manual control so that film can be analyzed one frame at a time or stopped on any frame. Approximately 2650 feet of motion picture film of aggressive play was made, and the examples of rhesus playfighting in chapter 3 and appendix 1 were selected from this film record. Field notes and film analysis were combined to construct the "typical" playfighting description.

Sampling

During each observation period, I observed the animals first encountered playing, assuming that if monkeys were encountered at random, aggressive play would be randomly sampled; it was not practical in a field situation with dense cover to sample rigorously. For example, I could not determine in advance which monkeys would be visible, nor was it possible to follow a given monkey for a specific length of time.

Beginning in early November, by which time I recognized all infants by sex, periodic censuses were made in order to assess the likelihood of sampling bias. Before each observation period to be censused a number between 1 and 10 was selected by shuffling a set of 3 x 5 cards and randomly selecting one. The number on the card stood for the beginning of a ten-minute segment of the observation period; for example, a 5 stood for the beginning of the 50th minute of observation. Then, if a 5 were selected, during the 50th and 51st minutes I would remain stationary, and record the sex of all infant monkeys and the identity of all noninfant monkeys that I could see.

In this report the following definitions are used: "infants" are animals born the preceding (1969) birth season; "juvenile-1s" are one and two years old;[2] "juvenile-2s" are three years old; an "adult female" is four or more years old; older males are either "central" or "peripheral," as discussed above. No C Group infants were tattooed either before or during the present study, and for approximately the first two months of the study I could not reliably identify all infants, even by sex. Therefore there are three "infant" categories in some tables: "male," "female," and "unknown." The "unknown" category shrank rapidly as I came to recognize infants by sex. It was not until nearly the end of the study, however, that I recognized all infants individually.

Tables 2.2, 2.3 and 2.4 indicate the frequencies with which age/sex classes were observed during the 21 two-minute censuses, averaging 29.7 monkeys per census, and the frequencies expected if sampling were random. Table 2.2 gives the census data for the entire group: $\chi^2 = 59.5$ (df = 8), and the probability that all C Group monkeys were randomly observed is less than .001. Clearly the greatest contribution to this χ^2 is the relatively small number of observations of peripheral males. Table 2.3 gives the census data and expected values on all animals except the peripheral males: $\chi^2 = 9.4$ (df = 7), and the probability that all "central" monkeys were randomly observed is .235. Table 2.4 gives the census data for the animals that engaged in the great major-

2. One- and two-year-olds are lumped for two reasons: First, they constitute a natural category in that they are similar in body size, frequency of play, and proficiency in play. Infants are almost always smaller, play less frequently, and are far less proficient than one- and two-year-olds, while three-year-old rhesus attain sexual maturity and are much less playful than one- and two-year-olds. Second, owing to the unbalanced sex ratio among yearlings, lumping facilities data analysis.

Table 2.2 Census: C Group

Class	N	N/76	No. Times Observed(O)	E=(N/76 ×623)	$(0-E)^2/E$
Male Infant	11	.145	100	90.3	1.04
Female Infant	7	.092	70	57.3	2.85
Male Juv.-1	5	.066	57	41.1	6.15
Female Juv.-1	10	.132	100	82.2	3.86
Male Juv.-2	1	.013	8	8.1	.00
Female Juv.-2	5	.066	46	41.1	.58
Adult Female	25	.329	197	205.0	.31
Central Male	2	.026	22	16.2	2.08
Periph. Male	10	.132	23	82.2	42.64
Total	76	1.001	623	623.5	59.51

$\chi^2=59.51$ (d.f. =8), $p<.001$ that all C Group monkeys were randomly observed.

Table 2.3 Census: Central Subgroup

Class	N	N/76	No. Times Observed(O)	E=(N/76 ×600)	$(0-E)^2/E$
Male Infant	11	.167	100	100.2	.000
Female Infant	7	.106	70	63.6	.644
Male Juv.-1	5	.076	57	45.6	2.850
Female Juv.-1	10	.152	100	91.2	.849
Male Juv.-2	1	.015	8	9.0	.111
Female Juv.-2	5	.076	46	45.6	.003
Central Male	2	.030	22	18.0	4.064
Adult Female	25	.379	197	227.4	.889
Total	66	1.001	600	600.6	9.410

$\chi^2=9.4$ (d.f. =7), $p=.235$ that central monkeys were randomly observed.

Table 2.4 Census: Central Infants and Juveniles

Class	N	N/39	No. Times Observed(O)	E=(N/39 ×381)	$(0-E)^2/E$
Male Infant	11	.282	100	107.4	.510
Female Infant	7	.179	70	68.2	.048
Male Juv.-1	5	.128	57	48.8	1.378
Female Juv.-1	10	.256	100	97.5	.064
Male Juv.-2	1	.026	8	9.9	.365
Female Juv.-2	5	.128	46	48.8	.161
Total	39	.999	381	380.6	2.526

$\chi^2=2.5$ (d.f. =5), $p>.7$ that central infants and juveniles were randomly observed.

ity of aggressive play, the "central" infants and juveniles: $\chi^2 = 2.5$ (df = 5), and the probability is greater than .7 that these animals were observed randomly. Therefore I conclude that quantitative differences in aggressive play between age/sex classes of "central" infants and juveniles (chapter 4) are not due to sampling bias but reflect real differences in the frequencies of behavior.

Chapter three

Description of Rhesus Aggressive Play

Aggressive play among rhesus monkeys is traditionally considered (e.g., Hansen 1966) to include two intergrading types of play: playfighting (rough-and-tumble play, contact play) and playchasing (approach-avoidance, noncontact play). This distinction is maintained in this report.

Because playfighting is so fast-paced and complex, a three-level approach is used to describe it: (1) Playfighting and its preliminaries are described in general terms. (2) Seven playfights (A through G) that were recorded on high-speed film are described in detail, the description presented in serially numbered lines. Playfight A follows the general description in the text and is illustrated with line drawings (figs 3.1–3.15) from individual frames of the film, while playfights B through G appear in appendix 1. The approximate temporal relationships of movements are indicated in these examples by the relative placement of descriptive paragraphs, but lines do not indicate duration or exact temporal relationships. The examples of playfights presented were selected for the following reasons: (a) the entire interaction was recorded on film; (b) various age and sex classes are represented; (c) long and short interactions are represented. (3) Each example is followed by notes that point out specific features of interest in the example and the ways in which the interaction illustrates general aspects of rhesus playfighting.

The general description is illustrated with photographs and with references to examples or to the notes to the examples. (For example, a general statement about rhesus play might be followed by the citation

(A, C6) which refers the reader to Example A, and to Example C, note 6.)

General Description of Aggressive Play

Preliminaries

Certain gaits, facial expressions, and postures regularly precede aggressive play and occur only in the context of play; some of these apparently function as invitations to play. Occasionally a play interaction is not preceded by any preliminary but is begun by one monkey grasping another from behind. Such initiations generally occur in the course of a series of playfights, when the monkeys already are playing, although not always with each other (C1, D1). It is more usual, however, for playfighting to be preceded by one or more of the following preliminaries.

Gaits. "Gamboling" and "staggering," unlike normal patterns of rhesus locomotion—running, walking, climbing, leaping—are observed exclusively in play. "Gamboling" is a bobbing, high-stepping gait in which the forequarters and hindquarters alternately are raised (photo 3.1, E1, G1). "Staggering" is a lurching gait in which the monkey may step sideways, arms highly flexed, hindquarters raised, and head on or near the ground (photo 3.2). In the extreme form of stagger the hand supports little or no body weight and drags palm upward on the ground, body weight is supported largely on the shoulder, and the hind foot steps in front of the hand on the same side (photo 3.3). The staggering monkey lurches forward, the shoulder on the ground leading (G1). Monkeys may gambol or stagger when approaching or moving away from a play partner or, occasionally, when not oriented to a specific partner during a sequence of play interactions.

Play-face. The only facial expression consistently associated with rhesus play is the relaxed open-mouth face, or play-face. It usually is given at the beginning of a play interaction, before contact occurs, and it may continue throughout the interaction (photos 3.3, 3.4, 3.8, 3.9, 3.10, 3.11, 3.13, 3.17, 3.21, 3.22, 3.23, 3.24, 3.25, 3.28, see also A3, B3, C3, D2, E2, G2).

In the analysis of motion picture film the play-face is an accurate

Photo 3.1 *Juvenile-1* (*rear*) *gamboling.*

Photo 3.2 *Juvenile-1 staggering.*

Photo 3.3 *Juvenile-2 exhibiting extreme stagger. Note playful approach by juvenile-1.*

Photo 3.4 *A mount between juvenile-1's about to become a playfight.*

Photo 3.5 *Juvenile-1 exhibiting head-down.*

Photo 3.6 *Juvenile-1 exhibiting roll-onto-back. Note playful approach by juvenile-1* (*right*).

predictor of playfighting and almost always is seen first in the monkey about to initiate a play interaction. For example, mounting sometimes precedes playfighting, which may be initiated by either the mounter or the mountee. The initiating monkey precedes a playfighting movement with a play-face: then, if the initiator is the mounter, it falls forward and bites the mountee's neck or back: if the mountee is the initiator it turns its head and forequarters and reaches back with one hand to grasp the mounter. The partner usually responds with a play-face immediately after the initial playfighting movement (photo 3.4), and playfighting ensues. When two monkeys playfight and a third observes them, the observing monkey gives a play-face before reaching out to grasp the playfighters and join the playfight.

A play-face merges into a playbite as the mouth moves onto the partner's body, although a play-face frequently is not directed at the partner and may be given by a playing monkey that is moving away from its partner (G5). In summary, play-faces reliably precede and accompany play and do not precede or accompany other rhesus activities. No other facial expression consistently occurs during play, although ear-flattening and eyelid exposure occur occasionally.

Postures. Postures frequently adopted by a monkey moving neither toward nor away from a play partner are "head-down," "crouch-stare," and "roll-onto-back." In the most complete form of "head-down" the head is placed on the ground, the forearms are almost on the ground, and the hindquarters remain elevated, the legs extended. The head-down monkey usually either looks at its partner's face directly (photo 3.5) or it looks at the partner through its legs, hindquarters toward the partner, with the top of its head against the ground (G4). In "crouch-stare" the limbs are flexed, the ventral surface is on or near the ground, and the partner is fixated visually (A1). The roll-onto-back frequently is preceded by a stagger, in which the head is brought onto the ground (photo 3.3). After the monkey rolls onto its back the limbs are relaxed, often waving, and the monkey may grasp its foot with its hand (photo 3.6; see also G1).

Invitation. Although there is no sharp distinction between gestures, postures, and gaits that accompany play or initiation of play and those that solicit (invite) play, an "invitation" can be defined as a movement given by a monkey who does not approach its partner that increases the probability of playful approach by the partner (A1, G1, G4). Invitation as a distinct phenomenon was not consistently recorded until late in the field study, and quantitative data therefore are few.

Of the 94 clear-cut invitations recorded in the field notes, 62 were successful and 32 were unsuccessful in eliciting playful approach by the partner. The field record is summarized below.[1] Two numbers are given in parentheses after each form of invitation listed, the first in-

1. During the 1975 shooting of footage for a 16mm motion picture, one monkey was observed to use "presenting" as an unmistakable play invitation.

dicating the number of times it was seen to succeed in eliciting playful approach, the second the number of times it was seen to fail.

Stare, then run (stagger, gambol) away (12, 5);
Look over the shoulder, then run (stagger, gambol) away, or run and then look over the shoulder (11, 12);
Run away (stagger, gambol) holding an object in the hand or mouth (9, 1);
Give play-face while standing and staring (3,0);
Give play-face, then run (stagger, gambol) away (2,0);
Ear-flatten while standing and staring (4,2);
Ear-flatten, then run (stagger, gambol) away (2,1);
Head-down, look back (usually preceded or followed by run or stagger) (3,6);
Roll-onto-back (12, 4);
Crouch-stare (2,1);
Crouch-stare with object in mouth (2,0);

Playfighting

The following description is based largely on detailed analysis of slow-motion film: activities that in reality are continuous, and often simultaneous, are broken up into their components, so that the narrative may give the misleading impression that playfighting is slow and deliberate. In fact, playfighting frequently is very fast-paced, and movements occur far too rapidly to represent conscious thought.

Approach. A playfight begins when one monkey approaches another or when they approach each other. The approach may be at a walk, run, gambol, stagger, or leap. Play may be initiated with an animal facing away from the approacher (C1, D1), but otherwise monkeys seem to look at each other's face during approach (A2, B1, C2, E7, F3, G3). A playfully approaching monkey may lower its head before making contact. When monkey A playfully approaches monkey B, B may give a passive or minimal response: that is, B may do nothing, or only close its eyes and remain lying, sitting, or standing; it may turn away from A (especially likely if A has lowered its head); it may walk or run away, or leap aside, or leap back from A.

Leaping. Either the approaching or the approached monkey may leap, and leaping may also occur during the playfight (e.g., B, C). If A initiates play by leaping at B, B may avoid contact by leaping back or

Photo 3.7 *Juvenile-1 leaping.*

Photo 3.8 *Juvenile-1 leaping, beginning 180 degree pivot (clockwise).*

by stepping around A, and B can then flee, circle around A, or take the offensive. If A leaps over B's head, B's response may be to raise its head, rear onto its hind feet and grasp and bite A (C11). In such a leap A frequently presses B's head or shoulders downward with one hand, making rearing and biting more difficult for B (photo 3.7, B6, C10). Unless the leaper is fleeing, a leap is accompanied by a 180-degree twist or pivot so that, as it lands, the leaper faces the leapee (photo 3.8, B7, C12).

Rearing. In relatively nonvigorous playfights one or both partners may maintain a sitting position (especially likely when the partners differ substantially in body size), but in almost all vigorous playfights, both monkeys rear onto their hind legs. This posture varies from a squat to a bipedal stand with legs almost fully extended. Rearing frees the hands for reaching and grasping and increases mobility (photo 3.9, A4, B2, C4, D6, E3, F10). A monkey that remains sitting when approached by a play partner usually is pushed over onto its back.

Reaching. Reaching toward the partner with the hands accompanies rearing at the beginning of a playfight and is a prominent fea-

Photo 3.9 *Juvenile-2s rearing.*

Photo 3.10 *Juvenile-1s grasping at beginning of playfight.*

ture of playfighting (e.g., A, B, C, D, E, F). Monkey A may approach B at a run, leap at and reach toward B with both hands, and dive into B (e.g., A, E). If A reaches toward B, B may use its hands to parry the reach (B4), may grasp A's hand and pull A off balance, or may step or lean away from A, or both. Rhesus sometimes hit during play, striking with the palm side of the open hand, but this is surprisingly infrequent. Furthermore, a hit is difficult to distinguish from a reach, parry, or push: if A reaches toward B, but misses (fails to grasp) B, this may look superficially like an attempted hit. Occasionally a monkey keeps its arm extended, holding the partner at arm's length, in a manner functionally similar to the left jab in boxing.

Grasping and Grappling. At the beginning of a playfight monkeys usually grasp each other with their hands, and mutual grasping continues through most of the interaction (e.g., photo 3.10, A, C, D, E, F). Initial grasps usually are on the partner's arm, torso, or head (A), and mutual grasping of forearms is common, both monkeys stepping, or even leaping, bipedally. As the playfight develops, monkeys constantly release and regrasp in response to the fluid situation.

Grappling is a continuous mutual shifting of grips. Each monkey is manipulating a constantly moving object, holding that object, and biting it (D3, F6). Grips apparently are shifted: as the partner shifts; as a hold is broken; and in order to break the partner's hold. If monkey A grasps B with one hand it may hold, push, or pull with that hand. Grasping facilitates biting, as in the following examples:

A approaches B. B rears. A lowers its head, rotating its forequarters in the transverse plane, the side of its mouth contacting B's ventral surface while A grasps B's arms or torso and bites B.

A approaches B, reaches toward B's head and grasps B's scalp, pulls B's head forward and downward, forcing B's face into the ground, grasps and holds B's shoulders, and bites the back of B's neck.

Grasping can control the partner's movement, put the partner off balance, put the partner in a position in which it is vulnerable to being bitten, and cause the partner to fall to the ground (A5, E11). The grasping monkey usually pushes or pulls in the direction in which the partner already is moving, using the partner's momentum to throw it to the ground (A6), as in the following example:

A approaches B rapidly, reaches toward B's head. B rears, reaches toward A and pushes up under A's chest. A is thrown completely over B's head.

A monkey's response to being pulled or pushed off balance is to step in the direction in which it is being pushed or pulled (A7).

During a playfight monkeys move by stepping, leaping, rolling, twisting, or pivoting to face their partner unless they are prevented from doing so or they are about to flee (A8, B8, C8, D4, E6, F1), and a monkey may place a hand flat on the ground and use it as a pivot (B5, C7, E15, F2). Forward movement of the body is halted by planting the feet wide apart, legs bent and spread (C9).

On-top and On-bottom Positions. A monkey is on-top if it is standing, squatting, or sitting, leaning over its partner and holding the partner with its hands, and the partner is lying on its back. The partner is, then, on-bottom (e.g., A, E). Not all interactions in which playfighting monkeys lie on the ground involve an on-top/on-bottom relationship: monkeys may lie side by side (photo 3.11) or may roll over and over on the ground.

As noted above, monkeys move to throw their partners to the ground. A monkey thrown to the ground rolls onto its back to face its

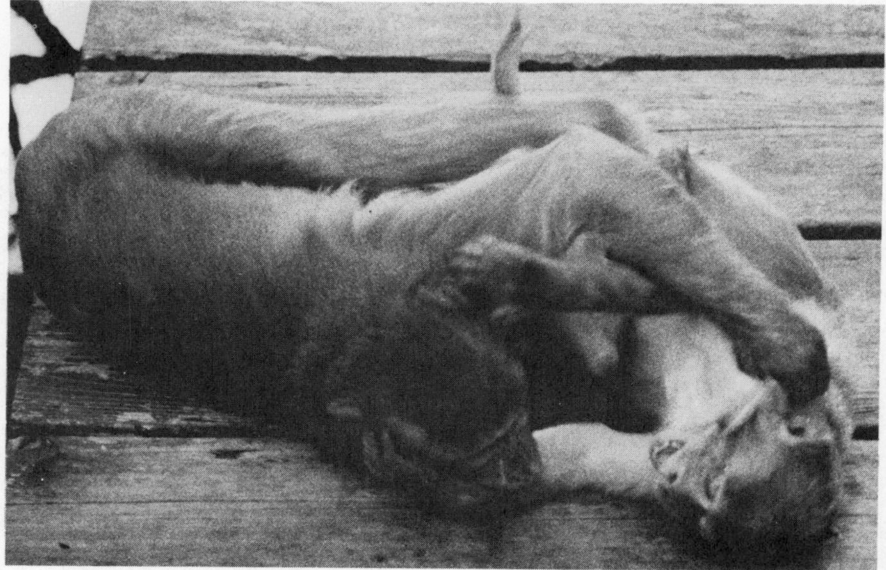

Photo 3.11 *Juvenile-2 (left) playfighting juvenile-1 lying side-by-side. Note grappling.*

partner (A8). Monkeys may actually adopt an on-bottom position in order to continue to face the partner, as in the following examples:

A approaches B, who is sitting, reaches and grasps B's shoulders and begins to walk bipedally around to the dorsal surface of B. B falls backward, and is on-bottom but facing A.

A is bipedal, grasping B with its hands (and possibly teeth) and dragging B across the ground. B twists and rolls onto its back.

The on-top monkey has the advantage over the on-bottom partner in leverage, mobility, and consequently in opportunity to playbite (A10, E16). This is documented in table 3.1, which summarizes the playbites recorded on all super-8 motion picture film of playfighting in which an on-top/on-bottom relationship existed. Expected values in table 3.1 are based on the null hypothesis that on-top and on-bottom monkeys are equally likely to playbite. On-top monkeys averaged four times as many bites as on-bottom monkeys, and this difference is highly significant.

Movements of the on-top monkey include: (1) On-top holds on-bottom with its hands, steps or leaps to keep its balance, and moves its face toward on-bottom's ventral surface and away from on-bottom's hands and feet (e.g., A, E). (2) On-top steps and/or leaps to on-bottom's side, then moves its head to on-bottom's abdomen, rather than moving directly over on-bottom's face or feet (A12, E21). On-top also may leap to avoid defensively deployed limbs of on-bottom. (3) If on-top leaps over on-bottom it twists or pivots 180 degrees and thereby continues to face on-bottom. (4) On-top pushes on-bottom with its hands, rolling on-bottom onto its side, and then bites on-bottom's exposed neck (photo 3.12).

Movements of the on-bottom monkey include: (1) On-bottom moves (rolls, twists) to face on-top (e.g., A, E, F). (2) If possible, on-bottom rises to its feet (A13, E8). (3) On-bottom pushes away on-top's face with a hand (photo 3.13), or curls its body ventrally and pushes with its feet (photo 3.14, E13–14). If A approaches B when B is sitting

Table 3.1 Number and Location of Bites by On-Top and On-Bottom Monkeys in 36 Filmed Playfights

Position of Monkey	Neck	Ventral Torso	Lateral and Dorsal Torso	Head	Hand	Arm	Foot	Leg	Total	Percent Total
On-Top	33	31	14	17	8	60	15	41	219	79.9
On-Bottom	4	7	2	18	3	17	3	1	55	20.1
Total	37	38	16	35	11	77	18	42	274	100.0

and B begins to topple over onto its back, the curling and pushing with the feet begin almost immediately, before it has fallen (photo 3.15). (4) On-bottom grasps and throws on-top (A5). (5) It is rare for monkeys in an on-top/on-bottom relationship to be head-to-tail, but in this situation there is mutual belly-biting and curling and pushing of the partner's head with the feet. (6) On-bottom develops rotational momentum by flailing, twisting, or rolling, breaking the on-top partner's grip, and on-bottom stands. Rolling while gripping the on-top partner can reverse the on-top/on-bottom relationship.

Behind and In-front Positions. A monkey is "behind" its partner if its ventral surface lies against or near the partner's dorsal surface and it grasps the "in-front" partner and prevents it from turning (photo 3.16, C). The behind partner makes virtually all bites, the in-front partner few or none (A17, C13).

Sometimes a monkey may be "semi-behind" its partner (E12), as in the following examples:

Photo 3.12 *Juvenile-1 (on-top) rolls infant (on-bottom) onto side and bites infant's neck.*

Photo 3.13 *Juvenile-1 (on-bottom) pushes away juvenile-1's (on-top) face.*

Photo 3.14 *Infant (on-bottom) attempts to push away juvenile-1's (on-top) face.*

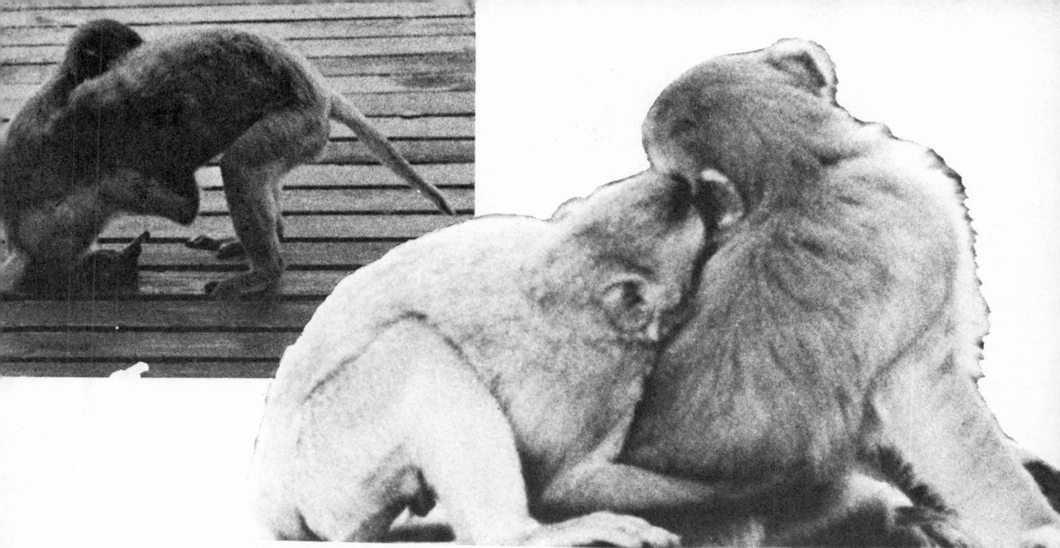

Photo 3.15 *Defensive use of feet by juvenile-1 about to be pushed over.*

Photo 3.16 *Behind/in-front relationship in juvenile-1 playfight.*

A and B face each other. A grasps B's head, pulls down, so that B's face is forced into the ground, and bites B on the back of the neck.

B stands quadrupedally, A stands bipedally beside B, arm across B's back, grasping B on the side opposite, and bites B on the back. (This also occurs if B flees and A catches it.)

One monkey may approach a second from behind, or the behind position may be achieved in the course of playfighting: that is, monkey A may step or leap (C10) to a position behind monkey B. Because playfighting monkeys move to face their partners, the behind position is far more difficult to attain than the on-top position, and the on-top position is attained about four times as often as the behind position.

Movements of the behind monkey include: (1) Behind holds in-front with its hands, preventing in-front from turning (A17, C5). (2) Behind steps or leaps to stay behind (C6). (3) Behind bites the dorsal surface of in-front. (4) If in-front partner rolls, attempting to face behind, behind may maintain its position by rolling as well, gripping in-front with all four limbs.

Movements of the in-front monkey include: (1) In-front creates momentum about its longitudinal axis by flailing, twisting, or pivoting, breaking behind's grip and turning to face behind (C8). (2) In-front twists its head back and attempts to bite behind (photo 3.16), or bites one of behind's hands. (3) In-front reaches back, grasps a grasping hand of behind and attempts to break behind's grip (C14). (4) (rare) A approaches B from behind and grasps B, B keeps hindquarters high, lowers forequarters, and A slides over B's back.

Playbiting. Playbiting, usually accompanied by eyelid closure just before contact, occurs when one monkey places its open mouth on the partner during playfighting. In the following description I use "biting" for "playbiting," with the understanding that all biting during play in inhibited. Although biting in play is inhibited, usually it is impossible to determine the degree of pressure being applied unless the skin is pulled away or a monkey actually drags its partner with its teeth. Biting and avoiding being bitten seem to determine the structure of playfighting (chapter 6).

Bites generally are aimed at the neck or the ventral surface (the ventral surface usually is the one exposed because of the tendency to face the partner) (e.g., A10, E9), but bites can be made anywhere on the partner's body. During vigorous playfighting a monkey bites whatever comes to mouth—hand, head, tail, or scrotum.

A neck bite often is preceded by rotation of the upper body in the transverse plane, which brings the teeth into biting position. A monkey biting its partner's throat is in a good strategic position, because the partner cannot counterbite until the bite is broken. On the other hand, by moving to bite the partner's throat, a monkey exposes its own. Frequently in vigorous playfighting monkeys feint with their heads while attempting to pull or push each other off balance, each apparently attempting to obtain a low-risk neck-biting opportunity. Once a neck bite is made, the biter attempts to keep its weight into the bite to prevent the partner from breaking free. While mutual neck biting is not possible, it is common for each monkey to bite simultaneously at the base of its partner's neck. One defense against neck biting is to grasp the back of the partner's head, neck, or upper back and pull the partner's face away from the bitee's neck (E10). This also exposes the partner's neck, and it may then be bitten (photo 3.17). The bitee may push the biter's face away with its hand or, if on-bottom, with its foot (photo 3.14, E13–14). A bite also may be broken or avoided when the bitee hunches its shoulders and lowers its chin, or when it interposes an arm between its body and the biter's teeth (A14, E17).

Photo 3.17 *Juvenile-1 grasps infant's scalp and pulls head back, exposing infant's throat.*

Photo 3.18 *Juvenile-2 rotating body in transverse plane to bite ventral surface of juvenile-1.*

Photo 3.19 *Juvenile-1 bites defensively deployed foot of on-bottom infant.*

Photo 3.20 *Juvenile-1 flees from playfight with juvenile-2.*

Photo 3.21 *Juvenile-1 (right) twists and pivots off left foot, preparing to flee from juvenile-2.*

A bite to the ventral surface sometimes is preceded by twisting of the forequarters, rotating the body in the transverse plane. This brings the teeth into biting position (photo 3.18, A16, E4). When the abdomen of the on-bottom partner is being bit, the on-top monkey moves, as the on-bottom monkey moves, to keep its face on or close to on-bottom's abdomen (A15, F8).

When a hand or foot is used to push a partner, the partner often turns its head toward the pushing extremity and bites it (photo 3.19, A11, E18), and the bitten limb usually is retracted (E19). Alternatively, a monkey may move its head away from a defensively deployed limb, and, once free of it, move its head back into biting position; or it may grasp the limb and push or pull it aside. On-bottom monkeys who use their limbs defensively to push the on-top partner's face away frequently get their extremities bitten. An on-top monkey may use its teeth to drag its partner across the ground, the biting monkey sometimes actually shaking its head, keeping on-bottom off balance. This effectively deters defensive tactics by on-bottom, but may prove so painful that the on-bottom partner flees, thus ending the playfight.

Fleeing. Playfighting may end when one monkey flees (photo 3.20) although playing monkeys frequently simply stop and sit. (When one monkey stops playfighting, its partner almost always stops as well, and they may separate or simply relax and hold each other.) Fleeing begins when a monkey orients away from its partner by rolling, twisting, pivoting, or turning (photo 3.21, B9, C15, D5, F11). Monkeys often pursue a fleeing partner (B11, D7, F13): if caught, the fleeing monkey is grasped on the flank or back and is bitten (D7). Monkeys usually flee to cover (C16, D8, F12). Many playfights are very brief (see chapter 4) consisting, for example, of approach, hold, bite, and flee, or approach, reach, grasp, and flee, or approach, reach-and-parry, and flee.

Playchasing

A playchase may precede, follow, or be dissociated from playfighting. Normal patterns of rhesus locomotion—running, climbing, leaping—are seen during playchases, although frequently a gamboling gait is used. Although free-ranging rhesus monkeys rarely manipulate or play with non-food objects, an object (usually a leaf or twig) occasionally is incorporated into chasing play, the chasee being the monkey holding the object; when the object changes hands (or mouths) so do the roles of chaser and chasee.

Variation in Play with the Terrain

Most play that I could observe completely and in which I could identify the participants occurred on open ground. Since playfighting most frequently took place in the open and playchasing in varying degrees of cover, playfighting was systematically recorded in greater proportion than its actual occurrence. But, with the exceptions of water and high grass, play occurred regularly in each type of terrain to be described. Except when the monkeys were resting or traveling deep within the

Example A

Monkey A: one-year-old male (I7)
Monkey B: two-year-old male (G6), A's brother
Location: bare ground
Time from line 16 to line 160: approximately 12 seconds

	A	B
1	Sits about 5′ high in a low,	Sits on ground, about 3′ from
2	bare tree.	trunk of tree, facing tree,
3		looking at A.
4	Climbs head first down trunk,	
5	grasps a horizontal limb with	
6	both hands, swings under it,	
7	and drops to ground, landing	
8	on hind feet, then dropping	
9	to all fours. He holds a	
10	leaf in his mouth.	
11		Leans forward so that his
12		forearms rest on the ground
13		lowering forequarters so
14		that chin comes to rest near
15		the backs of his hands. Looks
16		fixedly at A's face (crouch-
17		stare).

Figure 3.1

	A	B
18	Drops leaf from mouth, walks	
19	toward B, looking at B's face,	
20	play-face when about 1½ feet	
21	away.	
22		Play-face.
23	Reaches with right hand	
24	toward top of B's head.	
25		Raises forequarters by pres-
26		sing against ground with his
27		hands. Reaches toward A with
28		left hand.

Figure 3.2

Grasps A's chest and rears to bipedal position. (B's rear and reach have moved his head slightly to the right.)

Grasps B's left shoulder, instead of top of head where reach was aimed. Rears to bipedal position.

Pivots torso clockwise off left foot, stepping right with right foot and pulling A off balance in a clockwise direction. Several small bipedal steps as he pivots clockwise, about 270 degrees.

Figure 3.3

Takes large bipedal steps in direction he is being pulled, but falls, rolling onto his back with the momentum of the fall.

Stands bipedally anterior to A, leaning over him (on-top).

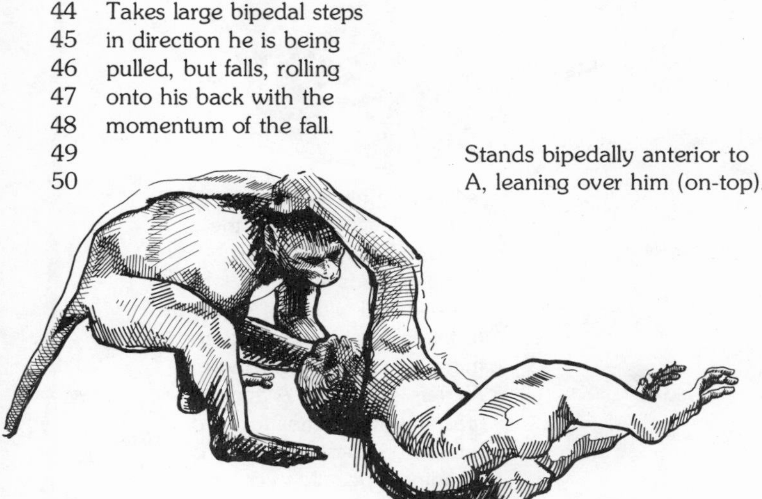

Figure 3.4

Figure 3.5

(Right hand has moved from B's shoulder to his head during the fall.) Right hand slips down, grasps B's right ear.

Turns head to right, bites A's right wrist.

Reaches back over head with left hand and grasps B's left side. (Now gripping B with both hands.) Pulls with both arms toward his own feet.

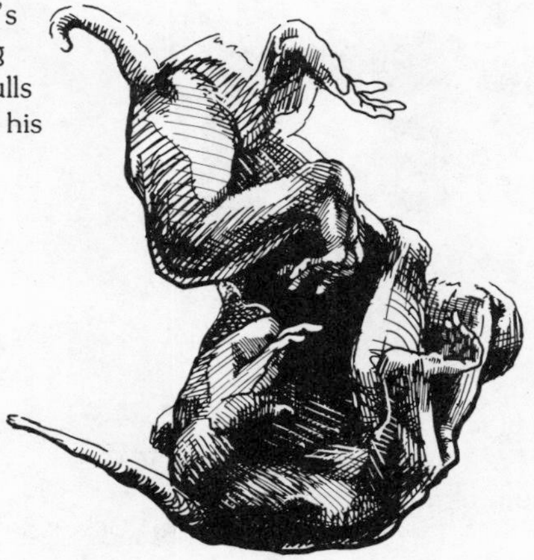

Figure 3.6

Is lifted off his feet and thrown, legs flying into the air. Briefly appears to be doing a headstand on A's belly. Legs spread wide. As he begins to fall, twists hindquarters so that his feet fall to ground to A's left, still facing A and grasping him. Leans forward, bites A on chest, once more standing bipedally over him (*on-top*). Takes two small steps for balance.

Rolls to left toward B, lies on left side, moving upper right arm between his chest and B's teeth. Makes uncompleted grasp with right hand at B's left shoulder.

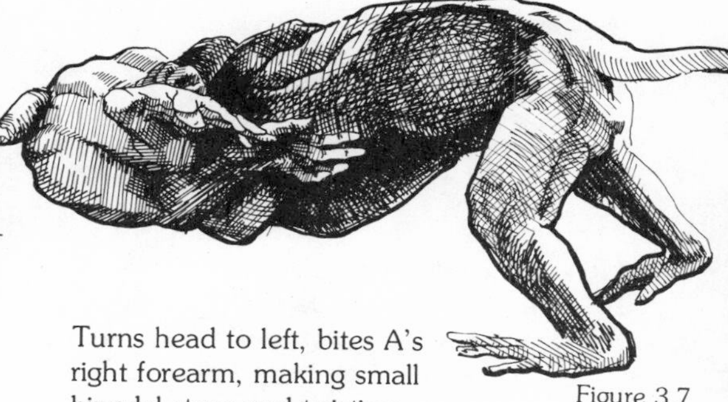

Turns head to left, bites A's right forearm, making small bipedal steps and twisting torso in response to A's movements.

Figure 3.7

Figure 3.8

(Inferred, movement hidden: pushes against ground with left hand.) Body rises from ground, twists hindquarters left and plants feet on ground, right side facing B.

Turns head to right, bites A's right shoulder. Continues to bite, raising, then lowering hindquarters with extension, then flexion of legs, in response to A's movement.

Figure 3.9

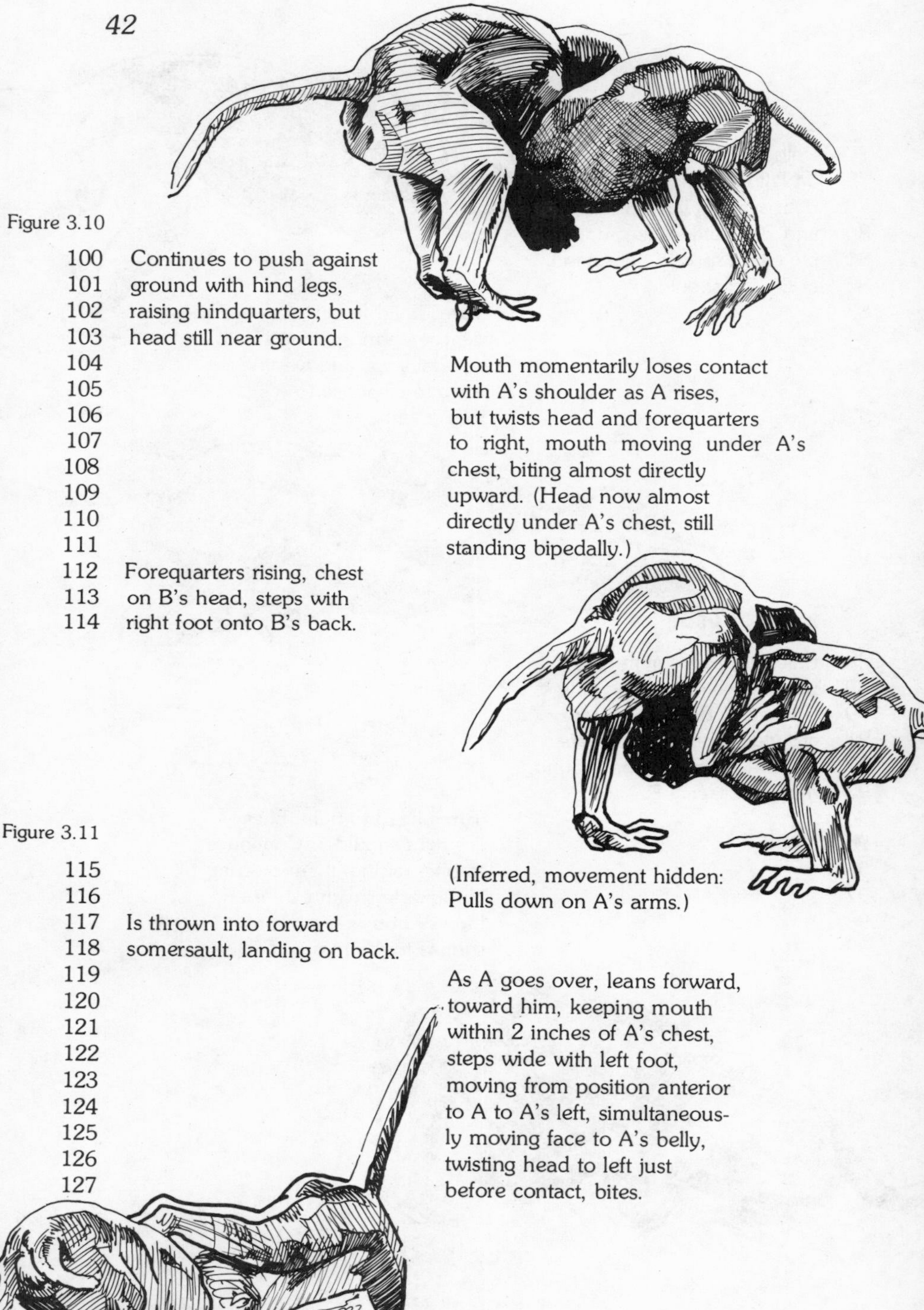

Figure 3.10

100 Continues to push against
101 ground with hind legs,
102 raising hindquarters, but
103 head still near ground.
104
105
106
107
108
109
110
111
112 Forequarters rising, chest
113 on B's head, steps with
114 right foot onto B's back.

Mouth momentarily loses contact with A's shoulder as A rises, but twists head and forequarters to right, mouth moving under A's chest, biting almost directly upward. (Head now almost directly under A's chest, still standing bipedally.)

Figure 3.11

115
116
117 Is thrown into forward
118 somersault, landing on back.
119
120
121
122
123
124
125
126
127

(Inferred, movement hidden: Pulls down on A's arms.)

As A goes over, leans forward, toward him, keeping mouth within 2 inches of A's chest, steps wide with left foot, moving from position anterior to A to A's left, simultaneously moving face to A's belly, twisting head to left just before contact, bites.

Figure 3.12

Figure 3.13

Pushes against ground with left hand, raising and twisting forequarters to the left, facing B. Now in a semi-sitting position. (Apparently used momentum of somersault to sit.) Bites B on B's left side, pushes against ground with hind legs, rising to a quadrupedal standing position.

Steps with right hind foot to A's left, now on left side of A, breaking A's bite. (Both monkeys now facing in same direction.) Throws right arm across A's back, grasps hair on A's right side and bites A on back of neck.

Figure 3.14

Figure 3.15

Pushes against ground with both hands and leans back, pivoting to right away from B and falling backward into a sitting position, wide play-face, arms waving.

Left hand moves to ground to prevent falling backward.

Leans backward, away from A, standing bipedally, wide play-face, steps backward bipedally and sits about 1 ½ feet from A. Looks to right, into mangroves.

Looks to left, into mangroves.

Notes to Example A

1. Playfighting is invited by crouching and staring at partner (B:11–17). Partner approaches, so invitation is successful (A:18–19).
2. Monkeys often look at partner's face at beginning of interaction (B:15–17; A:19).
3. Play-faces given at beginning of interaction (A:20–21; B:22).
4. Monkeys rear to bipedal position to facilitate reaching, grasping, and mobility (A:23–36; B:25–30).
5. Grappling monkeys move to throw partner (B:37–43, 115–16; A:58–63).
6. Momentum is utilized, both own (A:46–48, 133–34) and partner's (B:37–43).
7. Monkey pulled off-balance steps in direction of pull (A:44–46).
8. Thrown monkey rolls onto back to face partner (A:46–48). In general, monkeys move to face partner (B:41–43, 68–72; A:77–78, 128–34).
9. Older, but slightly smaller, monkey (B) scores two on-tops (B:50, 74–75) and is on-top for most of the interaction.
10. Bites are mostly made by on-top monkey (B:56–57, 73, 83–84, 94–95, 108–9, 125–27, 145–46).
11. Monkey bites limb which grasps him or moves toward him (B:56–57, 83–84).
12. On-top monkey moves to bite on-bottom monkey's ventral surface from the side rather than moving over on-bottom's face (119–24).
13. On-bottom monkey attempts to rise (A:88–93, 128–31).
14. Limb moved between partner's teeth and own body (A:78–80).
15. Monkey biting ventral surface of partner moves to keep face close to, or touching this surface if partner moves (B:94–99, 104–11, 119–26).
16. Rotation in a transverse plane is used to bite partner's ventral surface or to keep mouth in contact with partner's ventral surface if it moves (B:104–11, 125–27).
17. Monkey assuming a quadrupedal position during playfighting is held to prevent turning and bitten on the back of the neck (B:143–46).
18. Interaction terminated without fleeing (147–62).

mangroves, a variety of terrains—mangrove edge, trees, shrubs, and open ground—were available as settings for play; and during play, monkeys frequently moved from one type of terrain to another.

In general, playfighting and playchasing could only be imperfectly observed when they occurred in heavy cover, and individuals often could not be identified. I have not attempted to quantify the relative frequencies of play in terrain of various types, but because I observed thousands of play interactions at least partially, the variation of play with terrain can be described accurately.

Trees. As C Group spent most of its time near feeding stations, especially numbers 2 and 6 (fig. 2.1), play regularly occurred in mangrove trees and inland trees near feeders, primarily *Plumeria alba* and *Zysiphus jujuba* near station 6 and *Exostema caribaeum* and *Culubrina reclinata* near station 2. These trees generally are less than 30 feet high and are thickly branched with relatively small-diameter branches suitable for grasping by rhesus hands and feet. The only

Photo 3.22 *Infants playchasing. Note play-face given by infant below branch.*

Photo 3.23 *Leaping during juvenile-1 play.*

large tree in these locations was a hucar (scientific name unknown) directly east of station 6 which had widely spaced branches, and no branches at all within ten feet of the ground. Monkeys of all ages sat, groomed, and occasionally copulated in the hucar, but never played there. Were a monkey to have fallen while playing in this tree it would have had little chance of catching a branch before it hit the ground. Not surprisingly, monkeys also did not play on cactus, although sometimes they ate it. With these two exceptions, juvenile monkeys played throughout their habitat, while infants playfought mainly in parts of the habitat within five feet of the ground, although sometimes they playchased and engaged in solitary locomotor play in higher branches (photo 3.22).

In trees, much social play consisted of chases and leaps (up to 10–15 feet) toward or away from another monkey (photo 3.23). During these interactions monkeys were alert to their partner's preparatory jumping movements, and a monkey being leaped at usually jumped,

Photo 3.24 *Juvenile-1s grappling approximately fifteen feet above the ground.*

Photo 3.25 *Juvenile-1s grappling.*

Photo 3.26 (above) *Juvenile-1s grappling.*

Photo 3.27 (left) *Juvenile-1s grappling.*

Photo 3.28 (right) *Juvenile-2 about to dislodge juvenile-1.*

or dropped, to a lower branch before the leaper reached it. Since most trees were thick with foliage, usually it was not possible to follow a single interaction closely or to record meaningful quantitative data. Monkeys appeared on the exterior of a tree during a chase only to disappear into the foliage as the chaser appeared.

Monkeys could playfight sitting, or even lying, on top of a maze of branches that provided extensive horizontal support, but on a single branch, playfighting monkeys tended to fall under the branch, grasping it with their feet and using their hands to grapple (photo 3.24); but sometimes the reverse was true, and almost all possible combinations of grasping branches and play partners were seen (photos 3.25, 3.26, 3.27, F5). Monkeys playfighting in trees clearly attempted to dislodge each other (photo 3.28, F7) and to cause the partner to fall. Falling monkeys twisted to fall feet first and, when falling within the tree, reached out and grasped branches, either breaking or arresting their fall. Groups of juveniles sometimes playfought in terminal branches eight to twelve feet above the ground, pulling each other off, dropping to the ground, and running back up the tree. In these situations a good deal of the falling appeared to be intentional: that is, a monkey would drop from the branch after a minimal amount of playfighting or even at the mere approach of a second monkey. Sometimes a monkey dangling by its hands or feet from a branch appeared to wait for a second to approach before dropping to the ground. Only twice during the study were monkeys observed to playfight in trees so vigorously that they continued playfighting during the fall and hit the ground playfighting. In both instances the animals were juvenile males, one pair falling from about eight feet, the other from about ten feet. In the latter case the animals continued to playfight after landing; in the former the dominant juvenile (G2) threatened the subordinate, (I7), terminating the play. Juveniles, usually males, sometimes playfought 25 or 30 feet high in the mangrove interior, falling frequently, catching a branch, and climbing back to playfight again.

The infant equivalent of juvenile tree-play occurred on the mangrove edge (discussed below) and on thick, low shrubs covered with caro vine. Groups of infants moved and playfought on the surface of these shrubs, falling and catching terminal twigs and leaves, sometimes falling three or four feet to the ground, but always breaking their fall by grasping the surface of the shrub and by sliding down it.

Photo 3.29 *Infant falling during mangrove edge play.*

Photo 3.30 *Infant leaping to ground during mangrove edge play.*

Mangrove Edge. The inland border of mangrove was a favorite play location. Along the southwestern edge of La Cueva, from station 2 to station 6, mangrove branches grew six to twelve feet inland over bare ground, providing a rich play arena.

Certain specific places along the mangrove edge were especially popular play spots for infants. Each of these "special" places was a confluence of bare mangrove branches three to four feet from the ground which provided a fairly stable perch and handholds for several infants simultaneously and was low enough so that falling (photo 3.29) and leaping (photo 3.30) were not dangerous. These branches became a focus for play, monkeys converging there by climbing through the mangrove or by leaping and climbing up from the ground. Almost invariably, infants initiated this type of play, although juveniles sometimes joined in. As noted above, playfighting monkeys dangling below a branch attempted to dislodge each other from the branch. If one

Photo 3.31 *Juvenile-1 leaps at infant.*

Photo 3.32 *Juvenile-2 pulls juvenile-2 from low mangrove branch.*

monkey fell, its partner sometimes was able to scramble back to the branch, there to engage a new partner, pulling the new partner from the branch, or being itself displaced. Sometimes two playfighting infants attracted others, resulting in a small clump of dangling, grappling infants.

Monkeys sitting in these favored play branches, or hanging under them, provided a target for monkeys on the ground. An infant on the ground might leap repeatedly and unsuccessfully at another infant hanging from a branch only to have a juvenile come by, leap, grasp the dangling infant, and bring it to the ground (photo 3.31). Juveniles also leaped and pulled each other from low branches (photo 3.32).

When a monkey on the ground leaped at a second on a branch, the latter often immediately fell or leaped from the branch without actually being pulled. If the leaper then climbed onto the branch, the result was a rapid reversal of positions. If two infants hung from a branch grappling, a juvenile might leap, pull one off, then leap again to dislodge the second. Infants repeatedly initiated play with any juvenile arriving at a bare-branch play spot during an infant play episode. Once a two-year-old male (G2) was a target for six or seven infants who leaped on him, some falling to the ground and scampering back up, until the juvenile finally was dislodged and fell to the ground amidst a shower of infants.

Juveniles playing on the mangrove edge tended to chase and leap more than infants did, and juveniles rarely confined their play to a single spot. Typically a juvenile came out on a branch three or four feet above the ground and leaped off, usually at another juvenile on the ground. If a hit was scored, playfighting often ensued, but usually the monkey on the ground already was running into, rarely away from, the mangroves, and the leaper became a chaser. The direction of chases was into (photo 3.33) and then up the mangrove, the chasee then leaping off and running in again. Chaser and chasee roles often reversed. Juveniles also leaped at other juveniles on mangrove branches, the leapee usually jumping to the ground, or to another branch, before it was hit.

Shrubs and Stumps. A favorite play location was one that provided opportunities for different kinds of play. This was true of stumps and low shrubs with sparse foliage (especially *Brumelia krugii*) on bare ground, or ground covered only with grass or other low cover, if the shrub had enough open space beneath its foliage to accommodate monkeys. In these locations monkeys (1) playfought on the bare ground, (2) chased or playfought in the shrub, (3) displaced each other in the shrub or stump, and (4) chased around the trunk or up and down the shrub.

B. krugii was especially common north of feeding station 2 and there was a favorite stump in the station 2 clearing. When monkeys, playing on the mangrove edge, ran away from the mangrove instead of into it, they usually ran to one of these shrubs or stumps. Play was so frequent at several shrubs and stumps that they were circled by depressions, worn by the feet of playchasing immature rhesus monkeys (photo 3.34).

Photo 3.33 *Juvenile-1 turns into mangrove during a play-chase.*

Photo 3.34 *Juvenile-1's playchase around shrub.*

Male-male playchases around a shrub or stump sometimes were so fast-paced that the animals churned up dust as they struggled to stay in a circle three or four feet in diameter, and they sometimes grasped the trunk with their inside hands in order to keep to their circular paths. Playchases around shrubs or stumps often were quite slow, however, especially in female-female play. This was the only situation in which an extended playchase was conducted at a walk instead of a run.

The top of a stump was a focus for displacements, monkey A leaping onto the stump and monkey B leaping off or being pushed or wrestled off. Sometimes a monkey on the ground reared and pulled another off the stump. Low shrubs were similarly used, but were better avenues of escape from playfighting than a stump was. A good deal of the play under shrubs had the up-and-down character of play described above for the mangrove edge. Monkeys sometimes hung from a low shrub and dropped onto a pair of playfighting monkeys on the ground below, or leaped from the shrub onto a monkey on the ground. Such shrubs were too small to permit much sustained playfighting in their foliage, so that when A chased B up a shrub B usually leaped to the ground or ran to a terminal branch and rode it to the ground.

Grass. Crouching and freezing (remaining motionless) was a behavior pattern seen only in two situations: playchasing and as an occasional response to approach by humans (chapter 5). Freezing occurred during playchasing when animals played in terrain with enough ground cover to hide a small monkey flattened to the ground. In the following examples taken from field notes a single instance of freezing was incorporated into ordinary playchasing.

> November 6, 7:52 A.M., station 2. [17 has been chasing G6 in and out of the mangrove edge.] G6 appears at the edge of the mangrove about a foot above the ground, drops to the ground, partly concealed by mangrove leaves, crouches and freezes, looking up. About one second later I7 appears in the same spot that G6 appeared. I7 looks to the right and left, then looks down, sees G6, jumps at him, but G6 anticipates and has run into the mangrove.

In the following example, freezing successfully conceals the monkey:

> February 17, 5:30 P.M., station 6. G7 chases L2 down the trail, L2 darts off the trail into grass, crouches and freezes. G7 runs by.

In high grass, playchases consistently followed a crouch-freeze-chase pattern, although this behavior was seen occasionally in other terrain, such as low mangrove branches or scrubby grass. I observed play in high grass on only two occasions during the study, for a total of approximately two hours. One location was north of feeding station 3, the other the relatively barren, grass-covered southeastern end of La Cueva, both locations occupied infrequently by C Group. That high grass was not found in the areas C Group frequented probably explains the rarity of crouch-freeze-chase play.

The most intense instance of such play occurred November 25, 1969, at 5:22 P.M., behind feeding station 3. Almost every juvenile in C Group was involved, but observation was difficult because, unless they were very close, the monkeys were invisible in the three- to four-feet-high grass which grew in large clumps, creating a complex network of trails. Monkeys chased each other down these trails, one suddenly crouching and freezing, apparently remaining motionless until discovered or until seeing another monkey, and then chasing or being chased. Although it was not possible to be certain, there seemed to be virtually no playfighting, the pattern consisting of run, crouch-freeze, wait, and run. It was possible to follow some of the activity by watching the movement of grass as the monkeys ran through it, and the sudden cessation of grass movement when a monkey froze.

Water. The only bodies of water in which monkeys were seen to play were shallow salt-water pools completely enclosed by mangrove on the northern end of La Cueva. These pools were no more than 3 to 4 feet deep in the center, and at the periphery were shallow enough to permit wading. As with high grass, C Group spent very little time in the areas in which these pools were to be found, and this probably accounts for the rarity of play in the water.

Water activity began slowly and gradually increased in tempo. Initial entry into the pool was tentative, as juveniles slipped in from mangrove roots, swam or waded slowly, and then climbed out. Wading was generally quadrupedal, but on one occasion a juvenile female waded bipedally. Other monkeys sat on the edge of the pool and splashed the water with their hands, sometimes eating small objects they found in the water. Occasionally a monkey sat on the edge of a pool pulling out dirt, twigs, and leaves, smelling and then discarding them.

Climbing in from mangrove roots soon gave way to jumping, first from the roots and then from progressively higher branches. The only animals seen to jump were juveniles, and the only jumps of more than about ten feet were made by older juveniles—especially, but not exclusively, males—who sometimes jumped from as high as twenty feet. Jumping was strongly socially facilitated: as I approached a pool where juvenile monkeys were leaping and swimming frequently I heard staccato bursts of splashes interspersed with silence. Instead of leaping, monkeys sometimes hung by their hands or feet from a branch, and then dropped into the water. Monkeys usually leaped with limbs flailing but, even during rarely observed flips, twisted to land on all four feet.

Frequently a juvenile aimed its jumps at or near another juvenile who was swimming in the water, and occasionally scored a direct hit, pushing the swimmer under the water. Sometimes both monkeys disappeared beneath the surface and reappeared in a few seconds separated by several feet. In one case a three-year-old female (CO) sat on a branch watching a one-year-old female (L2) swimming across the pool in her direction. When L2 was directly below, CO leaped, scoring a direct hit and pushing L2 under the water; when L2 surfaced CO continued to cling to her back for a few seconds.

Monkeys swam both on and under the surface. Frequently a monkey jumped into a pool, disappeared beneath the surface, and reappeared perhaps twenty feet away on the other side, climbing out on a mangrove root. Swimming often was oriented to another swimming monkey. When one monkey swam toward a second, sometimes one or the other ducked under the surface just before contact would have been made and swam away under water. Occasionally monkey A would be seen swimming toward B; then, while still several feet from B, A would disappear under the surface and a few seconds later monkey B would suddenly disappear, suggesting that B may have been jerked under by A. Both monkeys would then reappear on the surface separated by several feet. Monkeys sometimes swam together, as well as toward and away from each other. Occasionally one monkey would reach and grasp a second, but nothing like real playfighting was seen among monkeys in the water.

Monkeys usually sat and rested between periods of swimming, often watching the monkeys in the water, but playfights and playchases did occur in the mangroves surrounding the pool. Sometimes the water was merely one more kind of terrain for playchasing, the monkeys bounding, high-stepping through the shallows, or, rarely, swimming. A branch at the edge of the pool sometimes became the focus for a series of displacements, as one monkey climbing toward the branch triggered a leap into the water by a second monkey on the branch, the displacer then being itself displaced by a third monkey.

Adults swam occasionally, but they did not leap into the water. They lowered themselves in, usually being careful to keep their heads out of the water. (An adult female once was observed to swim under water after she was already in.) Adults did not orient their swimming with respect to other animals, but paddled around quietly and then climbed out. They did not spend more than a minute or so in the water, and, once out, did not usually go back in. Adult females were seen swimming with infants clinging to their backs.

Chapter four

Aggressive Play in C Group

Play among Central Infants and Juveniles

Playfights (but not playchases) infrequently involved more than two animals simultaneously. When two monkeys playfought and a third or fourth leaped on them the play usually terminated quickly, or a new dyad formed.[1] When monkeys formed playgroups—which is to say, when they played in proximity and exchanged partners frequently—playfights nonetheless were generally dyadic. This section reports some quantitative aspects of these dyadic interactions among C Group's central infants and juveniles. Play involving peripheral males, adults, and members of other social groups is reported below, in separate sections.

Distribution of Playfights and Playchases

A playfight was considered to begin when the monkeys made contact and to end when they broke contact and any other activity, such as sitting, occurred. A playchase ended when one or both monkeys stopped or broke off the chase. Often I could not see the end of a playchase because the monkeys ran to cover. If, in a playchase, the chaser caught the chasee and a playfight ensued, or if a playfight resulted in a playchase, two interactions between that pair of monkeys (a playfight and a playchase) were recorded.

Tables 4.1. and 4.2 show the distribution among age-sex classes of 2194 playfights and 657 playchases respectively. As noted in chapter

1. A monkey joining an ongoing playfight in which there is an on-top/on-bottom relationship usually playattacks the on-bottom monkey.

Table 4.1 Playfights among Central Infants and Juveniles

	Infant			Juvenile-1		Juvenile-2	
	Sex Unknown	Male	Female	Male	Female	Male	Female
Sex Unknown	56	6	0	50	48	5	14
Infant							
Male		211	72	137	164	11	11
Female			22	7	35	0	2
Juvenile-1:							
Male				397	487	53	56
Female					205	10	85
Juvenile-2:							
Male						—	36
Female							14
Total = 2194							

2, the greater frequency of observations of playfights probably reflects the greater visibility of playfighting and not a greater frequency of occurrence. These tables include interactions involving infants whose sex was not known.

Some age-sex classes were seen to play together frequently, others very infrequently. This could, however, be a function of differing numbers of monkeys in age-sex classes. To investigate this possibility, table 4.3 shows the total participation (total participations equal twice the total number of interactions) for each age-sex class. For the purposes of this table the "infant" class is distributed between "male in-

Table 4.2 Playchases among Central Infants and Juveniles

	Infant			Juvenile-1		Juvenile-2	
	Sex Unknown	Male	Female	Male	Female	Male	Female
Sex Unknown	3	0	0	22	9	1	1
Infant							
Male		30	5	55	33	2	1
Female			2	2	9	0	0
Juvenile-1:							
Male				127	157	17	26
Female					96	1	43
Juvenile-2:							
Male						—	10
Female							5
Total = 657							

Table 4.3 Participation in Playfights and Playchases of Central Infants and Juveniles

Class	N	Observed Participation	Expected Participation	$(0-E)^2/E$	Mean	Sex Ratio of Means
			Playfighting			
Infant Male	11	1020	1237.6	38.3	93	3.3/1 (Infants)
Infant Female	7	198	787.6	441.4	28	
Juv. 1 Male	5	1584	562.6	1854.4	317	2.6/1 (Juv. 1s)
Juv. 1 Female	10	1239	1125.1	11.5	124	
Juv. 2 Male	1	115	112.5	.1	115	2.5/1 (Juv. 2s)
Juv. 2 Female	5	232	562.6	194.3	46	
Total	39	4388	4388.0	$\chi^2=2540.0$	113	2.7/1
			Playchasing			
Infant Male	11	191	370.6	87.0	17.4	5.1/1 (Infants)
Infant Female	7	24	235.8	190.2	3.4	
Juv. 1 Male	5	533	168.5	788.5	106.6	2.4/1 (Juv. 1s)
Juv. 1 Female	10	444	336.9	34.1	44.4	
Juv. 2 Male	1	31	33.7	.2	31.0	1.7/1 (Juv. 2s)
Juv. 2 Female	5	91	168.5	35.7	18.2	
Total	39	1314	1314.0	$\chi^2=1135.7$	33.7	2.4/1

χ^2 (playfighting) = 2540.0, (playchasing) = 1135.7 (d.f. = 5), p's < .001.

fant" and "female infant" in the same proportion that these classes were seen to play (i.e., it assumes that unidentified infants were seen in the same sex ratio as infants whose sex was known). Table 4.3 also shows the number of monkeys in each class, the sex ratio of average play participations for infants, juvenile-1s, and juvenile-2s, and expected participations if participation in play for a class is simply a function of the number of animals in that class. A χ^2 of 2540 for playfighting and of 1136 for playchasing (df = 5) suggest that this hypothesis can be rejected. Males play about 2.5 times as frequently as females, and juvenile-1s are much more playful than infants and juvenile-2s. The most playful class by far is the juvenile-1 male. These conclusions are the same for playfighting and playchasing. The male-female difference actually is greater than table 4.3 indicates since, as described below, males also play with peripheral males and males from other groups, and females do not.

One also may inquire whether monkeys "distribute" their play randomly: that is, does a class of monkey play with other classes only on the basis of the degree of playfulness of the classes involved, or is there selection or rejection between classes? Tables 4.4 and 4.5 inves-

Table 4.4 Playfights among Central Infants and Juveniles (Infants Lumped, Expected Values in Parentheses)

	Infant	Juvenile-1 Male	Juvenile-1 Female	Juvenile-2 Male	Juvenile-2 Female
Infant	367 (169.0)	194 (439.7)	247 (343.9)	16 (31.9)	27 (64.4)
Juvenile-1:					
Male		397 (285.9)	487 (447.3)	53 (41.5)	56 (83.7)
Female			205 (174.9)	10 (32.5)	85 (65.5)
Juvenile-2:					
Male				—	36 (6.1)
Female					14 (6.1)

Total Observed = 2194
Total Expected = 2192.4

tigate this question for playfights and playchases respectively. (Infants are lumped into one class because of the existence of unidentified infants and because of the small amount of female infant play. No juvenile-2 male vs. juvenile-2 male interactions were possible because only one central male (C4) existed in this class.) Each cell shows the observed (0) number of play interactions between a pair of age-sex classes and the expected (E) number (parenthetically) if play occurs between classes only on the basis of degree of playfulness of the class,

Table 4.5 Playchases among Central Infants and Juveniles (Infants Lumped, Expected Values in Parentheses)

	Infant	Juvenile-1 Male	Juvenile-1 Female	Juvenile-2 Male	Juvenile-2 Female
Infant	40 (17.6)	79 (87.2)	51 (72.7)	3 (5.1)	2 (14.9)
Juvenile-1:					
Male		127 (108.1)	157 (180.1)	17 (12.6)	26 (36.9)
Female			96 (75.0)	1 (10.5)	43 (30.8)
Juvenile-2:					
Male				—	10 (2.2)
Female					5 (3.2)

Total Observed = 657
Total Expected = 656.9

Table 4.6 Playfights among Central Juveniles (Expected Values in Parentheses)

	Juvenile-1		Juvenile-2	
	Male	Female	Male	Female
Juvenile-1:				
Male	397 (359.7)	487 (513.4)	53 (51.2)	56 (106.1)
Female		205 (183.2)	10 (36.6)	85 (75.7)
Juvenile-2:				
Male			—	36 (7.6)
Female				14 (7.8)

$\chi^2 = 150.5$ (d.f. = 8), $p < .001$.
Total Observed = 1343
Total Expected = 1341.3

Table 4.7 Playchases among Central Juveniles (Expected Values in Parentheses)

	Juvenile-1		Juvenile-2	
	Male	Female	Male	Female
Juvenile-1:				
Male	127 (106.9)	157 (185.1)	17 (13.2)	26 (41.9)
Female		96 (80.1)	1 (11.4)	43 (36.3)
Juvenile-2:				
Male			—	10 (2.6)
Female				5 (4.1)

$\chi^2 = 50.4$ (d.f. = 8), $p < .001$
Total Observed = 482
Total Expected = 481.6

and there is no selection or rejection (appendix 2 shows the calculation of E).

Infants tended to play much more frequently with each other than expected and much less frequently than expected with other classes. Infants preferred other infants (or were rejected by juveniles) so consistently, and they played so frequently, that expected values for noninfant interactions might be deflated for these reasons alone. Therefore expected values are recalculated (tables 4.6 and 4.7) to include juvenile play only. The results are similar for both playfights and playchases and may be summarized briefly: (1) each class of monkey plays more frequently than expected within itself; (2) males play more frequently than expected with males of all ages; (3) females play more frequently than expected with females of all ages; (4) juvenile-2s of both sexes play more frequently than expected with other juvenile-2s.

Initiation of Playfights

Sometimes it was possible to determine the initiator (approacher) of a playfight. These data are summarized in table 4.8 for 1222 initiations. (Infant-infant initiations usually were not recorded because most

Table 4.8 Initiation of Playfights among Central Infants and Juveniles

	Initiator				
		Juvenile-1		Juvenile-2	
	Infant	Male	Female	Male	Female
Initiatee					
Infant	—	90	101	3	9
Juvenile-1:					
Male	61	283	161	29	11
Female	67	162	133	2	25
Juvenile-2:					
Male	8	7	3	—	9
Female	3	15	25	10	5
Total = 1222					

infants were not recognized individually, and therefore infant-infant initiations are not shown.) This table suggests that infants initiate play with juveniles less frequently than juveniles initiate play with infants.

Table 4.9 shows the data for juveniles only and expected values based on the null hypothesis that initiations are simply a result of number of monkeys in a class (χ^2 is not calculated for it would simply reflect what already is known: some classes of monkey play more frequently, and therefore initiate more frequently, than others.) Table 4.9 is remarkable for its symmetry. Most juvenile age-sex class pairs initiated playfighting with each other at about the same frequency, whether the total amount of initiation between them was high or low. The only exception is the relationship between juvenile-1 males and the juvenile-2 male, C4. Although these classes played together more frequently than expected, C4 initiated more frequently, and the

Table 4.9 Initiation of Playfights among Central Juveniles (Expected Values in Parentheses)

	Initiator			
	Juvenile-1		Juvenile-2	
	Male	Female	Male	Female
Initiatee				
Juvenile-1:				
Male	283 (247.8)	161 (170.9)	29 (21.8)	11 (26.5)
Female	162 (170.9)	133 (117.8)	2 (15.0)	25 (18.3)
Juvenile-2:				
Male	7 (21.8)	3 (15.0)	—	9 (2.3)
Female	15 (26.5)	25 (18.3)	10 (2.3)	5 (2.8)

Total Observed = 880
Total Expected = 878.0

younger males initiated much less frequently, than expected. Table 4.10 summarizes the frequency of juvenile initiation of playfights. Clearly initiation of playfights follows a pattern similar to that of play itself: males initiate more frequently than females and juvenile-1s initiate more frequently than juvenile-2s.

Monkeys sometimes refused attempted play initiation: that is, a monkey ignored or moved away from another monkey who made a playful approach or contact. Table 4.11 shows these data, along with the number of successful initiations observed between the classes of monkey. The numbers in most cells are too small to permit calculation of a meaningful χ^2. Therefore table 4.12 examines the refusal relationship only among the large-sample classes, juvenile-1 males and females: "O" is the number of refusals observed and "E" is the number expected if refusals are simply a function of number of initiation attempts. $\chi^2 = 18.6$ (df = 3), $p < .001$: males refuse fewer, and females refuse more, initiations than expected, and females are especially likely to reject initiation attempts by other females.

Termination of Playfights

Although I assume that most playfights do not end because of a simultaneous mutual decision, in the field it is usually not possible to be certain which monkey is responsible for termination of a playfight.

Table 4.10 Frequency of Initiation of Playfights among Central Juveniles

Class	N	No. of Initiations	Mean	Sex Ratio of Means
Juv. 1 Male	5	545	109.0	3.1/1 (Juv. 1s)
Juv. 1 Female	11	389	35.4	
Juv. 2 Male	1	27	27.0	2.3/1 (Juv. 2s)
Juv. 2 Female	5	58	11.6	
Total	22	1019	83.2	2.7/1

Table 4.11 Refusal of Attempted Play Initiation among Central Infants and Juveniles (Number of Successful Initiations in Parentheses)

	Initiator				
		Juvenile-1		Juvenile-2	
Refuser	Infant	Male	Female	Male	Female
Infant	—	7 (90)	6 (101)	0 (3)	1 (9)
Juvenile-1: Male	1 (61)	32 (283)	11 (161)	3 (29)	0 (11)
Juvenile-1: Female	9 (67)	29 (162)	37 (133)	0 (2)	3 (25)
Juvenile-2: Male	0 (8)	0 (7)	0 (3)	—	0 (9)
Juvenile-2: Female	0 (3)	5 (15)	6 (25)	0 (10)	1 (5)

Total Refusals = 151

Table 4.12 Refusal of Attempted Play Initiation among Central Juvenile-1s (Expected Values in Parentheses)

	Initiator	
Refuser	Male	Female
Male	32 (40.6)	11 (22.1)
Female	29 (24.5)	37 (21.9)

$\chi^2 = 18.6$ (d.f. = 3), $p < .001$.
Total Observed = 109
Total Expected = 109.1

Table 4.13 Termination of Playfights by Fleeing among Central Infants and Juveniles

	Terminator				
		Juvenile-1		Juvenile-2	
Partner	Infant	Male	Female	Male	Female
Infant	—	5	6	0	0
Juvenile-1:					
Male	23	40	42	1	4
Female	42	19	31	0	10
Juvenile-2:					
Male	0	8	2	—	3
Female	8	8	8	0	1
Total = 261					

Often the monkeys simply stop playing and sit. Sometimes, however, one monkey flees from the playfight. Table 4.13 summarizes data on fleeing (infant-infant terminations were not systematically recorded). Clearly infants are far more likely to flee from playfights with juveniles than juveniles are to flee from infants. Since the observed values in some cells are too small to permit calculation of a meaningful χ^2 on the entire matrix, table 4.14 shows the data on termination only for juvenile-1 males and females. Expected values were obtained from the total number of playfights recorded between each class, based on the null hypothesis that the amount of playfighting is the only factor determining the number of terminations by fleeing, and that males and females are equally likely to flee. $\chi^2 = 11.99$ (df = 2), $p < .004$: females flee from playfights more frequently, and males less frequently, than expected regardless of the partner's sex.

Table 4.14 Termination of Playfights by Fleeing among Central Juvenile-1s (Expected Values in Parentheses)

	Terminator	
Partner	Male	Female
Male	40 (48.2)	42 (29.5)
Female	19 (29.5)	31 (24.8)

$\chi^2 = 11.99$ (d.f. = 2), $p < .004$.
Total Observed = 132
Total Expected = 132.0

In summary, not only do females flee from playfights with females, as well as with males, more frequently than expected, but also they avoid more attempted initiations and they especially avoid other females. About 20 percent of observed juvenile female–juvenile female play initiation attempts failed because the potential partner refused to play.

Play Ending in Aggression

One possible explanation for female avoidance of play and fleeing from play is suggested by analysis of playfights that resulted in an agonistic interaction, either fighting or threatening. Playfights among central animals were observed to end in aggression only 19 times during the field study, less than 1 percent of all recorded playfights.

Table 4.15 Playfights of Central Juveniles that Ended in Aggression

	No. Obs. Playfights Between Classes	No. Obs. Playfights /1343	E = Column #2 × 19	0 = Interactions Ending in Aggression	$(E-0)^2/E$
Male vs. Male	450	.335	6.4	3	1.806
Male vs. Female	589	.439	8.3	6	.637
Female vs. Female	304	.226	4.3	10	7.556
Total	1343	1.000	19.0	19	9.999

$\chi^2 = 9.999$ (d.f. = 2), p = .007.

Table 4.15 shows these data for male-male, male-female, and female-female playfights. It includes only juveniles, because infant play never was observed to result in aggression. Expected values are based on the null hypothesis that playfights become agonistic in proportion to the number of playfights between the classes. $\chi^2 = 9.999$ (df = 2), $p = .007$: a playfight is more likely than expected to become agonistic if a female is involved and less likely if a male is involved.

Since male-male play is much more fast-paced and vigorous than female-female play, these results are surprising. They are, however, supported by the data above on the avoidance and fleeing of playfights and by my general impressions in the field. Juvenile females often seemed to avoid each other in subtle ways, difficult to quantify, although some cases were especially clear. For example, the small, one-year-old daughter (127–68) of C Group's alpha female (127) was the second-ranking immature monkey in C Group, outranked

Table 4.16 Participations of Individual Juvenile-1s in Playfights and Playchases

	Playfights		Playchases	
	Male	Female	Male	Female
	501(G2)		171(G2)	
	420(H1)		139(H4)	
	323(H4)			135(F7)
		299(F7)	91(G6)	
	237(G6)		86(H1)	
		171(G1)	75(I7)	
	139(I7)			52(G1)
		122(L6)		45(I4)
		113(I4)		39(L3)
		112(G7)		38(L6)
		102(L2)		38(G7)
		95(L3)		34(125-68)
		87(127-68)		33(L2)
		73(125-68)		22(127-68)
		65(J4)		19(J4)
Total	1620	1239	562	455
Mean	325.0	123.9	112.4	45.5
Standard Deviation	143.4	68.2	40.9	32.9
Coefficient of Variation	.44	.55	.36	.72

only by her older brother, C4. This yearling played very infrequently and other monkeys seemed to avoid her. Her older brother was the only juvenile observed to threaten her and she regularly exerted her dominance over other juveniles and infants. Of the thirteen playfights in which she participated (playfights with her brother excluded) in which I could determine which monkey initiated play, 127-68 initiated eleven times. Other females seemed reluctant to play with her.

Another suggestive line of evidence with respect to avoidance of play is the relative frequency of observed participations in playfights and playchases by individual juvenile-1s, summarized in table 4.16. Although, as discussed in chapter 2, there is reason to believe that age-sex classes of central infants and juveniles were equally likely to be observed, since sampling was not systematic, it cannot be assumed that *individuals* were equally likely to be observed, and this limits the interpretations of data on individuals. Nonetheless, these data suggest: (1) that the high frequency of juvenile male play relative to females is the result of frequent play by all males, and (2) that there is more variability in the frequency of play among females than among males. Furthermore, the male coefficient of variation probably is overestimated because the two-year-old male G6, and his one-year-old brother I7, almost certainly were observed less frequently than most other animals. The mother of these males was exceedingly shy of humans, and her sons to some extent shared this characteristic. If I had been able to sample rigorously, and observe each animal for the same amount of time, I suspect that all males would have been observed to play more frequently than all females, with the possible exception of the two-year-old female F7. F7's frequency of play was very high in large part because she played regularly with the smallest juvenile male, the two-year-old G2. As shown below, G2 was consistently bested in playfights with the other, larger males, and he may have preferred F7 as a play partner for this reason. One contribution to the large female coefficient of variation may be the reluctance of juveniles to engage in play with certain females who outrank them.

The data suggesting that males are unlikely to flee from playfights or refuse attempted play initiations may, in part, result from focusing on juvenile-1s. There are few data on interactions involving juvenile-2 central males because C4 was the only animal in this class, but most playfights between juvenile-1s and C4 were initiated by C4 and terminated by the younger animals. C4 played roughly, and on three occasions juvenile-1 males reacted fearfully to playful approaches by C4: the juveniles grimaced, raised the shoulder closest to C4, leaned away, and turned their heads away, as if preparing to flee. On two of these occasions, however, when C4 grasped the younger animals so that they could not flee, they responded with playfighting and not with crouching and screaming as they would have if C4 had attacked them. The most dramatic case of fearful response to attempted play initiation occurred between the largest juvenile-1 male, H1, and C4. C4 seemed especially rough with H1 and, as shown below, consistently outplay-fought H1. On one occasion H1 responded to C4's playbiting by screaming, grimacing, and finally by clinging to the belly of his three-year-old sister (C5), who was only slightly larger than H1 himself. C4's movements were relaxed, relatively slow, and clearly not preparatory to attack; and he made no threat gestures. Nonetheless, apparently he either hurt or frightened H1, and H1 did not respond playfully.

Duration of Playfights

The duration of 496 playfights was determined by stopwatch to within a few tenths of a second. A playfight was considered to begin with contact and to end when both monkeys stopped moving or when contact ended. (Momentary breaks in contact, as in leaping, during the playfight were ignored.) Playfights between juveniles and infants so frequently ended with the juvenile holding the infant that a meaningful duration could not be determined.

Table 4.17 Duration of 496 Playfights to the Nearest Second

Seconds	Infant-Infant (178 playf.)	Juv. Fem-Juv. Fem. (37 playf.)	Juv. Male-Juv. Fem. (128 playf.)	Juv. Male-Juv. Male (153 playf.)
0–5	61.8%	51.3%	48.6%	51.7%
6–10	25.3%	29.7%	23.4%	24.2%
11–15	7.3%	13.5%	13.3%	17.0%
16–20	4.5%	5.4%	6.3%	2.0%
21–25	1.1%		5.5%	3.3%
26–30			0.8%	0.7%
31–35			1.6%	
36–40				
41–45			0.8%	
46–50				0.7%
51–55				
56–60				0.7%
Total	100.0%	99.9% [a]	100.3% [a]	100.3% [a]

[a]Figures do not add up to 100 owing to rounding off of decimals.

Table 4.17 reveals little difference in duration of playfights among age-sex classes. The median duration of infant-infant playfights was almost exactly four seconds and the median duration for all juvenile-juvenile playfights was almost exactly five seconds. All juvenile-juvenile playfights of more than 19 seconds, however, involved at least one male.

Attainment of Advantageous Positions

As discussed in chapter 3, two positions stand out as advantageous for biting and not being bitten: on-top monkeys make about four times as many bites as do on-bottom partners. In the field I recorded the existence of an on-top or a behind only if these positions were achieved

Table 4.18 On-Top–On-Bottom Relationships in Central Juvenile Playfights (Expected Values in Parentheses)

	On-Top				
	Juvenile-1		Juvenile-2		Total
	Male	Female	Male	Female	
On Bottom					
Juvenile-1:					
Male	119 (90.6)	12 (55.6)	29 (6.1)	3 (6.5)	163 (158.8)
Female	87 (55.6)	27 (46.8)	4 (1.1)	7 (9.7)	125 (113.2)
Juvenile-2:					
Male	1 (6.1)	0 (1.1)	—	1 (4.2)	2 (11.4)
Female	10 (6.5)	0 (9.7)	6 (4.2)	0 (3.1)	16 (23.5)
Total	217 (158.8)	39 (113.2)	39 (11.4)	11 (23.5)	306 (306.9)

in the course of playfighting, not if they began the interaction. For example, if monkey A was lying on the ground and B approached and initiated play, B was not recorded as on-top. Similarly, if A was mounting B and fell forward and began to playbite the back of B's neck, A was not recorded as behind.

Table 4.18 summarizes the on-top/on-bottom relationships among the juvenile classes, and Table 4.19 does the same for behind/in-front relationships. In interactions between infants and juveniles, infants were on-top only if they were pulled there by a juvenile; no infant could wrestle to an on-top or behind position against a juvenile,

Table 4.19 Behind–In-Front Relationships in Central Juvenile Playfights

	Behind				
	Juvenile-1		Juvenile-2		Total
	Male	Female	Male	Female	
In Front					
Juvenile-1:					
Male	16	0	5	0	21
Female	41	5	0	0	46
Juvenile-2:					
Male	0	0	—	0	0
Female	0	1	2	1	4
Total	57	6	7	1	71

Table 4.20 On-Top—On-Bottom Relationships in Central Juvenile-1 Playfights (Expected Values in Parentheses)

	On-Top		
	Male	Female	Total
On Bottom			
Male	119 (89.4)	12 (54.8)	131 (144.2)
Female	87 (54.8)	27 (46.1)	114 (100.9)
Total	206 (144.2)	39 (100.9)	245 (245.1)

$\chi^2 = 70.0$ (d.f. $= 2$), $p < .001$.

and these data therefore were not recorded. Table 4.18 shows expected values based on the null hypothesis that the number of on-tops is simply a function of the number of playfights between or within age-sex classes, and that between any two classes the number of on-tops is equal. Some expected values are too small to permit a meaningful χ^2 to be calculated, but note that the juvenile-2 male C4 was on-top of juvenile-1 males 29 times and on-bottom only once.

Tables 4.20 and 4.21 consider the large-sample classes, juvenile-1 males and females. The results are similar for both on-tops and behinds, and may be summarized as follows: when males playfight with females the males are far more likely to achieve an on-top or behind

Table 4.21 Behind–In-Front Relationships in Central Juvenile-1 Playfights (Expected Values in Parentheses)

	Behind		
	Male	Female	Total
In Front			
Male	16 (22.6)	0 (13.9)	16 (36.5)
Female	41 (13.9)	5 (11.7)	46 (25.6)
Total	57 (36.5)	5 (25.6)	62 (62.1)

$\chi^2 = 72.4$ (d.f. $= 2$), $p < .001$.

position than the females are. In this sense males are superior to females at playfighting. Females achieve fewer than expected on-tops and behinds when playing with other females. This may be a quantitative expression of my strong impression that females are much less vigorous playfighters than males are and do not "try" so hard as males do; female-female play contains more passive holding than male-male play does.

Since playfighting monkeys attempt to face their partners (chapter 3), the behind position is much more difficult to attain than the on-top;

Table 4.22 Individual Juvenile Male On-Top–On-Bottom Relationships (Estimated Body Weight in Parentheses)

	On-Top						
	(6 lb.) G2	(7 lb.) G6	(7 lb.) H4	(7 lb.) I7	(9 lb.) H1	(12 lb.) C4	Total
On Bottom							
G2	—	19	11	2	18	3	53
G6	2	—	0	4	24	0	30
H4	0	1	—	0	11	0	12
I7	0	14	0	—	1	0	15
H1	1	5	6	0	—	26	38
C4	0	0	0	0	1	—	1
Total	3	39	17	6	55	29	149

306 on-tops and 71 behinds were observed, a ratio of 4.3/1. (For juvenile-1's only, 245 on-tops and 62 behinds were recorded, a ratio of 4.0/1.) This may explain why there are fewer male-male behinds than expected, and why in the entire study I did not observe a single instance of a female achieving a behind position during a playfight with a male.

To explore further the achievement of advantageous positions in playfighting, tables 4.22 to 4.27 summarize on-top and behind relationships among individual juveniles. Tables 4.22, 4.23, and 4.24 show on-tops for male-male, male-female, and female-female dyads respectively, and tables 4.25, 4.26, and 4.27 do the same for behinds. In these tables animals are listed in order of estimated body weight.[2] Weight is not completely dependent on age and sex; some older animals are smaller than younger ones, some females larger than same-aged males. These analyses by individual enrich the picture shown by class-analysis in the following ways:

2. Body weights estimated by Victor Bracero.

Table 4.23 Individual Juvenile Male vs. Individual Juvenile Female On-Top–On-Bottom Relationships (Estimated Body Weight in Parentheses)[a]

	Males						
	(6 lb.) G2	(7 lb.) G6	(7 lb.) H4	(7 lb.) I7	(9 lb.) H1	(12 lb.) C4	Total
Females							
(5 lb.)							
127–68						0/2	0/2
I4	0/3	0/2	3/11		0/1		3/17
L3			0/1	0/1		0/2	0/4
125–68			0/1				0/1
J4		0/1	1/7				1/8
(7 lb.)							
L6	1/4		0/1	0/1	0/2		1/8
L2	0/2						0/2
G7	0/1				0/4		0/5
F7	5/19		0/5		0/8		5/32
(8 lb.)							
D5					0/1	1/2	1/3
G1					2/12		2/12
(11 lb.)							
B7	1/0				1/0		2/0
D9							0/0
C5					0/9	0/4	0/13
C0					1/0		1/0
Total	7/29	0/3	4/26	0/2	4/37	1/10	16/107

[a] No. above slash indicates female on-top, no. below slash indicates male on-top.

Table 4.24 Individual Juvenile Female On-Top–On-Bottom Relationships (Estimated Body Weight in Parentheses)

	On-Top															
	(5 lb.)					(7 lb.)				(8 lb.)		(11 lb.)				
	127–68	I4	L3	125–68	J4	L6	L2	G7	F7	D5	G1	B7	D9	C5	C0	Total
On-Bottom																
127–68	—															0
I4		—							1							1
L3	1		—					1		2			1			5
125–68		2		—					3							5
J4					—							1				1
L6						—									2	2
L2							—	4			5	2				11
G7								—			6					6
F7						2			—						1	3
D5								1	1	—						2
G1											—					0
B7												—				0
D9													—			0
C5														—		0
C0															—	0
Total	1	2	0	0	0	2	0	6	5	2	11	3	1	0	3	36

Table 4.25 Individual Juvenile Male Behind–In-Front Relationships (Estimated Body Weight in Parentheses)

	Behind						
	(6 lb.) G2	(7 lb.) G6	(7 lb.) H4	(7 lb.) I7	(9 lb.) H1	(12 lb.) C4	Total
In Front							
G2	—	2	7		3		12
G6		—			1		1
H4			—				0
I7				—	1		1
H1			2		—	5	7
C4						—	0
Total	0	2	9	0	5	5	21

Table 4.26 Individual Juvenile Male vs. Individual Juvenile Female Behind–In-Front Relationships (Estimated Body Weight in Parentheses)[a]

	Males						
	(6 lb.) G2	(7 lb.) G6	(7 lb.) H4	(7 lb.) I7	(9 lb.) H1	(12 lb.) C4	Total
Females							
(5 lb.)							
125–68	$^0/_3$						$^0/_3$
I4			$^0/_6$				$^0/_6$
L3					$^0/_1$		$^0/_1$
127–68							$^0/_0$
J4		$^0/_1$					$^0/_1$
(7 lb.)							
L6	$^0/_2$			$^0/_1$			$^0/_3$
L2	$^0/_1$		$^0/_2$	$^0/_1$			$^0/_4$
G7					$^0/_1$		$^0/_1$
F7	$^0/_9$		$^0/_2$		$^0/_6$		$^0/_{17}$
(8 lb.)							
D5							$^0/_0$
G1					$^0/_5$		$^0/_5$
(11 lb.)							
B7							$^0/_0$
D9							$^0/_0$
C5							$^0/_0$
C0						$^0/_2$	$^0/_2$
Total	$^0/_{15}$	$^0/_1$	$^0/_{10}$	$^0/_2$	$^0/_{13}$	$^0/_2$	$^0/_{43}$

[a] No. above slash mark indicates female behind, no. below slash indicates male behind.

Table 4.27 Individual Juvenile Female Behind–In-Front Relationships (Estimated Body Weight in Parentheses)

	Behind															
	(5 lb.)					(7 lb.)				(8 lb.)		(11 lb.)				
	127–68	I4	L3	125–68	J4	L6	L2	G7	F7	D5	G1	B7	D9	C5	C0	Total
In Front																
127–68																0
I4																0
L3																0
125–68																0
J4																0
L6																0
L2											2					2
G7											2					2
F7																0
D5			1													1
G1									1							1
B7																0
D9																0
C5										1						1
C0																0
Total	0	0	1	0	0	0	0	0	1	1	4	0	0	0	0	7

(1) They suggest that within the female class and within the male class the achievement of favorable positions is largely a function of size and weight: bigger monkeys usually succeed against smaller monkeys, and the achievement of advantageous positions within dyads of approximately the same weight is variable, as might be expected of well-matched opponents. Note, for example, that the small two-year-old male G2 achieved on-top position only three times against other juvenile males while they achieved the on-top position against him 53 times. H1, the large two-year-old male, achieved the on-top position 54 times against the smaller males, while they achieved only 12 against him. H1 achieved only one on-top against C4, the three-year-old, but C4 achieved 26 on-tops against H1.

Although both are listed as seven pounds, the two-year-old male G6 was slightly smaller than his one-year-old brother I7. No behinds were recorded for this dyad, but G6 achieved 14 on-tops to I7's four. Example A (chapter 3) presents a detailed description of a complete playfight between these two monkeys recorded on motion picture film. G6 is on-top for almost the entire interaction. Close examination will reveal that although the two monkeys employ similar tactics, G6 seems to be the more skillful. Between animals of different ages and approximately the same size, the older may have the advantage.

(2) The second conclusion suggested by the record of individual on-tops and behinds is that males are superior playfighters to females in that they achieve favorable positions independent of weight (see tables 4.23 and 4.26). This is difficult to establish firmly, since the males in C Group were usually larger than females of the same age, but there are some exceptions. For example, the two-year-old male G2 was smaller than females L6, L2, G7, and F7, and yet he achieved 26 on-tops against them to their six against him. The two-year-old male H1 was smaller than his three-year-old sister C5, and yet he achieved nine on-tops to her zero. Similarly, G2 achieved 12 behinds against L6, L2, and F7, but they did not achieve a behind against him.

Play Involving Peripheral Males

On 15 observation days, 106 play interactions involving peripheral males were recorded. On two other days photographs were made and field notes were not recorded, but observations were summarized later.

Every central juvenile male was observed playing with a peripheral male at least three times, and with a minimum of two peripheral partners. The mean number of interactions was 12.7 with an average of 2.5 peripheral male partners. No female of any age was seen playing with a peripheral male. Of the 106 interactions, 76 (72 percent) were between a central and peripheral male, the rest between two peripherals; 82 (77 percent) involved only animals under four years of age; 95 (90 percent) involved at least one animal under four years of age. CA, a castrated male, was the only fully adult male I observed playing in the course of the study.

The eleven interactions I observed between monkeys of four years old or older were an interesting contrast to the play of younger males. Playchases involving animals of this age were not observed. I observed seven playfights between the four-year-old peripherals C6 and B2. These were long interactions, but they were extremely slow and unvigorous. The monkeys lay together on a dock, holding each other and playbiting gently, remarkably like two females. They did not chase, roll, or leap, and did not use their feet defensively; at times they were almost motionless, but large play-faces were given constantly. These unvigorous playfights were interspersed with periods of mutual grooming. The remaining older male playfights were between B2 and CA. B2 initiated all of these and CA was mostly passive, apparently frightened of B2, as the following field notes suggest:

> Oct. 9, 5:33 P.M. dock at F3. [Peripheral males B2 and C6 have been lying together on the dock grooming.] CA walks down the dock approaching the spot where C6 grooms B2. When CA is about 3 feet from them he jumps off the dock, walks past them on the mangrove roots, then jumps back onto the dock. He sits on the end of the dock and grooms himself. C6 stops grooming B2 and lies in front of B2, apparently soliciting grooming. B2, however, also lies down, so they are lying back to back. B2 walks down the dock to CA, grasps CA's left arm and playbites CA's left shoulder for about two seconds. CA gives a very wide play-face, looking straight ahead, not at B2. CA makes no further response. B2 releases CA's arm, and walks back down the dock to C6. [This interaction was considered to be a "playfight" because CA did not move away and did give a play-face.]

When three-year-old males played with younger males their play resembled that of two-year-old males; it was vigorous and complex, contained some very long sequences, and was characterized by frequent on-top/on-bottom relationships. When three-year-old males played with older males, their play resembled that of the older males in being less vigorous, generally attenuated, involving few movements and positions. The form and frequency of male playfighting appeared to alter significantly after the age of three. When three-year-old males played with each other the encounters were short, sometimes tense, with strong avoidance tendencies. For example:

> Oct. 21, 5:15 P.M., trail north of F2. [C4 has initated four short playfights with peripheral three-year-old E5.] C4 turns toward E5, E5 raises his shoulder, leans away from C4 and grimaces, then moves away from C4.

Good examples of the difference between three-year-old male play among themselves and their play with younger males were seen when the two three-year-old peripherals E4 and E5 played with central two-year-old male H4. It was during these episodes that all of the play interactions between E4 and E5 were seen.

E4 and E5 were constant companions and were natal to the same group. I never observed a threat between these monkeys, and was not able to ascertain which was the dominant. When all the peripheral males were together in one place, redirected aggression sometimes flashed down the hierarchy, but when it reached E4 or E5 at the bottom they always threatened me, not each other.

Play interactions between E4 and E5 were very rare, brief, and attentuated, and the monkeys gave obvious and continuous play-faces. When E4, E5 and H4 playfought together, all the long, complex, and vigorous playfights occurred between E4 or E5 (or both) and H4. One of these episodes consisted of a long series of playfights about 30 feet high in mature mangrove. H4 fell frequently, but always caught a branch before he had fallen more than 10 feet and then climbed back. E4 and E5 fell occasionally, but only when H4 fell as well. Almost all the interactions were E4 vs. H4 or E5 vs. H4. Three brief interactions occurred between E4 and E5, each seemingly aborted; the monkeys made wide playfaces and put their mouths on each other, but then simply held, or moved away to playfight with H4.

In all the interactions I observed between H4 and E4 or E5 (46 recorded in my field notes and many more on the two occasions photographs instead of field notes were made), H4 was dominated: he was always on-bottom, never on-top; he was pulled out of low trees and shrubs and thrown to the ground; occasionally he was able to bite E4 or E5, but usually the three-year-olds got past his defensively deployed feet and bit his belly; sometimes he was dragged along the ground in their teeth; he squealed on several occasions until they released him, but never caused his partners to squeal. Yet H4 always returned for more, and sometimes initiated the play. At no time did fights or threats result from these interactions; in fact, neither fights nor threats were precipitated by an intragroup playfight involving a peripheral male.[3]

Play Involving Adult Females

I observed fourteen episodes (constituting about 25 play interactions) involving an adult female (that is, a female of four or more

3. Because this study was conducted almost entirely during the mating season the frequency of play among sexually mature males (three years old and older) probably was underestimated, since they are reported to play less frequently during the mating season (Sade 1966), and the lack of vigor of such play may have been overestimated. Males are much more aggressive during the mating season (chapter 9) and this may reduce the intensity of their playfighting. During the shooting of a 16mm motion picture film on La Cueva during the nonmating season in early summer, 1975, some very vigorous play among large peripheral males was observed and recorded on film.

years). No adult of either sex was observed playing with another adult. Of the 14 episodes, eight consisted of an adult female playing with an infant, and six with a female juvenile. In four of the eight female-infant episodes the female was the infant's mother, in two an older sister, and in two the animals were unrelated. Female-infant play interactions were brief and gentle, the female holding the infant and playbiting its head and shoulders, sometimes getting the infant's head almost entirely within her mouth. Occasionally this gentle mouthing was a response to the infant's leaping onto, or walking on, its mother.

Of the six episodes of adult female–juvenile play, two were with a daughter, one with a younger sister, and three between unrelated animals. The mother-daughter episodes occurred between the adult female 270 and her two-year-old daughter F7. Play was initiated by F7's leaping on her mother and playbiting her neck; 270 responded playfully and gently. On one occasion 270 lay on a dock holding her infant (270-69). F7 repeatedly attempted to touch the infant, but 270 always pushed her hand away. F7 responded by initiating grooming and play with her mother, letting her hands wander toward the infant. This interaction ended when 270 got up and walked toward the feeder, F7 following.

The three episodes in which an adult female played with an unrelated juvenile involved two four-year-old females (A8 and 309) and the ovariectomized adult female 211. The juveniles involved were a two-year-old female (G1) and a yearling female (I4). These episodes were brief, but involved both playchasing and playfighting. On one occasion 211 initiated play with I4 and her infant brother (181–169). This was the only adult female–juvenile play observed in which the initiator was the adult.

Intergroup Play

Members of C Group were seen playing with members of other groups on 11 observation days. Intergroup play usually occurred when two groups had settled down for the night next to each other, especially near Feeding Station 2. In three of these episodes I recorded the occurrence of many playfights but, because the animals were partly concealed by shrubs or mangrove, interactions could not be counted. Thirty-one interactions were seen clearly and approximately twenty were seen partially. With one exception, described below, intergoup play occurred between two- and three-year-old males of C Group and two-, three-, and four-year-old males from the other three groups on La Cueva (A, E, and I). Playchasing was observed only five times; the remaining interactions were playfights.

Intergroup play often was very vigorous and generally was accompanied by continuous and obvious play-faces. On one occasion the soft panting, or grunting, that sometimes can be heard during rhesus playfights seemed significantly louder than usual. In only one instance did intergroup playfighting turn into fighting:

> September 16, 5:26 P.M. trail north of F2. [C4 and A0 (a four-year-old peripheral male of A Group) playfight.] There is a sudden increase in vigor of movements, C4 screams, gives an open-mouth threat at A0. Both monkeys stand stiffly, approximately six feet apart staring at each other, not vocalizing but slapping the ground. C4 turns away and initiates a vigorous playfight with H1.

This example also illustrates what might be considered displaced aggression, except that aggression was "displaced" as playfighting, not attack or threat; C4, in a standoff agonistic encounter with A0, did not attack his subordinate, H1, but playfought vigorously with him. Sometimes young C Group males reacted to the presence of extragroup males by playfighting vigorously with members of their own group, a technique that seemed designed to avoid intergroup play:

> November 14, 5:36 P.M. small trees and grass east of F6. [H4 and H1 have had a long series of vigorous playfights.] I6 [a large four-year-old E Group male] appears. H4 gives open-mouth threat at I6, then approaches H1 and they playfight again, both giving large play-faces. . . . I6 approaches, initiates playfighting with H4, approximately two seconds, H4 screams and runs up a small tree. I6 walks toward H4, H4 drops out of the tree and moves away. . . . H4 climbs another tree, I6 moves toward him, H4 runs down the tree, I6 approaches through the grass, H4 moves back to H1. [H4 and H1 then engage in a series of very vigorous playfights.]

Although I6 either hurt or frightened H4, and H4 seemed reluctant to play, H4 did not flee as he would have done if I6 actually had attacked him.

In the first example C4 reacted to a fight with playfighting directed at a subordinate. In the second case H4 reacted to a play attempt with "displaced play." Displaced aggression as a response to play also was observed:

Feb. 9, 7:20 A.M. south of F6. U8 [a three-year-old I Group male] holds G6 down and playbites his belly. G6 leaps away and scream-threatens H1, who stands nearby. H1 moves away.

Nothing in the movements and gestures of I6 and U8 indicated that either was acting aggressively, although doubtless they were acting roughly. There were no vocalizations, stalking, or rapid movements suggesting fighting or threat.

Several intergroup play encounters occurred between the three-year-old peripheral male E4 and the two-year-old A Group males H2 and G5 (E4's younger brother). These interactions were seen on three different occasions when A Group was settling down for the night next to C Group in the Feeding Station 2 area. At these times E4 and E5 returned to the interior of A Group (their natal group) and E4 groomed and was groomed by his mother and a four-year-old A Group female.

The single instance of intergroup play that included an animal not in the juvenile male class occurred between H5 (four-year-old A Group male) and an infant C group male (289-69). In this interaction, which lasted approximately three minutes, H5 held the infant, walked holding the infant to his ventral surface, playbit the infant about the head and neck, playbit the infant's scrotum, and, when the infant attempted to move away, pulled it back by the tail. When H5 did release 289-69, the infant walked behind H5 and began to groom him. At no time did the infant show any sign of fear or pain.

In general, intergroup play seemed more tense than intragroup play. One indication of tension is the general lack of grooming interspersed with play, a common feature of intragroup play. Grooming between males of different groups was seen only once (except for the grooming just described) when a two-year-old male (G5) from A Group joined a two-year-old C Group male (H4) in grooming a four-year-old C Group peripheral (C6). Younger males sometimes avoided the playful advances of older extragroup males, but this occurred within the group as well. It was always clear that the monkeys were playfighting, not fighting. When the playfight between C4 and A0 suddenly became a fight and then threat, the change was dramatic and unmistakable.

Chapter five

The Structure and Function of Playchasing and Play Above the Ground

During playfights on the ground, monkeys respond primarily to the partner's position and movements; during playfights in trees or shrubs, and during playchases, movement patterns are determined in large part by the nature of the terrain.

Monkeys observed on La Cueva playfighting in trees or shrubs were constrained by the necessity to use one or more extremities to grasp a branch. They often began playfights standing quadrupedally on top of a branch, but almost immediately fell beneath it, usually grasping the branch with their feet, and using their hands to grapple. Sometimes a monkey grasped the branch with its hands and used its feet to grapple. As in playfights on the ground, a major goal of playfights in trees is to bite while not being bitten (see chapter 6) but in trees an important secondary goal is to cause the partner to fall. Monkeys hanging and grappling beneath a branch attempted to dislodge their partner by pulling it off the branch, and monkeys on the ground often leaped repeatedly at another monkey in a low tree or shrub, grasped it, and attempted to dislodge it.

Infants are not skilled at falling, and generally confined their playfights to parts of the environment (usually within five feet of the ground) where a fall was not dangerous. Infants frequently playfought on shrubs densely covered with vines, probably because they provided maximum opportunity to break a fall as the infants slid down the almost solid surface of these shrubs, grasping the readily available terminal branches, leaves, and vines. Juveniles rarely playfought on such shrubs.

Juveniles regularly playfought high in thickly branches trees, falling frequently, catching a branch, and climbing back up to playfight again, males sometimes playfighting up to a height of 30 feet in mature mangrove. Monkeys were not observed to playfight in a large tree with widely spaced branches that was available to them, where a fall probably would have been to the ground. By the time they are juveniles, rhesus monkeys have become extremely skilled at falling, rarely falling more than a few feet before catching a branch. No monkey was observed to be injured by a fall.

Attempting to pull a play partner from a branch and cause it to fall has also been reported in Lowe's guenon (*Cercopithecus campbelli*) (Bourliere et al. 1970), in spider monkeys (*Ateles geoffroyi*) (Richard 1970), and frequent falling has been reported during the play of Nilgiri langurs (*Presbytis johnii*) (Poirier 1970).

The direction of a playchase is determined by the chasee, but the required behaviors are determined by the substrate over which the monkeys travel. Playchasing monkeys move through their environment at high speed, climbing tree trunks, running along the ground and branches, and leaping from the ground into trees or shrubs, from trees or shrubs to the ground, from branch to branch, and from branch to water. The chaser often leaps at the chasee on the ground, on a branch, or in the water, but the chasee usually anticipates these leaps and flees before it is hit. Infants and juveniles swim on, and sometimes under, the surface of small, enclosed pools. Rhesus swimming also has been reported by Koford (1963a), Southwick et al. (1965), and Sade (1966). Simonds (1965) observed swimming during play among bonnet macaques (*Macaca radiata*), where it was primarily a male activity.

As Aldis (1975) remarks, there is a certain simplicity to playchasing, since it consists of one animal fleeing and another chasing. The complexity of these chases becomes apparent, however, when one considers the problems of moving rapidly through intricate arboreal pathways. During playchases rhesus run swiftly along, and occasionally under, branches that vary continuously in diameter and flexibility while avoiding other branches that loom to block their path and make rapid, precise, and sudden turns and leaps without losing momentum. They must judge distance accurately, since leaping too far is as ineffective and potentially dangerous as not leaping far enough. They must anticipate which branches will support their weight and which will not, and this varies according to the weight of the animal, its velocity, and the distance leaped. When springing from a flexible branch monkeys must utilize the whip of the branch to augment the jump and when landing on a flexible support they must ride the rebound of the branch as they continue the chase. If they fall, they must twist to fall feet first, grasp a branch, climb on top, and resume running.

Sometimes rhesus playchases on the ground followed a circular path around a tree trunk or stump. Circular playchases also have been reported in the stumptail macaque (*Macaca speciosa*) (Bertrand 1969) and chimpanzee (*Pan troglodytes*) (Lawick-Goodall 1968). Far more common, however, are noncircular playchases, and in these the chasee almost invariably runs to cover. On La Cueva, mangrove trees grow inland over bare ground, and immature rhesus frequently playchased along the edge of the mangroves. The chasee almost always turned into the mangroves, not away toward open ground, and climbed or leaped into the branches. Ripley (1967) reports that in langur (*Presbytis entellus*) playchases the chasee usually flees to the cover of trees.

If there was sufficient available cover, such as low mangrove branches or high grass, sometimes a monkey being chased during play would suddenly crouch low to the ground and freeze, thereby concealing itself from the chaser. When rhesus on La Cueva played in open terrain covered with high grass a specialized kind of chasing play was observed in which a playchasing monkey would suddenly crouch and freeze in the grass, remaining motionless until discovered by a play partner and then resuming the chase, crouch, and freeze pattern. Little or no playfighting occurred at these times. Struhsaker (1967a) describes a very similar "hide and seek" play pattern among vervet monkeys (*Cercopithecus aethiops*) which also occurs only in high grass:

> Two or more monkeys leaped and bounded in an exaggerated manner through the tall, green grass as they chased and counter chased. Either the chaser or chasee would suddenly crouch low and remain motionless, thus concealing itself in the tall grass. The "hider" remained motionless and concealed until the "seeker(s)" either came very close or actually jumped upon him, whereupon the chasing and counter chasing would resume. . . . (p. 33).

In summary, during playchases immature rhesus monkeys regularly exhibit behavior that is infrequently observed in adults: running, climbing, and leaping at high speed; falling, freezing in high grass, and fleeing to cover. Playchasing is not a random activity but, on the contrary, one that mimics the behavior required to survive the emergencies of predation and intraspecific aggression.

Emergency Locomotor Behavior

I did not observe a monkey fall in any context except play, but they undoubtedly fall on occasion during high-speed aggressive chases and during escape from predators in natural environments. Richard (1970) reports that spider monkeys and howling monkeys (*Alouatta palliata*) sometimes fall during aggressive encounters, and Struhsaker (1967b) notes that falling (dropping) is a typical vervet response to a major avian predator.

On La Cueva, adult rhesus were observed to run with amazing speed and precision through the maze of the mangrove interior when chasing, or being pursued by, other adults during aggressive interactions. Although there were no predators on La Cueva, the monkeys frequently became alarmed when on open ground and the typical response, as during play, was immediate and swift flight to the mangroves. Flight to the safety of trees is an anti-predator pattern common among primates that spend time on the ground such as langurs (Ripley 1967), baboons (Saayman 1971, Altmann and Altmann 1970), and vervets (Struhsaker 1967a).

Monkeys occasionally responded to my approach by crouching and freezing in the grass, remaining motionless but watchful. If I ignored the monkey it would continue to freeze until I had passed. If I looked directly at it as I approached it would stop freezing, but would not necessarily move away. During the course of my field work a four-year-old rhesus male fell into an acre enclosure containing a group of vervets, and I was able to observe his response to the humans who attempted to capture him. Although the male was sitting in a fairly high tree, upon seeing men with monkey-catching nets approaching, he ran down the tree, across the enclosure, and froze in the grass, where he was not visible even from a distance of a few feet. Freezing in high grass as a response to danger has been reported in several terrestrial monkeys including baboons (Altmann and Altmann 1970), patas (Hall 1965), and vervets (Struhsaker 1967b).

Conclusions

The design of playchasing, then, and its striking similarity to behavior seen during intraspecific aggression and predator avoidance, suggests the following hypothesis: The adaptive function of playchasing is to rehearse, or practice, and thereby perfect the specific locomotor skills used during emergencies.

The literature on animal play supports this hypothesis. In prey animals, such as deer, most social play mimics escape behavior (Müller-Schwarze 1968). Wilson and Kleiman (1974) note that locomotor movements in animal play appear to be related to antipredator behaviors, and that the amount of such movement in the play of a particular species correlates well with the level of predation on that species. For example, they point out that the giant panda (*Ailuropoda melanoleuca*) has no major predators and little locomotor play, while rodents and seals are preyed upon by larger carnivores and frequently exhibit locomotor play.

Moreover, descriptions of locomotor play in many species suggest that they mimic the specific techniques of predator avoidance of that species. Ewer (1966), for example, describes the play of the African ground squirrel (*Xerus erythropus*), most of which is locomotor play. During "jinking play," the squirrels run rapidly with frequent reversals of direction, a pattern also seen when they flee from danger to their burrows. Ewer also describes a type of play in which a squirrel jumps vertically into the air and turns in midair to land facing a different direction. The same response is made to a noise close at hand, in which case the squirrel makes a short dash upon landing. This vertical leap, turn, and dash apparently is adapted specifically to snake evasion and, according to Ewer, is the only behavior likely to avoid the bite of a striking snake.

The nonhuman primate literature also suggests that noncontact play mimics emergency behavior, and that the form of play in a given species is similar to adult behaviors in that species (Dolhinow 1971). For example, during play an immature patas monkey at full gallop hurls itself into a sapling or small bush, catapults itself sideways and gallops off. This display is used by adult male patas to divert predators (Hall 1965) and during intergroup encounters (Struhsaker and Gartlan 1970). Hall (1965:89) interprets patas playchasing as an adaptation for rehearsing emergency behavior: "The surplus energy of the young patas is almost entirely spent in social play interactions which involve a most vigorous exercising or practising of speed and agility of ground locomotion which can be readily seen as an adaptation for survival from day-hunting predators. . . ." Ripley (1967) notes that during playchases young langurs leap back and forth over the pathways between trees used by adults and that the tendency of immature langurs, fleeing in play, to run to cover anticipates the adult need to find safety in the trees. Juvenile male langurs move through the trees during playchases at speeds seen in adult males only when they are about to engage another troop in a fight or when they are chasing another adult male.

Locomotor play and playchasing frequently have been said to function to acquaint the player with its environment. Loizos (1967:185) objects to this hypothesis:

> It is simply not necessary to play in order to learn about the environment. The animal could explore as, in fact, some mammals that do not appear to play certainly do; for example, the rat. Of course it is inevitable that during play, or during any activity, an animal will be gaining additional knowledge about what or who it is playing with; but if this is the major function of play one must wonder why the animal does not use a more economical way of getting hold of this information.

But high-speed locomotion during aggression or predator avoidance is the most difficult locomotor task in the life of a rhesus monkey and probably in any animal species, and only in playchases do specific emergency behaviors occur without benefit of an actual emergency. During playchases a monkey receives information not only about the environment but about the environment-player relationship.

Rhesus skills in arboreal locomotion are acquired first in the solitary, or self-motion (Mears and Harlow 1975), play of infants, and with increasing age there is improvement in speed, timing, and precision, in the economy and ease of movement, and in the distance and gracefulness of leaps. It is chasing or being chased in play, however, that provides the incentive for the sustained high-speed running, and the climbing, falling, and accurate leaping that are required to perfect emergency locomotor skills. As Ripley (1967:150) remarks: "Locomotor skills are ranges of complex skills which must be learned and practiced."

Chapter six

The Structure and Function of Playfighting

The examples and general description of playfights in chapter 3 and appendix 1 indicate that rhesus playfighting is a complex but structured activity with the following apparent design: each monkey attempts simultaneously to bite without being bitten. Thus a playfighting monkey succeeds in achieving its goal to the extent that its partner fails. It is the participants' pursuit of opposed goals that makes playfighting more complex than any rhesus social activity except fighting.[1]

Playfighting rhesus simultaneously use all four limbs (pushing, pulling, and grasping), their heads and faces (turning and biting), their torsos (twisting, turning, curling, and pivoting), and assume almost every possible spatial orientation. The resulting diversity of positions, movement combinations, and relationships to the partner are most unlikely to be reduced meaningfully to a series of discrete "motor patterns." Unlike most animal social behavior, playfighting is not stereotyped; it has not been shaped by natural selection for clear and unambiguous communication. Despite its complexity, however, playfighting is constrained insofar as there are apparently a limited number of useful tactics, and these seem to develop similarly in all rhesus monkeys.

Most of the movements that occur during playfights are clear-cut ex-

1. That playfighting is a competitive activity does not imply that success alone is rewarding: on the contrary, in playfighting the striving or competition appears to be its own reward, as can be seen when a smaller monkey repeatedly initiates playfights, in which it is almost sure to be bested, with a larger monkey. Why this should be the case is discussed in detail in chapter 7.

amples of biting and/or not being bitten. A monkey lying on its back and being bitten on the neck may grasp the skin on the back of the biter's head and pull the biter's head back; it may curl and use its feet to push the biter's head away; it may push the biter's head away with a hand; it may roll or twist to one side or attempt to interpose a hunched shoulder between its neck and the biter's teeth. Whether or not they succeed, these movements are designed to break the bite. Nontactical moves are conceivable but seldom occur; a monkey being bitten could, for example, grasp the biter's tail, which would have little direct effect on the bite. Occasionally, however, monkeys do not respond, or respond minimally, to being bitten in play.

During most playfights monkeys behave as if playbites were potentially injurious. But since playbites in fact are inhibited, playfighting monkeys, unlike fighting monkeys, do not risk injury if they fail to respond vigorously, and sometimes playfights are very relaxed. This is especially true of playfights that do not involve a male and those in which the partners differ substantially in size. For example, a juvenile may roll onto its back when playfighting with an infant although it was not, and could not have been, forced into that position. A juvenile may not strenuously resist an infant's bites, and an infant is physically incapable of successful defense against a juvenile's bites. In addition, during nonvigorous playfighting monkeys do not necessarily pursue every potential "opening." The most vigorous, advantage-seeking play occurs between well-matched male partners.

Many playfighting movements comprise both offensive and defensive aspects; they simultaneously increase the probability of biting and decrease the probability of being bitten. For example: (1) Necks are bitten frequently, perhaps in part because a neck bite makes retaliation difficult until the bite is broken. (2) If monkey A, being bitten on the neck by monkey B, grasps the skin on the back of B's head and pulls B's head back, A simultaneously breaks B's bite and exposes B's throat, which A then may bite. (3) A monkey in the on-top position, standing anterior to its on-bottom partner, regularly steps or leaps to on-bottom's side before it moves forward to bite on-bottom's ventral surface. The on-top monkey's move to bite is basically offensive, but its initial move to the side of the on-bottom monkey is a defensive tactic that avoids the danger of moving directly over the on-bottom monkey's face. Moreover, as the on-top monkey moves in to bite on-bottom's ventral surface, on-top usually rotates its head and torso away from on-bottom's head (and teeth), thereby exposing the back of its neck, not its throat. Thus, although in a given playfight one monkey may make mostly defensive moves and the other mostly offensive moves, defense and offense are inseparable, and rhesus playfighting cannot usefully be considered to consist of offensive and defensive "roles."

Many of the movements observed during playfights seem designed to achieve positions that facilitate biting and avoid positions that increase susceptibility to being bitten. The most favorable position a monkey can achieve is to get behind the partner, and grip it to prevent its turning; a monkey in the behind position can bite without hindrance and cannot be bitten. The next most favorable position is on-top of the partner: because of their greater leverage and mobility, on-top monkeys score, on the average, four times as many bites as their on-bottom partners. One of the most consistent features of rhesus playfighting is that monkeys move—by stepping, turning, twisting, pivoting, or rolling—to face their partners, and the on-top position is therefore achieved far more frequently than the behind position. When a monkey is thrown to the ground during play it rolls onto its back, from which position it can undertake vigorous defense.

The nonrandom attainment of favorable positions supports the hypothesis that rhesus monkeys seek advantage during playfights: larger animals are generally successful against smaller animals and males are generally successful against females. In each of the detailed examples of playfighting given in chapter 3 and appendix 1, one of the playfighting pair clearly is the superior playfighter.

Advantage-Seeking in Mammalian Play

I identify biting without being bitten as the fundamental objective of rhesus playfighting (Symons 1973, 1974) and similar analyses have been arrived at independently by other students of play. According to Gentry (1974:393), the apparent goal of Stellar sea lion (*Eumetopias jubatus*) play (which consists mostly of biting, grappling, pushing, lunging and parrying), is "to bite without being bitten and to best the opponent in pushing contests." On the basis of seven hours of super-8 film of play in a variety of zoo-living mammals, Aldis (1975) concludes that the final objective of wrestling is to mouth and not be mouthed, and the secondary objectives are to get past the partner's defenses, hold the partner to prevent its escaping, and attain a favorable position from which to mouth. Carpenter (1964:114) describes advantage-seeking in the play of two captive gorillas (*Gorilla gorilla*): "While wrestling, each animal seemed to strive for that position of advantage which would allow him to bite at the nape of the other animal's neck. This seemed one of the main objectives toward which the behavior was directed." Schaller (1963) reports that free-ranging gorillas also aim playbites at the angle made by the shoulder and neck, and Poirier (1970) makes a similar observation about Nilgiri langur play. Fox (1971) notes that in many species of canid, playbites are often aimed at the throat or cheek and that much of the behavior seen during a wrestling sequence is aimed at gaining such a hold.

While published descriptions of playfighting are rarely analyzed in terms of strategy and tactics, many of these descriptions, as well as published line drawings and photographs, demonstrate that mammals seek advantage during playfighting and that many of the discernible tactics are similar to those used by rhesus monkeys.

Throwing the partner to the ground and thereby attaining a position "on-top" of the partner appears to be a fundamental tactic in mammalian play. Among Steller sea lion pups "a common maneuver is to 'lock' necks and attempt to wrestle one another to the side or down to the ground" (Farentinos 1971:431). Hall's (1965:90) description of the attempt of patas monkeys (*Erythrocebus patas*) to throw each other is reminiscent of rhesus play: "each player on hind legs, facing each other, a grappling with hands around the shoulders and arms, then sometimes one, sometimes both, rolling over on the ground; two juveniles wrestled thus for two minutes, trying to 'throw each other.' . . ." Among gibbons that spend time on the ground, during playfights "one or another participant usually strives to gain an uppermost position by straddling, lying or sitting on the other" (Baldwin and Teleki 1976). The on-top/on-bottom relationship apparently occurs in several rodent species (Wilson and Kleiman 1974), African ground squirrels (*Xerus erythropus*) (Ewer 1966), Columbian ground squirrels (*Spermophilus columbianus*) (Steiner 1971), crab-eating macaques (*Macaca fascicularis*) (photograph in Angst 1975), and stumptail macaques (Bertrand 1969). The photograph in Angst (1975) clearly shows the defensive use of a foot by the on-bottom monkey to push away the teeth of the on-top monkey. Schenkel (1966) and Schaller (1972) note the existence of on-top/on-bottom relationships between playfighting lion (*Panthera leo*) cubs, and also that playbites frequently are aimed at the throat. Line drawings in Schaller (1972) show defensive use of the paw by an on-bottom lion, and biting of such defensively deployed paws by the on-top lion. Poole (1966) finds that an on-top/on-bottom relationship is usual in the aggressive play of European polecats (*Putorius putorius*), and notes that the older, larger animal is usually on-top, and that the paws of the on-bottom polecat are used defensively.

Baldwin (1969:52) describes a relationship commonly seen between playfighting squirrel monkeys that is similar to the behind/in-front relationship seen occasionally in rhesus play: "The dorsal-ventral position was the most common holding position during contact play, perhaps because when it was reached the under-animal was somewhat limited in what it could do to counter the other."

Bertrand (1969) describes "leaping over" in the stumptail macaque in two contexts: leaping over is seen during normal locomotion, when one animal passes another animal or an object on a narrow, elevated support, and it is also seen during play. Bertrand notes that leaping over in play differs from ordinary leaping over in that during play the leaper often puts one or both hands on the animal over which it is leaping. The significance of this movement probably is the same as in rhesus macaques: one may press down on the top of the head of the animal over which it is leaping, thereby preventing that animal from rearing and biting. Henry and Herrero (1974) observed neck biting, attempting to pin the partner down, pawing at a partner's arms to block an attack, rearing, rolling and hind-leg clawing, and attempts to maneuver into biting position in the American black bear (*Ursus americanus*):

> Once the social partner is pushed or pulled into a vulnerable position, a playbite or neck-bite-hold is frequently delivered. The bitten animal then rolls over and may hind-leg-claw in order to break the neck-bite-hold. Once freed, both bears frequently return to the rearing-pushing-pulling phase until one of the bears once again becomes vulnerable to a bite or clawing action (p. 382).

Henry and Herrero interpret the differences between bear and canid playfighting as resulting from the double-weapon system of bears (biting and clawing) compared with the single-weapon system of canids (biting). McGrew (1972) and Aldis (1975) describe wrestling among human male children as an attempt to achieve the on-top position. McGrew (1972:105) writes: "Each individual apparently tries to 'control' the other, that is, limit the other's movements, move the other's body, or keep the other on bottom while remaining atop him." Based on the analysis of super-8 film, Aldis (1975) describes the tactics used by on-top and on-bottom boys. Unlike all other mammals of which I am aware, the on-bottom boy attempts to roll onto his stomach, not onto his back. The difference between human and nonhuman playfighting may result from the absence of biting as a goal in human playfights; a boy, turning onto his stomach and attempting to rise to his feet and to break the hold of the on-top boy, presumably does not risk being bitten. Far more hitting and kicking occur during human playfights than during the playfights of nonhuman animals (see Aldis 1975).

This brief review suggests that advantage seeking is a general characteristic of mammalian playfighting and that the specific form of playfighting is a function of the physical capacities and limitations of the species and the nature of its weapon system. Thus, mobile, arboreally adapted macaques leap over their partners during playfighting while sea lions use their weight to advantage in pushing contests. Animals that fight mainly with their teeth attempt to achieve positions favorable for biting during play, while bear and felid tactics are based on the double weapon system of teeth and claws. Certain tactics, such as getting on-top of the parnter, seem to be of such fundamental advantage in increasing biting opportunities that they appear in the playfights of virtually all playing mammals.

Soliciting Play and "Metacommunication"

In chapter 3 a variety of rhesus gestures, postures, and gaits were described whose function appears to be to solicit (invite) a potential partner to play or to communicate intent to play. These gestures, postures and gaits lend aggressive play its unmistakable "playful" appearance. While they are not genuinely discrete categories, a signal may be considered to *solicit* play if it is given by a stationary monkey or one moving away from the solicited partner, and to communicate *intent* to play if it is given while approaching the intended partner or during the course of play. No patterns were observed to be used exclusively by an approaching monkey, but some, by their nature, preclude approach.

Soliciting Play

One of the most frequently observed soliciting devices occurs along a continuum: in the mildest form, the soliciting monkey adopts a staggering, or lurching gait, in which the arms are bent in an exaggerated manner; in a more extreme version, the forearms actually come to rest on the ground; still more extreme, the soliciting monkey puts its shoulder to the ground, and finally, may shoulder-roll onto its back, limbs waving in a relaxed manner. Other frequently observed soliciting signals include: crouch-stare; placing the head and forearms on the ground with the hindquarters elevated, looking at the solicited partner; looking over the shoulder at the partner and then running away, sometimes carrying an object. Some of these gestures, such as fleeing or lying on the back, may succeed because they put the solicitor at an initial disadvantage. (The head-down position often precedes fleeing.) This interpretation is supported by Aldis's (1975) observation that a play-soliciting mammal may actually put one of its limbs in the intended parnter's mouth. Frequently a monkey solicited play with one of these signals but, as soon as it succeeded in getting the partner to chase or to approach, the soliciting monkey turned and counterchased or otherwise took the "offensive."

There are several indications that the behavior patterns described are specialized play soliciting signals: they are almost always oriented to a potential play partner; regularly, although not invariably, they are followed by the partner's playful approach; they are almost entirely confined to the context of play. (The only exceptions were ear-flattening and eyelid exposure, which were given occasionally by a play-soliciting monkey. Although these gestures occur as components of certain communicative signals observed in non-play contexts neither, by itself, is known to have a communicative function outside of play [see Symons 1974].) Also, the signals occur in a variety of permutations and combinations, so that if one fails to solicit play, another may be attempted; there are clear-cut similarities in play-soliciting signals in many mammalian species, where they are similarly confined to the play context.

The head-down, looking at the partner either sideways or through the legs position is reported in squirrel monkeys (DuMond 1968, Baldwin 1969) and baboons (Owens 1975a). Lowering the forequarters with the hindquarters elevated is seen in play-soliciting canids (Fox 1971, Bekoff 1972, 1974) and lions (Schaller 1972). Rolling onto the back and waving the limbs solicits play in stumptail macaques (Bertrand 1969), baboons (Owens 1975a), lions (Schaller 1972), giant pandas (Wilson and Kleiman 1974), and in a variety of mammals studied by Aldis (1975). Looking over the shoulder and running away solicits play in chimpanzees (Lawick-Goodall 1968). Nilgiri langurs were observed to solicit play by running with, or dragging, an object (Poirier 1970). Play soliciting signals reported in the nonhuman primate literature that were not observed among rhesus monkeys in the present study include bouncing on the same spot, a signal used by patas monkeys (Hall 1965) and Sykes's monkeys (*Cercopithecus mitis*) (Dolan 1976), and possibly the "play duck" of Sykes's monkeys (Dolan 1976).

Play Intention Signals and "Metacommunication"

Four behavior patterns occur before and/or during rhesus playfights and playchases that seem to function as play intention signals: (1) as can be seen in most of the photographs in chapter 3, the relaxed open-mouth face, or play-face, is the most consistently observed of these patterns; (2) a high-stepping, gamboling, gait frequently is adopted during playchases and when initiating playfights; (3) a play approach may be accompanied by rotation of the torso in the transverse plane. This was identified as possible "metacommunication" by Sade (1973); (4) during vigorous playfights a distinct panting is sometimes audible.

Each of these signals is apparently an exaggerated element of playfighting or playchasing. The play-face is derived from opening the mouth in preparation for delivering a playbite (Redican 1975) and, during the course of playfighting, play-faces merge smoothly into playbites. Gamboling seems to be an exaggeration of the relaxed run at which most playchases are conducted. Aldis (1975) suggests that play vocalizations evolved by exaggerating the panting of normal exertion. I was not usually aware of panting during playfights, and when I was aware of it, I could not reliably distinguish it from panting caused by exertion, although occasionally it seemed exaggerated. Aldis (1975) argues that whether vocalizations are heard during playfighting depends primarily on the observer's distance from the playing animals and the intensity of play, the probability increasing with proximity and intensity. Since many, and perhaps most, species of mammal may have specialized play vocalizations (Aldis 1975), it is possible that rhesus monkeys do as well. Transverse rotation may be a derived exaggeration of the torso rotation that frequently brings an approaching monkey's mouth into biting position.

There are several indications that these patterns are specialized play-intention signals: Bekoff (1975b) provides evidence that, among coyotes, such signals have the effect of altering response probabilities to subsequent signals; the patterns are most evident at the beginning of a playfight when such gestures might be supposed to be most useful; the patterns are most exaggerated in the play of older rhesus males where an element of fear and avoidance seems to be present; the patterns are confined to the play context; there are clear-cut similarities in these patterns in many mammalian species, where they are similarly confined to the play context.

The primate play-face has been discussed extensively (Altmann 1962b, Goodall 1965, Loizos 1967, Hooff 1967, 1972, Lawick-Goodall 1968). This gesture also is reported in playing canids (Fox 1971, Bekoff 1972), lions (Schaller 1972), and bears (Henry and Herrero 1974). Students of play seem unanimous in the conviction that this gesture communicates play intent or a playful mood.

A gamboling gait during play is reported in bonnet macaques (Simonds 1965), vervet monkeys (Struhsaker 1967a) and chimpanzees (Lawick-Goodall 1971), and this gait may be a play signal in most terrestrial primates. Schaller (1972) describes a similar gait in lion play, and Bekoff (1974) in canid play.

A "play peep" is said to function as a play signal in squirrel monkeys (Winter 1968), as is a "squeak" in ground squirrels (Ewer 1966). On the basis of his observations of play in a variety of mammals Aldis (1975) speculates that vocalizations may be the most important play signals in most mammalian species, and the only signals likely to be of use during the course of a playfight.

The hypothesis that communication about communication, or

"metacommunication," is a necessary feature of playfighting originates with Bateson (1955:41):

What I encountered at the zoo was a phenomenon well known to everybody: I saw two young monkeys *playing,* i.e., engaged in an interactive sequence of which the unit actions or signals were similar to but not the same as those of combat. It was evident, even to the human observer, that the sequence as a whole was not combat, and evident to the human observer that to the participant monkeys this was "not combat."

Now, this phenomenon, play, could only occur if the participant organisms were capable of some degree of meta-communication, i.e., of exchanging signals which would carry the message "this is play."

While Bateson's notion is useful and has been widely accepted (e.g., Altmann 1962b, 1967, Bekoff 1972 [but see Bekoff 1976a], Henry and Herrero 1974, Poole and Fish 1975, Dolan 1976), I believe that his formulation makes unnecessary assumptions and has led to needlessly convoluted interpretations of animal behavior.

Bateson maintains that a "play signal" contrasts what is happening (or what is about to happen) with a similar activity that might be happening but isn't. He writes that the statement "this is play" means: "These actions in which we now engage, do not denote what would be denoted by those actions which these actions denote" (p. 41). For example, "The playful nip denotes the bite, but it does not denote what would be denoted by the bite" (p. 41). In addition, "the bite itself is fictional. Not only do the playing animals not quite mean what they are saying but, also, they are usually communicating about something which does not exist" (p. 43).

That the playful nip denotes the bite to *Bateson* is not evidence that it denotes the bite to the *monkeys.* Monkeys can communicate about what they are doing without communicating about what they are not doing. When a monkey nips playfully it probably means precisely that, and when it emits a specialized signal before or during playfighting, that signal may refer to the playfighting, and may function to reduce the probability of aggression, without contrasting playfighting with nonexistent or fictional entities. Monkeys engaged in sexual activities emit signals that function to coordinate and integrate their behavior, and probably to reduce the likelihood of aggression; but the signals are not interpreted to mean "this is 'not combat.' "

The word "play," in almost every one of its many meanings, implies contrast. "Play" is used to describe certain patterns of animal behavior because *observers* distinguish these patterns from other, similar patterns in the species' repertoire, but the *animals* need not make this distinction. In other words, "play" may be a useful category for humans without necessarily being a category for playing nonhuman animals. By describing the signals he observed as carrying the message "this is play," Bateson merely assumes what he purports to demonstrate.[2]

Playfighting is inhibited compared with fighting; a playbite and a bite are not the same thing, and do not necessarily require another signal to distinguish between them. Thus, although Altmann (1962b:279) writes: "preceding and accompanying play encounters, rhesus monkeys went through certain motions . . . that signaled to the other members of the play group that any aggressive behavior in the play situation would not be 'real' aggression," in fact, aggression rarely occurs in the play situation. When it does occur, playfighting terminates immediately. Altmann himself goes on to make this point: "the playing monkeys mouthed and nipped each other but did not bite, even though their dentition and jaw musculature were mature enough to do so." By considering that playfighting requires "metacommunicative" signals, Altmann (1962b:279) makes unnecessary assumptions in interpreting rhesus behavior: "not infrequently a play situation became so rough that an infant no longer accepted it as play; the metacom-

2. I believe Bateson's analysis is misleading in another way. He considers a bite delivered during combat to be a signal, and to "denote" something, apparently adopting a definition of "communication" similar to Altmann's (1967:326): "in a communication process, the behavior [the message] of one individual . . . changes the probability distribution of the behavior [the response] of the other." Accordingly, a bite delivered during combat certainly is a message, since it changes, indeed changes drastically, the opponent's probability of response. On the other hand, by considering such a bite to be a message, or signal, we ignore a fundamental difference between it and behavior patterns that, through ritualization and stereotypy, are specialized adaptations to permit or facilitate communication (Moynihan 1970). If signals are defined as "behavioral, physiological, or morphological characteristics fashioned or maintained by natural selection because they convey information to other organisms" (Otte 1974:385), then a bite delivered during combat is not a signal, and does not denote anything, because its function is not to convey information but to harm the opponent. The transference of information is an incidental effect. After all, a bite delivered in combat may be lethal. To consider a lethal bite to be a "message" is the equivalent of subscribing to the proposition that "Death is simply Nature's way of telling us to slow down." If someone fires a warning shot across my bow, I shall get the message and doubtless change the probability distribution of my behavior; on the other hand, if someone fires a "warning" shot into my brow, an observer may remark subsequently, "He got the message," but his remark will be ironical.

municative message, 'this is play,' broke down. The infant squealed. Its mother quickly approached and threatened her infant's playmates, who then fled." It seems to me superfluous to posit a breakdown in metacommunication; a more straightforward interpretation is that the infant squaled because it experienced pain. I doubt whether any amount of metacommunication would prevent a bitten monkey from interpreting a bite delivered with maximum force as attack, and responding accordingly.

The cues an observer has used to distinguish playfighting from fighting need not be the cues that the animals use. If a blindfolded immature rhesus monkey, knowing that a second immature monkey was approaching with an open mouth, were to predict the second monkey's intent based on probability alone, it would predict "playbite," since immature monkeys regularly playfight and rarely fight. For every bite an infant experiences and delivers it probably experiences and delivers a thousand playbites. Furthermore, playbites are not preceded or accompanied by agonistic threat signals that precede and accompany rhesus combat, and the absence of agonistic signals—indeed, the absence of a "bone of contention"—may be at least as important as the presence of play signals in identifying the activity. Play occurs in relaxed circumstances; a major outbreak of aggression in the group may terminate play for hours.

The Function of Playfighting

Playfighting interactions among rhesus monkeys thus constitute two kinds of behavior patterns: play soliciting and intention signals; and playfighting itself. Playfighting is a structured activity in which the apparent goal is to bite without being bitten, achieved in part by gaining positions favorable for biting and avoiding positions that increase susceptibility to being bitten. Although, compared with fighting, playfighting is inhibited, and self-handicapping is evident when partners are mismatched, the nonrandom attainment of favorable positions—behind and on-top—provides additional evidence that playfighting monkeys seek advantage.

A detailed description of rhesus play reveals design, and functional hypotheses of rhesus play must take account of this design. Since playbites do not inflict damage, there is no obvious reason why monkeys should avoid being bitten during play or, indeed, why such effort should be expended getting past the partner's defenses, or into favorable positions, in order to inflict playbites. Adult rhesus monkeys, however, sometimes are involved in serious, and occasionally lethal, fights (chapter 9). The negative effects on fitness of being bitten are obvious; it is adaptive for a monkey involved in a fight to avoid being bitten by its opponent. The positive effects on fitness of biting the opponent are less obvious and immediate, but that monkeys fight at all indicates that biting the opponent is adaptive as well. Unless monkeys could sometimes increase their fitness by biting, selection would always favor monkeys who fled from, or otherwise avoided, a fight. Fighting incurs serious risks to fitness, and selection favors risk-taking only when there exist potential compensatory payoffs in reproductive success. This point is elaborated in chapter 9.

Given the existence of adult combat, the functional hypothesis that seems to explain the design of rhesus playfighting most economically is that playfighting is the process whereby monkeys develop fighting skills. An interaction in which two animals simultaneously attempt to inflict and to avoid inhibited bites is the sort of interaction that is most likely to develop such skills. Similar functional interpretations of aggressive play have been made by other observers, particularly those who have emphasized detailed description of behavior (e.g., Rasa 1971, elephant seals; Gentry 1974, sea lions; Owens 1975b, baboons; Aldis 1975, mammals in general.) Ewer (1968:300) makes a more guarded suggestion about the relationship between playfighting and fighting among *Thryonomys:*

> Youngsters show all the adult fighting patterns in play fights: nose pressed against nose they push, strain, twist their heads in the "boring" movement, leap away and thwack each other with their rumps. Watching the performance it is difficult to believe that this experience will not be useful to them in the genuine fights that lie ahead. They know in advance what it feels like to be pushed back, how to utilise their weight effectively in a well aimed rump thwack or brace themselves to receive one.

Ewer, a member of the "experiment" school of functional hypothesis testing, goes on to caution that, although this view of the function of playfighting is a reasonable one, it is untested.

The hypothesis that fighting skills are practiced in playfights generates the prediction that animals deprived of playfighting experience subsequently will exhibit fighting skills inferior to nondeprived animals but, even in the absence of such experiments, the design of playfighting is itself strong, and necessary, evidence for adaptive function. To be given serious consideration, alternative hypotheses regarding the function of aggressive play must satisfactorily account for its design.

In the following two chapters I shall consider critically the reasons why the hypothesis that the adaptive function of play is to practice and perfect specific skills has not been generally accepted.

Chapter Seven

Play and the Development of Skill

That by playing animals practice and perfect specific skills would seem so obvious as to be nearly beyond dispute to many observers of animal play (e.g., Aldis 1975, Gentry 1974, Owens 1975b, Symons 1973). This is one of the oldest and most persistent explanations for the existence of play (Groos 1898); yet, as Bekoff (1974, 1976a) and Vincent and Bekoff (in press) point out, it is not widely accepted and many students of play maintain that there is good evidence against it.

Some of this disagreement probably results merely from different interpretations of the word "practice," which Webster defines as "to do repeatedly in order to learn or become proficient." If the phrase "in order to" is understood in an evolutionary-adaptive and not a psychological sense, this definition seems to reflect the views of most observers who support a theory of play as practice. This definition of "practice" implies that some qualities of the performance of an activity change as a result of repetition; it does not imply that adequate performances are impossible without repetition, nor does it imply that the practice repetitions must have any specified degree of similarity to the resulting proficient performance. Thus, although Bekoff (1974:338) writes that the practice theory "has not been supported in various mammalian groups," he goes on to say: "What appears to be the case is that play experience increases the "smoothness" of carrying out certain sequences of behavior, but that it is not necessary for achieving the consummatory phase of the sequence (e.g., the killing of prey)." If Webster's definition of practice is accepted, Bekoff cannot be numbered among the implacable foes of the practice theory.

Semantic issues aside, however, substantive issues remain. The practice theory has been rejected for two quite opposite reasons: (a) that play patterns are so *similar* to the "serious" patterns they mimic that play cannot improve subsequent performance; and (b) that play patterns are so *dissimilar* to the "serious" patterns they mimic that the primary function of play cannot be to practice these "serious" patterns.

Play and Nonplay as Too Similar

The first sort of criticism seems to have its origin in ethological tradition. For example, Lorenz (1956:636) writes: "we do not believe that instinctive motor patterns need practising or are susceptible to improvement through practice." This position is supported by Poole (1966, 1967) who studied both playfighting and fighting among polecats. Because he did not observe a gradual change or development in the form of the motor patterns, Poole (1966:32) concluded that the function of playfighting is not to practice fighting skills:

> Observations on aggressive play show that it consists almost entirely of instinctive patterns of behavior which develop in sequence; the basic patterns of the neck bite and rolling over appear even before the eyes are open. The patterns of aggressive play emerge one by one in a completed form and at first appearance resemble the adult behavior pattern, so that they do not appear to be modified by experience as the animal grows older.

I believe that Poole's observations provide insufficient support for his conclusions. Beer (1975:50) has recently written, "Preoccupation with aspects of form, part of the inheritance of ethology from the past of zoology, has had a tendency to keep attention away from the full complexities and intricacies of function." By neglecting the complexities of function, students of animal behavior have insufficiently considered the development of skill. Even patterns considered to be classic examples of "innate" behavior may improve in many ways with practice. For example, laughing gull chicks trigger the adults' response of regurgitation by pecking at the tip of the adult's beak. This "begging" response is innate in the sense that it is made preferentially to stimuli that resemble adult beak tips the first time it occurs. Nevertheless, pecking efficiency rapidly increases as chicks become better at judging the distance between themselves and the beak tip and as they come to discriminate, through trial and error, appropriate stimuli at which to peck (Alcock 1975).

The nature of "proficiency" and the development of skills are rarely considered in the literature on animal play; investigations into the origins of skilled performances have concentrated on humans. Many of the principles elucidated in these investigations, however, probably apply to nonhuman animals as well, especially to playful mammals with substantial learning abilities. I propose, therefore, to review briefly some ways in which human proficiency increases with practice, emphasizing what happens and postponing speculations on mechanisms until chapter 8. I shall also draw analogies between the skills of nonhuman animals and human skills in sports. Such analogies may prove useful in elucidating biological principles (see Williams 1966 and Maynard Smith 1972) and are offered not as proofs but as hypotheses or illustrations.

Human proficiency improves through practice in the following ways: (1) Strength increases, and movements become potentially more vigorous or intense. (2) The accuracy or precision of movements increases. (3) Speed of performance increases as extraneous movements are eliminated (Bruner 1970, Connolly 1970). (4) Reaction time decreases, the magnitude of the effect being directly related to the uncertainty whether a given stimulus will occur in a particular situation. If the stimulus can be anticipated, reaction time approaches zero (Fitts and Posner 1967). (5) Timing (the ability to coordinate movements appropriately with external events) increases as a result of increased efficiency in the flow from component to component of a complex activity (Bruner 1970). (6) As anticipation improves, the ability to choose among an array of components to achieve the overall objectives of the activity increases (Bruner 1970). (7) The components of a complex activity no longer require conscious attention for their performance and become automatic, or reflex-like (Fitts and Posner 1967, Bruner 1970) and the speed of reaction becomes independent of the number of possible stimuli (Fitts and Posner 1967). Once the components of a complex activity are mastered and have become automatic, conscious attention is freed to monitor larger groupings of components (Bruner 1970, Connolly 1970) and the overall objective or strategy of the activity (Kay 1970, Bruner 1972). The unit of response enlarges, so that eventually whole component groups can be triggered off automatically (Kay 1970).

The issue, then, is not whether reasonably normal adult behavior will occur without prior play; it probably will. The issue is proficiency. In the operation of natural selection, small differences can be crucial. Although an unpracticed polecat, lacking playfighting experience, might exhibit all the motor patterns of fighting and inflict damage on rival polecats, previous playfighting experience might, on the average, mean the difference between winning and losing. In a competitive activity like fighting, skill is relative. An animal's performance can be judged only in relation to the performance of its opponent; no matter how skilled an animal may be, if it loses, it was not skilled enough.[1]

In this regard I should point out that, although my description of rhesus playfighting and playchasing probably is accurate in that independent observers, given the same data, would provide similar descriptions (an experienced wrestler could perhaps provide better description), I have almost certainly failed to identify many significant features of rhesus aggressive play.

This point may be illustrated by analogy with the sport of handball. A lay observer at a handball match may understand the rules and objectives of the game as well as the strategies and tactics commonly used to achieve these objectives, but it is extremely unlikely that the lay observer will be able to determine the behavioral sources of skilled performance. For example, the observer sees a player running to inter-

1. The significance of increments of skill in determining the outcome of competitive activities is not generally understood. Consider two athletes, A and B. Assume that both are experienced players, so that the reliability of their performances is high, and that a layman might therefore notice little difference between their performances. Assume, however, that B is judged by experts to be 90% as proficient as A. (In part, this judgment could be verified independently by measuring a relatively small number of component abilities [Fleishman 1966].) Now, it is not the case that A will win ten matches for every nine that B wins; if both players are highly motivated to win, and if the sport is one, such as handball or track, in which short-term chance or luck is of minimal significance, A will win virtually every time. The relatively small margin in skill assures victory. (Because a single "lucky" bite might profoundly influence the outcome, short-term chance effects may play a larger role in animal combat than they do in many human sports.)

It is doubtful whether a human could discriminate levels of skill by observing animals fighting. Experimental determination of the effects of playfighting on subsequent fighting performance would require experienced animals to be pitted against inexperienced animals. Success is the criterion. (I do not, however, advocate such experiments, which would not appear to differ, in their ethical underpinning, from cock fighting.)

cept the ball while simultaneously drawing back an arm, and then striking the ball with his hand. The observer is aware that the player is attempting to cause the ball to strike the front wall of the court before it strikes the floor and then rebound from the front wall in such a way that it will be difficult or impossible for the opponent to retrieve before it has bounced twice. But the observer probably will not be able to see that the power in the good player's shot comes not from the easily observed swing of the arm, as does the power in the lesser player's shot, but rather from the legs, hips, and wrist, and from the transfer of body weight at the moment of impact. The observer probably will not be able to see that the good player watches the ball until just before the moment it strikes his hand, while the lesser player loses sight of the ball when it is a few feet from his body.

If the observer films the players and then analyzes the film he will discover far more about the mechanics of skilled handball performance than is possible through unaided observation, but he will not learn everything. Highly experienced players—who know what to look for—while observing the match will note many of the subtle features of the performances. But even they can rarely determine through observation alone exactly what movement patterns differentiate the champion's play from their own, and therefore they occasionally suspect divine intervention on behalf of the champion.

When a human observes nonhuman animals engaged in vigorous, complex, competitive activities using anatomical structures the observer does not possess to attain goals with which the observer has no first-hand experience, some important features of the activity inevitably must remain unappreciated.

Play and Nonplay as Too Dissimilar

Many critics believe that although play may have the effect of improving subsequent performances, it cannot be explained as an adaptation to practice specific skills. Loizos (1967:184–85) writes:

> None of this is to deny that practice or rehearsal of many forms of behaviour is likely to improve the efficiency with which they are performed in adult life. But it has yet to be shown that it is the *playful* execution of these particular patterns in infancy or childhood that is crucial to their later perfection, as opposed to their *non-playful* execution at whatever level of maturity the animal is then

operating. Quite simply, it is not necessary to play in order to practise—there is no reason why the animal should not just practise.

Criticisms of this sort have their origins in attempts to characterize or identify play patterns of immature animals, and to set off play as a distinct behavioral category, by comparing these patterns to similar adult patterns. The following characteristics of play were compiled from Meyer-Holzapfel (1956), Loizos (1966, 1967), Marler and Hamilton (1966), Ewer (1968) and Miller (1973). In each case, the authors contrast play patterns with behavior patterns observed in other functional contexts: (1) the motor patterns observed in play are similar to those observed in other functional contexts; (2) play patterns may be incomplete; (3) play patterns may be inhibited; (4) certain behavior patterns are unique to the play context; (5) play patterns may be exaggerated or uneconomical; (6) play occurs in different situations or as a result of different stimuli; (7) patterns may be repeated more during play; (8) play patterns may be relatively unordered; (9) patterns from different functional spheres may alternate during play; (10) play is characteristic of immature animals.

Fagen (1974) describes this approach, which emphasizes the form, appearance, and temporal patterning of play, as the "structuralist" approach, and distinguishes it from the "functionalist" approach which emphasizes the causes and adaptive significance of play. But structure and function are inseparable, and "structuralists" such as Loizos have, in fact, drawn functional inferences based on their characterizations of the structure of play.

Williams (1966) argues that the evolutionary purpose of a mechanism (e.g., playfighting) can be determined only by examining the machinery (e.g., the details of playfighting), and arguing that these means are appropriate to particular ends (e.g., the development of fighting skills). Fagen (1974:850) writes that it is difficult to verify practice hypotheses "because they fail to specify particular psychological and evolutionary mechanisms that could result in adaptive behavior having 'playful' characteristics." But it is equally true that structuralists who reject practice hypotheses fail to show why adaptive behavior could *not* be expected to have "playful" characteristics. Rather, they assume that the differences between play patterns and the similar non-play patterns somehow render practice theories suspect *prima facie.*

The fallacy in structuralist arguments against the practice theory of play is that a logically necessary step has been omitted. Loizos argues: (1) play has structure X; (2) the similar "serious" adult activities have structure Y; (3) therefore, play cannot be explained as an adaptation to improve performances of "serious" adult activities. But whether play has been designed by natural selection to serve a practice function cannot be answered simply by comparing play and non-play behavior patterns. In addition, it is necessary to have criteria for determining whether a given behavior pattern is designed appropriately for improving subsequent performances. The practice theory can be rejected confidently only after it has been demonstrated that play does not meet these criteria.

To my knowledge, criteria for identifying behavior patterns designed by natural selection to improve specific skills through practice have not been developed. Nevertheless, it is worthwhile to examine each of the ten characteristics of play listed above in order to consider their consequences for practice theories given our present, imperfect, understanding of playfighting, of fighting, and of how skilled performances develop.

(1) *The motor patterns observed in play are similar to those observed in other functional contexts.* The notion of "practice" implies that repetitions must in some respects structurally resemble the behavior whose proficiency is to be improved. With one exception, discussed below, the patterns of playfighting exhibited by a species of mammal resemble the fighting patterns of that species. For example, goats (*Capra hircus*), blacktail deer (*Odocoileus hemionus*) and domestic cattle butt with their heads in play (Brownlee 1954, Müller-Schwarze and Müller-Schwarze 1969, Chepko 1971). The similarity between polecat playfighting and fighting already has been noted (Poole 1966, 1967). Steiner (1971:259) writes of Columbian ground squirrels:

> During the breeding season, soon after coming out of hibernation, mature males fight fiercely and intensively, using basically the same patterns and hitting the same body parts—but with "high intensity"—as juveniles do in playfighting. This fact is clearly confirmed by the wounds and scars frequently found on the body parts of big males during the breeding season.

Fighting has not been studied in detail in rhesus monkeys or in any other species of nonhuman primate. (Such a study would require the analysis of motion picture films of many fights.) It is therefore impossible to compare rhesus playfighting and fighting in detail, although the few fights I have witnessed suggest striking similarities. One difference can be noted: at low intensities, or when combatants are mutually fearful, slapping is observed frequently during rhesus agonistic interactions (Bernstein et al. 1974a, Southwick et al. 1974, personal observations). While occasional "sparring" occurs during rhesus playfights, I could not distinguish it reliably from reaching and parrying, and it is not an important feature of playfighting. Apparently much more sparring occurs in the play of baboons (Owens 1975a).

Owens (1975b) reports that baboon playfights resemble the "mutual" fighting characteristic of adult males and for this reason he suggests that playfighting provides fighting practice. Henry and Herrero (1974) find that the playfights of American black bears closely resemble fights, although the rearing and pawing matches observed in play are not observed in fights. Gentry (1974) notes that playfighting among sea lions resembles adult fighting, and he writes: "The continuity between behavior of the young, or juveniles, and of adults is obvious" (p. 392). Farentinos (1971) also reports a marked similarity between sea lion playfights and fights, citing the lack of wounding in the former as the major difference.

Wilson (1974) describes play in the common seal (*Phoca vitulina*) and compares it to the grey seal (*Halichoerus grypus*). Immature grey seals playfight by lunging at each other and by rearing and lunging at each other's cheeks, the same patterns used by adult grey seals during breeding-season fights. Groups of immature common seals "haul out" together on a rock during play, which Wilson interprets as mimicking anti-predator behavior, and also engage in a pattern of dyadic play in which the animals make nose-to-nose or nose-to-face contact and then somersault over each other while maintaining contact, a pattern Wilson terms "rolling." Common seals are exceptional in that this pattern does not resemble any adult pattern; they have never been observed to fight.

Members of a sibling species of the common seal, *Phoca kuruensis,* do, however, fight during the breeding season using a pattern similar to the rolling play of *P. vitulina,* except that they bite. Wilson suggests that the fighting patterns of *P. kuruensis* may have been derived from the rolling play patterns typical of *P. vitulina,* which, she suggests, function to acquaint individuals with one another. It strikes me, however, as extraordinarily improbable that a behavior pattern designed to meet only the very general requirement of acquainting individuals with one another would, by chance, turn out to have the specific features required to be an effective fighting pattern. It seems more likely that the recent common ancestor of *P. vitulina* and *kuruensis* fought, and that fighting patterns have been retained in *kuruensis* and in similar form in the play of *vitulina.*

In general, then, mammalian playfighting patterns resemble fighting patterns closely enough to make a practice hypothesis tenable and, to many observers, compelling.

(2) *Play patterns may be incomplete compared with patterns observed in other functional contexts.* Because it lacks stereotyped agonistic signals, playfighting is characterized frequently as "incomplete" compared to behavior observed during agonistic encounters.

The overwhelming majority of agonistic encounters among rhesus monkeys involve signals of threat and submission, not fighting. In fact, most rhesus communication functions to mediate agonistic, but nonfighting, interactions (Hinde and Rowell 1962, Rowell and Hinde 1962, Altmann 1962a). On the other hand, rhesus playfighting lacks agonistic signals, including loud vocalizations and piloerection. Sade (1967:100) describes an "intense" rhesus agonistic encounter:

> . . . the attacking monkey charged, roaring and batting at another, then grabbed and held the victim while biting him on the back. As the attack began, the victim cowered away, grimacing and shrieking, presenting his hindquarters to the attacking monkey at the same time. Almost immediately the victim leapt away and fled, still shrieking and grimacing, and finally escaped after being bitten.

But playfighting rhesus monkeys do not roar, cower, grimace, shriek and present: a monkey "attacked" in play responds with play "counterattack." As described in chapter 3, playfighting rhesus move to face their partners; lack of submission is the *sine qua non* of playfighting.

Playfighting, then, mimics only the most extreme, unritualized form of aggression. Loizos (1969:42) makes a similar point in her report on play among captive chimpanzees:

> That grabbing, pulling, biting and wrestling occur most frequently in a nondispersal play situation may be accounted for by the fact that the vast majority of adult chimpanzee agonistic encounters consist of threat alone; they rarely fight. An analysis of only those dispersal agonistic encounters involving actual

attack might have produced a different picture, in which no action patterns correlated significantly with either dispersal or non-dispersal, and all occurred equally often in either context.

The absence of stereotyped agonistic signals as a distinguishing feature of playfighting has been noted in stumptail macaques (Bertrand 1969), patas monkeys (Hall 1965), baboons (Owens 1975a), sea lions (Farentinos 1971), polecats (Poole 1966, 1967), blacktail deer (Müller-Schwarze 1971), and black bears (Henry and Herrero 1974), although Steiner (1971) occasionally observed an arched back threat as a play preliminary in Columbian ground squirrels. The absence of agonistic signals is almost certainly a general characteristic of mammalian play (Aldis 1975); in fact, Bekoff (1972) cites the absence of passive-submissive behaviors as part of his definition of play.

Far from rendering suspect the practice hypothesis, the lack of agonistic signals is evidence in its favor. Since it is generally adaptive for animals to avoid fights, stereotyped signals evolved to mediate agonistic encounters by indicating intent to attack or flee. But it is not generally adaptive for animals to avoid playfights, and attack, avoidance, and passivity make playfighting impossible. Selection can be expected to eliminate agonistic signals, which produce these responses, from a practice fighting context. This view is supported by instances in which agonistic signals do occur in the course of a rhesus playfight: the playfight stops immediately, or becomes an agonistic interaction, usually involving other monkeys. Threat and submissive signals also terminate playfights in coyotes (Bekoff 1974) and black bears (Henry and Herrero 1974).

(3) *Play patterns may be inhibited compared to patterns observed in other functional contexts.* Playfighting could not exist if playfighting movements were as intense as fighting movements; the risk of damage would be so great that animals would avoid playfights as they avoid fights. The relative inhibition of playfighting movements has been noted by many observers (e.g., Marler and Hamilton 1966, Steiner 1971, Bekoff 1972, Washburn and Strum 1972, Miller 1973, Aldis 1975, Owens 1975a). Although rhesus playbites are clearly inhibited, there is substantial variation in the degree of inhibition; in some cases a "bite" involves merely placing the open mouth on the partner's body, while in other cases the partner is dragged across the ground or lifted into the air in the biter's teeth.

If the function of playfighting is to practice and perfect fighting skills, each animal can be expected to "adopt a strategy" enabling it to maximize the development of its skills. The more playfighting movements are inhibited the less they will approximate real fighting, the less a playing animal will succeed in biting and gaining advantageous positions, and the less useful will be the practice. On the other hand, the more uninhibited playfighting movements become, the more the animal risks being attacked or avoided. Perhaps playfighting animals strike a compromise between advantage-seeking and inhibition.

Fox (1971:152) shows that domestic dog and wolf pups must learn to inhibit bites in order to engage in playfights of long duration:

> The gentleness of the bite of a four-month-old wolf or dog contrasts with the often painful bite by the same animal at six weeks of age. Pups that have been hand-raised and not allowed to play with each other until twelve or sixteen weeks of age seem to lack bite inhibition when first put together. Play fighting is of short duration because one or both pups bite too hard and one escapes or retaliates and actual fighting breaks out. After a few days they soon learn to control their bite, and play sequences are of longer duration.

Occasionally rhesus playfights turn into real fights (chapter 4, Sade 1966, Lindburg 1971), as do playfights among adolescent male chimpanzees (Lawick-Goodall 1968), suggesting that these primates sometimes may regulate the intensity of their movements close to the maximum tolerable limit.

This point of view is supported by observation of the choice of play partners. The only actual fights an animal is ever likely to engage in are with opponents of approximately equal ability. If there is an obvious disparity in ability, the less capable animal will flee to avoid the interaction, or, if caught, become passive or submissive. To derive the maximum benefit from playfighting, animals can be expected to choose partners of similar ability most frequently. This is borne out among rhesus monkeys (chapter 4), crab-eating macaques (Fady 1969), bonnet macaques (Simonds 1965), chimpanzees (Goodall 1965), and baboons (Owens 1975a).

The phenomenon of "self-handicapping," wherein animals are more inhibited playfighting partners much smaller than themselves than they are playfighting partners more nearly their own size, provides an additional line of evidence that animals adjust the intensity of their playfighting movements to a level tolerable to their partners. This has been noted in rhesus monkeys (this study, Altmann 1962b), baboons (Owens 1975a), and may be a general mammalian characteristic (Aldis 1975).

(4) *Certain behavior patterns are unique to the play context.* In rhesus monkeys, and probably in all mammals that playfight, some movements occur in the context of playfighting that do not appear in the context of fighting. Most of these appear to function as signals of play solicitation (invitation) or play intention (chapter 6, Marler and Hamilton 1966, Bekoff 1974, Gentry 1974, Henry and Herrero 1974, Aldis 1975).

Fighting among nonhuman animals is not known to be solicited, and, by definition, fighting cannot include a play-intention signal. Signals of intention and invitation increase the probability that fighting skills will be practiced without harm to the participants by indicating playfighting intent and by encouraging partners to play. There is, however, a danger here of circular argument: if every movement that could not be explained as practice fighting were assumed to be a play signal, the practice theory of play would be rendered less vulnerable to disproof. Nevertheless, several independent lines of evidence (see chapter 6) indicate that nearly all of these movements are specialized play signals.

In the intervals between playfights rhesus occasionally exhibit novel behaviors that seem neither to be oriented to a play partner nor to have a signal function. Examples are reaching back with one hand and grasping a foot, whirling around, and walking a few steps bipedally, arms waving and head thrown back. Such movements are probably incidental effects of the relaxed attitude often adopted by monkeys between playfights. During relaxed playfights between an infant and a juvenile, the juvenile, in a sitting position, occasionally leaned backwards and threw its head back. While their existence does not favor the practice theory, such movements occur too infrequently to pose much of a challenge to it. The great majority of movements unique to the playfighting context apparently are specialized signals.

(5) *Play patterns may be exaggerated or uneconomical compared with patterns observed in other functional contexts.* As Henry and Herrero (1974) remark, this description is vague and difficult to test. During episodes of rhesus playfighting, some movements occurring between playfights appear to be exaggerated. If, as I have argued,

these movements are mostly specialized play signals, exaggeration is to be expected, since most specialized signals exaggerate movements in the species' repertoire. Playfighting itself appears to be unexaggerated (inhibited) compared with fighting. Using duration of three acts (body bite, stand over, and scruff bite) among eastern coyotes (*C. latrans*) as a measure of exaggeration, Hill and Bekoff (cited in Bekoff 1976a) found that for one of the three acts there was no significant difference between play and aggression and for two of the acts play was less exaggerated than aggression.

Even if some playfighting movements were demonstrated to be exaggerated compared with the fighting movements they mimic, this demonstration would not have clear-cut consequences for the practice theory. In the development and teaching of sports skills, exaggeration of some movements frequently is an effective tool.

(6) *Play occurs in different situations, or as a result of different stimuli, from the behavior it mimics.* Play is low in the "hierarchy of functional systems" (Müller-Schwarze 1971), appearing in the absence of immediate survival needs such as those for food, water, or escape from danger, and environmental discomforts such as very hot or rainy weather (Aldis 1975). As I have already pointed out, competitive situations that render rhesus fighting likely render playfighting unlikely, and an outbreak of serious aggression in the troop may terminate play for hours. These features seem completely compatible with a practice theory.

(7) *Patterns may be repeated more during play than during the nonplay activity it resembles.* By definition, play does not have the biological goal of the activity it resembles (Leyhausen 1973). Mutual fighting is extremely dangerous; even a short fight may result in wounding or death, and Pyrrhic victories may be won. Once a fight has begun, it is to the advantage of both combatants to terminate as soon as it becomes clear which animal will win. If this can be determined without fighting, it is to their mutual advantage not to fight at all. As playfights are not dangerous, different constraints obtain on their structure. In fighting, selection favors animals that succeed with minimum injury. If the practice theory is correct, in playfighting, selection favors animals that increase their fighting skills.

Owens (1975b) found that contact between baboons was greater during playfights than during aggression, presumably resulting in more repetitions during play. When Henry and Herrero (1974) compared playfighting and fighting among black bears they found some motor patterns that were repeated more frequently during playfights. Since playfights occur much more frequently than fights, the *total* repetitions during playfighting will, of course, be much greater than during fighting.

Repetition is precisely what is required to develop high levels of skilled performance. In the development of human skills, whether it is desirable to practice components of an activity together or separately varies with the activity (Fitts and Posner 1967) and presumably with age; similar considerations may determine how selection operates on play patterns of nonhuman animals.

(8) *Play patterns may be relatively unordered compared with similar patterns observed in other contexts.* Meyer-Holzapfel's (1956) suggestion that playing animals tend to be active in any way whatsoever conjures up images of animals moving about like gas molecules. In a similar vein, Loizos (1967:179) writes: "It is suggested that play has no formalized sequence of events, such that action A will always be followed by actions B, C or D. In play, depending upon the feedback from the object or the social partner, A may be followed with equal likelihood by B or by Z." Bekoff (1974) speculates that order of movements during playfights may differ from the order during fights as a metacommunicative signal identifying play. While this hypothesis may be correct, certainly it is not necessary, since many features of playfighting differentiate it clearly from fighting. As Millar (1968:80) has written, "all that needs to be assumed is that the . . . [animal] has learned to discriminate the many different cues which distinguish friendly from hostile situations."

Variability in rhesus behavior is found in the form of individual movements and in the ordering of these movements into sequences. Variability in movement form unquestionably declines with age as extraneous moves are eliminated; goals are attained with increasing economy and precision as movements become more like those of an adult. But the question of variability in the order in which movements occur is more complex. Whether or not the order is variable probably depends on the nature of the activity and the goal of a social interaction.

Animal social interaction can be considered to be of two types. Most frequently, the participants pursue the same goal; there is an identity of interests, the animals cooperate, and there is mutual facilitation of movement. Less frequently, the participants pursue opposite goals; there is a conflict of interests, the animals are antagonistic, and there is mutual countering of movement. Selection can be expected to operate on these types of interaction in opposite ways. Pursuit of identical goals leads to simple, relatively inflexible, stereotyped interactions, in which the order of movements is relatively invariant and predictable. Pursuit of opposite goals leads to complex, relatively flexible, unstereotyped interactions in which the order of movements is relatively variable and unpredictable.

As a result of natural selection and individual learning, most signals that animals emit, such as an infant giving a "lost" call or an estrous female presenting to a male, elicit responses that, on the average, benefit both the signaler and the responder. Competitive interactions usually are mediated by stereotyped signals, and the participants can be considered to be cooperating in avoiding physical conflict. Thus, agonistic signals are mutually beneficial insofar as they reduce the likelihood of fighting by communicating intent. Even the ritualized "herding" neckbite that an adult male hamadrayas baboon delivers to a female member of his harem can be considered to benefit the female because, by subsequently following the male, she avoids a more serious bite. But a bite delivered in combat has precisely the opposite effect: the bitee's response is to employ defensive and offensive tactics that are both highly constrained by the biter's behavior and are directly contrary to the biter's interests.

Almost all animal behavior commonly called "play" mimics antagonistic, not cooperative, interactions: in fighting, chasing, fleeing, predation, and anti-predator behavior the participants pursue opposed goals.[2] In such interactions it is advantageous to have the option of selecting from alternate movements, both to respond with maximum precision to the exact demands of the instant and to prevent the opponent from anticipating and countering the move, and a variable order of component movements is to be expected.

2. Kruuk (1975:119) notes that only very recently has it become clear how closely adjusted the anti-predator behavior of a prey species is to the hunting strategies of its predators and how complex is "the defense system which a predator must penetrate in order to eat."

The order of movements during playfights is one of the most important considerations in evaluating the practice theory of play. The most fundamental question, however, is not whether movements occur during playfights in the same order that they occur during fights, but rather: Are playfighting movements ordered *appropriately* to improve fighting performance? In chapters 3, 4, and 6 I argue at length that rhesus playfighting is highly ordered in that monkeys attempt to bite while not being bitten, but the order of movements cannot be compared with rhesus fighting, which has not been studied.

Müller-Schwarze (1968) and Müller-Schwarze and Müller-Schwarze (1969) report that major groupings of elements in the play of blacktail deer occurred in a definite order. Bekoff (in press) reports that coyote play sequences were more variable than agonistic sequences in terms of the distribution of transitional probabilities. Aldis (1975) notes that animals emphasize defense rather than offense both in fighting and playfighting, but he perceives a "random element" in playfighting that fighting lacks. Henry and Herrero (1974) find that, while playfighting black bears tend strongly to bite the partner on the side of the face and on the neck, fighting bears tend even more strongly to bite these areas, indicating that biting is somewhat more variable during playfights than it is during fights.

A greater variability in playfighting movements is precisely what is to be expected if fighting skills are developed during playfighting; variable movements are the raw materials from which efficient responses are shaped. Without variability, there can be no improvement. Serious athletes in all sports practice some movement patterns outside the game itself. Such practice is useful because it permits concentrated repetitions of a single pattern that may occur infrequently during the actual game, but it is useful also because it allows the athlete to vary, and perhaps thereby improve, the pattern. Since most variations can be expected to be dysfunctional, athletes are unlikely to risk experimenting during the game itself.

Poole and Fish (1975) report that the elements of aggressive play in the laboratory rat (*Rattus norvegicus*) were organized into structured sequences that differed from sequences of elements in aggressive behavior. For example, although social play resembled adult fighting it lacked elements indicative of high levels of attack and fear such as catalepsy, freeze, and uninhibited bite. In addition, rat aggressive behavior can be divided into either entirely flight-motivated or entirely fight-motivated types, but in aggressive play frequent transitions between the two types of behaviors occurred. These data seem consistent with the practice theory: a behavior pattern that functions to develop fighting skills need not have the same sequential order of elements as an actual fight, in which it is adaptive to damage the opponent quickly and to submit or flee as soon as defeat becomes probable.

To evaluate the practice theory with respect to the order of movements it is necessary to have a theory of skill development in addition to evidence about the details of playfighting and fighting. Still more to the point, it is useful to have studies of the ontogeny of playfighting and fighting. There may be, for example, more variability during playfights than the practice theory can account for, and some tactics developed and perfected during playfights may be dysfunctional in fights. But the available evidence suggests that the order of movements during playfights is probably adaptive in developing skilled fighting performance.

(9) *Patterns from different functional spheres may alternate in play although they do not alternate in non-play contexts.* A general feature of mammalian play is that patterns mimicking aggression, copulation, and capture of prey may all occur during a single play sequence (Müller-Schwarze 1968, 1971, Aldis 1975). Among immature rhesus, for example, a mounter and a mountee frequently begin to playfight, whereas adult rhesus mountings virtually never become fights. Columbian ground squirrels sometimes simultaneously exhibit elements of mounting and wrestling, which Steiner (1971) terms "mosaic behavior." In the present study, very young rhesus infants occasionally were observed to make pelvic thrusts while wrestling, but such "mosaic behavior" was never observed, except briefly in transitions from mounting to playfighting, among older infants and juveniles. (Note that in the detailed examples of rhesus playfights in chapter 3 and appendix 1, no elements of copulation or grooming occur.) Mosaic behavior has not been reported in other mammals.

"Serious" behavior patterns occur in appropriate circumstances; animals flee, for example, when menaced by a predator. As discussed above, circumstances apparently are appropriate for play when animals are not hungry, hot, frightened, etc., and if several types of behavior are susceptible to improvement through repetition, it is not surprising that, in these circumstances, immature animals sometimes alternate between different types of behavior.

The practice theory can account for some features of the alternation of behavior. Studies of humans have shown that frequent repetitions interspersed with frequent rest periods are more efficient in increasing skill than are long, continuous repetitions without rest periods. "This is particularly true where the skill requires much motor activity, since the tendency to practice incorrect response patterns may increase as the muscle groups involved tire" (Fitts and Posner 1967:13). Among rhesus monkeys, the median length of playfights is four to five seconds for all age-sex classes, and sitting, standing, slow walking or climbing are the most common activities during intervals between playfights. Alternation between activities of different types might rest particular muscle groups even if all the activities were strenuous.

If play patterns have been designed by natural selection for efficient skill acquisition, the frequency with which an activity occurs in play can be expected to be determined by: (a) intensity of selection pressure on the performance of the similar activity in its "serious" context; and (b) difficulty of mastery of the activity. As discussed above, since one animal succeeds in a fight only to the extent that its opponent fails, combatants work at cross purposes to each other, and fighting therefore is far more complex, fast-paced, and unpredictable than activities such as copulation. In a fight, whether the animal survives or dies may be a matter of fractions of inches and seconds; fighting, although it is relatively infrequent, is difficult to master and is a critical agent of natural selection.

Owens (1975a) estimates that 2 to 5 percent of baboon social play is "sex play" and the remainder is aggressive play. Henry and Herrero (1974) report that black bear social play consists of 2 percent sexual patterns and 98 percent aggressive patterns. Aldis (1975) estimates that in the mammals he observed, aggressive play is 50 to 100 times as frequent as immature sexual behavior, and a similar figure probably is valid for rhesus monkeys.

Washburn and Hamburg (1965a:5) point out that animals must be able to respond both to daily needs and to occasional crises; a primate is "more playful than there is any need for on the average day. . . . survival requires coping with the rare event." If activities were practiced by immatures in proportion to their frequency of occurrence in adult life, a juvenile male rhesus monkey would spend almost all of his waking hours practicing sitting (see Fisler 1967). The practice theory predicts that animals will playfight far more frequently than they will exhibit sexual patterns, and the evidence bears out this prediction.

(10) *Play is characteristic of immature animals.* While adults of some species playfight occasionally, playfighting is much more frequently and uniformly observed among immature animals in all species that play. This characteristic is predicted by the practice theory of play. As the level of skill increases with practice, the rate of improvement for the same amount of effort constantly declines; at very high levels of skill an enormous investment of time and energy is required to effect small increments of improvement in performance (Fitts and Posner 1967). Playfighting involves a substantial investment of time, energy, and risk of exposure to injury and predators, and the investment per unit of time probably increases with age because larger animals require more calories and because older, highly skilled animals pose a greater threat to each other if a playfight turns into a fight. It is to be expected, then, that at some point in the life histories of members of a playful species the investment (in fitness) required to add increments of skill will outweigh the benefit, and selection will favor animals that cease to play at that point.

To summarize the argument, many students of play reject the practice theory because it fails to explain the differences between play activities and similar activities mimicked by play. These critics do not deny that the performance of many behaviors may improve as a consequence of playing, but they interpret improved performance as an incidental effect, since, in their view, play does not seem designed to produce it. As Loizos remarks, "it is not necessary to play in order to practise—there is no reason why the animal should not just practise." Although Loizos does not define "practice," or specify how practice can be identified and differentiated from play, it is reasonably clear that she, and other critics of the practice theory, believe that a behavior pattern designed to be "practice" would lack many of the ten features enumerated above.

I argue, however, that it is incorrect to suppose the practice theory to be refuted as a direct function of the number of differences between play and the "serious" patterns play mimics. We do not conclude that, because batting practice differs in many respects from a baseball game, it is not designed to improve subsequent baseball performances; on the contrary, we know that batting practice is evidence of serious intent to improve baseball performances, and that players who confine their practice to playing baseball are less serious about the game and are less likely to improve. By considering each feature in which play patterns contrast with the "serious" patterns they mimic I have tried to show that not only are these features in harmony with the practice theory, but many are predicted by it.

What is Play?

At this point it is appropriate to return to the question, originally posed in chapter 1, of what constitutes "play." Many of those who discuss animal "play" do not attempt to define it, but regard it nonetheless as a natural category of behavior because, it is claimed, there is high interobserver reliability in identifying "play" (Lorenz 1956, Loizos 1966, 1967, Miller 1973). Mason (1965:530), for example, writes: "In spite of the difficulties in arriving at an acceptable and comprehensive definition of play, the fact remains that observers show considerable agreement in judging 'playful behavior.' . . . The problem of a comprehensive definition is more serious in theory than in practice." Although observers reliably distinguish aggressive play from genuine aggression—which, considering the number of differences between them, is not surprising—there is not, in fact, general agreement in identifying play. Some students regard immature sexual patterns as "play" (e.g., Altmann 1962a), while others insist that these patterns are not "play" (e.g., Aldis 1975); Lancaster (1971) considers the infant-caretaking patterns of juvenile females to be "play," but Ghiselin (1974) disagrees.

Consider the following definitions, or characterizations, of play: Müller-Schwarze (1971:233) defines motor play as

> . . . the performance of a mixed sequence of mostly stereotyped behavior patterns by an immature animal. These patterns belong to different functional systems and do not serve their usual functions. The patterns occur often in a social situation, under moderate general arousal, but low specific motivation.

To Bekoff (1972:417) social play is

> . . . that behavior which is performed during social interactions in which there is a decrease in social distance between the interactants, and no evidence of social investigation or of agonistic (offensive or defensive) or passive-submissive behaviors on the part of the members of a dyad (triad, etc.), although these actions may occur as derived acts during play. . . . In addition, there is a lability of the temporal sequence of action patterns, actions from various motivational contexts (e.g., sexual and agonistic) being combined.

Fagen (1974:850) characterizes play as

> . . . active, oriented behavior whose structure is highly variable, which apparently lacks immediate purpose, and which is often accompanied by specific signal patterns.

Aldis (1975:126) describes playchasing and playfighting:

> Almost everyone would agree that chasing and play fighting in young animals is play. The serious counterparts of these behaviors may be broadly classified as agonistic behaviors—predation, aggression, and flight. In play, these behaviors are usually accompanied by play signals and are modified in certain ways (lower intensity, relaxed muscle tone) from their serious counterparts. In addition, some serious behaviors may be omitted, new behaviors may be added, and the order may be changed. The causation of play may also differ from that of serious behavior.

The essential common features of these varied definitions are not immediately evident, but their defining characteristics may be pared down in several ways. First, we might leave aside characteristics prefaced by "often" and "may," which suggest they are variable or optional. Second, we might leave aside characteristics that should have been optional: for example, playfighting is easily recognizable and identifiable without being "mixed" with patterns from other functional contexts. Rhesus monkeys may engage in a series of playfights and simply sit, stand, or walk in the intervals between them. Henry and Herrero (1974) found that sexual patterns occurred in only 3.9 percent of black bear play episodes; the remainder consisted of patterns of playfighting and playchasing only. Third, we might leave aside characteristics, such as being "oriented," that, while unarguable, do not seem to be essential in distinguishing "play" from other kinds of behavior. Fourth, we might leave aside characteristics, such as having a "variable structure," that are vague or arguable.

The essential features of those definitions seem, then, to be that "play" patterns differ from similar patterns in the species repertoire, and either lack immediate function or, at the least, lack the function of the patterns they resemble. (Clearly, the decision about what constitutes immediate function rests with the observer; one assumes that to the animals, all activity has immediate benefit. Millar (1968:99) writes: "The felt benefits of rushing to and fro may be quite as immediate as those of feeding.") "Play," then, exists in contrasts: playfighting contrasts with fighting; immature sexual patterns contrast with mature sexual patterns; the infant caretaking activities of juvenile females contrast with the infant caretaking activities of mothers.

It is because the existence of "play" depends thus upon contrasts that some students of the ontogenetic development of animal behavior consider "play" to be a useless category and concept. They point out that behavior patterns develop from simple to complex, from rudimentary to complete, and that the activities of immature animals cannot be understood by contrasting them with adult activities; juvenile behavior is appropriate to the needs of juveniles, adult behavior is appropriate to the needs of adults (Welker 1971, Lazar and Beckhorn 1974). In this view, the behavior patterns of immature animals are not mixtures of incomplete, exaggerated, or repeated adult patterns: the opposite is true; adult patterns are a *product* of immature patterns (Lazar and Beckhorn 1974). Welker (1971) points out that behavior patterns of weanling rats, generally considered to be "play," are presaged at earlier ages by simpler, more rudimentary responses, such as turning toward the source of body contact, and these early precursors are never considered to be "play." These writers conclude, then, that "play" is neither a valid class of behavior nor a scientifically useful concept. Rather, behavior develops ontogenetically by progressive differentiation and integration of patterns, and it is this developmental process, not an undefinable and arbitrary component, "play," that is the proper unit of study.

While in many respects this is a compelling point of view, it seems to be open to objections of three sorts: (1) It assumes that the behavior patterns of immature animals have developmental adaptive significance, and not all biologists are willing to make this assumption. For example, Ghiselin (1974) considers "play" to be a nonarbitrary category of behavior whose adaptive significance is not developmental at all; rather, Ghiselin believes that play serves immediate, nondevelopmental functions in that, by playing, immature animals are protected from genuinely competitive interactions. (2) By assuming that immature behavior patterns are appropriate for the level of development at which they occur, this formulation does not lend itself readily to the question: "appropriate toward what end, or for what purpose?" Those who believe that the function of "play" is to produce abnormal, or novel, behaviors probably will not grant the assumption that the normal behavior of immatures is designed to produce the normal behavior of adults. (3) The most serious objection is that "play" is not invariably defined by contrasting immature and mature activities; in some cases, it is defined by contrasting two potential modes of activity in the same animal. Immature animals that playfight, playchase, and play at capturing prey can also fight, chase, and capture prey (Ewer 1968, Bekoff 1974), although not necessarily so skillfully as adults do. Similarly, although most adults rarely or never playchase or playfight, some do (chapter 11, Leyhausen 1973, Bekoff 1974).

The Ontogeny of Rhesus Behavior

The development of play in laboratory-reared rhesus monkeys is discussed by Rosenblum (1961), Hansen (1962, 1966), Hinde, Rowell, and Spencer-Booth (1964), Harlow and Harlow (1965), Hinde and Spencer-Booth (1967), Harlow (1969), and Suomi and Harlow (1971). The Wisconsin studies divided rhesus peer-related development into four "stages": (1) *reflex,* a laboratory artifact resulting from the absence of the infants' mothers (Harlow 1969); (2) *exploration,* in which peers are explored visually, orally, and tactually (Harlow 1969); (3) *peer utilization* or *social play,* including playfighting (rough-and-tumble play) and playchasing (approach-withdrawal play) (Harlow 1969); and (4) *aggressive play,* which emerges near the end of the first year: "The monkeys cry out in dismay from time to time as the wrestling, grabbing and biting become rough and tumble for real and not merely for fun" (Harlow 1969:347), and "the intensity of playfighting increases, barking and piloerection occur, and play may be one-sided, the non-participating animal making frantic efforts of escape" (Hansen 1962).

Apparently on the basis of a developmental model similar to that of the Wisconsin studies, Hinde (1971:47) implies that the playfighting of immature rhesus is simply a developmental stage in the ontogeny of fighting:

> The relation among the tentative sexual patterns of monkeys in their early months, the near-complete patterns shown by adolescents, and the complete adult patterns, does not seem to differ in kind from that between the various aggressive patterns seen at similar ages. The label "play" is equally suitable or unsuitable for the earlier stages.

The "aggressive play" stage, however, like the "reflex" stage, seems to be a laboratory artifact; in free-ranging rhesus monkeys of all ages playfighting is silent or almost so, and piloerection does not occur (this study, Bernstein and Mason 1963, Sade 1966).

Although nonhuman primates sometimes avoid attempted play initiations (this study, Lawick-Goodall 1968) and may indicate tension by directing threat away from play (this study, Lindburg 1971), both the human observer and other monkeys can almost always distinguish playfighting and fighting. A playfight that becomes a fight is marked by sudden piloerection, loud vocalizations, increase in the speed and vigor of movements, interference by other animals, and rapid termination of the interaction.

Playfighting reaches a peak of frequency, complexity, and vigor in one- and two-year-old males and then declines; the playfighting of four- and five-year-old males is slower-paced, less vigorous, less varied, more "stylized," and resembles fighting less than does the playfighting of younger males. I observed relatively few playfights among older animals, perhaps because the study was conducted almost entirely during the breeding season, when such play is known to be relatively infrequent (Sade 1966), but it has been reported in other studies of rhesus monkeys (e.g., Kaufmann 1967), and available descriptions seem to support the above conclusions. Sade (1966) describes the play of older males as "more sedate" and Lindburg (1971) notes that all adult play bouts are brief.

Kummer (1968) writes that the play of three-year-old hamadryas baboon (*Papio hamadryas*) males is "more inhibited" than the play of younger males. Simonds (1965:190) describes the play of adult male bonnet macaques:

> There were no threat gestures used, and no signs of attack, no biting to break the skin, no growling or screeching, nor the lunging and slapping that takes place during a threat sequence. These males were clearly playing and their

Photo 7.1 *A two-year-old female holds her infant sister. Their mother is in estrus and has formed a consortship with a male.*

preliminary gestures were like those used by juveniles and subadult males in an approach to a play situation. . . . There was no tenseness in the action of either male.

Like mature rhesus monkeys, immature monkeys eat, drink, sleep, use a variety of resting and locomotor patterns, groom, communicate with stereotyped signals, and exhibit recognizable patterns of sexual behavior, chasing, fleeing, and fighting. Because juveniles' nervous systems are not fully mature, and because they lack experience, all their behavior patterns probably differ, at least in subtle ways, from adult patterns, and yet not all are called "play." Grooming, for example, is never called "play," presumably because it is thought to serve the same immediate functions as adult grooming. Sexual patterns sometimes are called "play," however, because they lack a consummatory response and cannot result in impregnation. Juvenile females (and juvenile males as well) sometimes hold and carry infants (photo 7.1), a behavior pattern occasionally called "play," apparently because it is performed by juveniles and not by mothers. Nevertheless, immature sexual and infant-care patterns, like immature grooming patterns, seem to be the precursors of typical adult behaviors, and to become increasingly competent with age. After an adolescent male's first intravaginal ejaculation it permanently exhibits the normal adult copulatory pattern (Michael and Wilson 1973).

Some writers apparently consider immature sexual patterns to be "play" because they occur in a "play context." While rhesus monkeys often exhibit sexual patterns during intervals between playchases and playfights, they also exhibit these patterns in indistinguishable form at other times (also see Owens 1975a). Moreover, grooming, standing, sitting, walking, and climbing also occur in intervals between playfights and playchases, and yet these are never called "play."

Juveniles occasionally exhibit patterns of fighting and chasing and, in addition, regularly exhibit similar patterns which contrast with fighting and chasing in that they are relatively inhibited, lack specialized agonistic signals (including vocalizations and piloerection), and frequently are accompanied by specialized signals of their own. Adult monkeys may also exhibit this inhibited mode, but they do so rarely. Because individual animals possess both aggressive and aggressive-like patterns which are not simply successive developmental stages, most observers use the label "play" to identify the inhibited mode.

The practice theory of play is part of a general expectation that the behavior of immature organisms is designed for day-to-day survival and for developing skillful performances of species-typical activities. While criteria have not been developed for identifying behavior patterns designed by natural selection to provide practice in specific skills, the uncritical comparisons between behavior patterns of mature and immature animals, and the failure to consider obvious opportunities and constraints in the lives of young animals, have sometimes made juvenile behavior appear unduly mysterious. Juvenile monkeys do not practice grooming on tree trunks or other "inappropriate" objects, because more appropriate objects (other monkeys) are readily available; neither is there need for an inhibited, "play" mode of grooming incorporating specialized "playgrooming" signals and differing systematically from "serious" grooming. Similarly, although the sexual behavior of prepubescent monkeys obviously cannot fulfill all adult functions (although it may fulfill some of them), it is not associated with superfluous "playcopulation" signals and does not occur in a "playcopulation" mode, but develops from the rudimentary patterns of infants to complete copulation in three-year-olds.

Patterns of fighting, chasing, and predator avoidance, however, cannot be practiced efficiently or safely in the same way that grooming and sexual patterns are practiced. A monkey that waited for the "appropriate" stimulus situation to practice predator avoidance would receive far less experience than would a monkey that used similar patterns regularly during intraspecific interactions. Thus, although "freezing" during playchases is "inappropriate" in that the chaser is a juvenile monkey and not a predator, it seems entirely appropriate as practice in anti-predator behavior. Similarly, as I argue above, monkeys cannot "just practice" fighting. A behavior pattern that is designed appropriately to develop fighting skills must differ systematically from real fighting: relative inhibition, self-handicapping, lack of agonistic signals, presence of specialized "play" signals, occurrence during relaxed circumstances, and attempting to bite while not being bitten all seem to be appropriate design features for practice fighting.

Joslyn (1973) found that when juvenile female rhesus were injected with androgen the frequency of their aggressive behavior increased substantially but the frequency of their aggressive play did not, which suggests that aggression and aggressive play depend in part on different neural mechanisms. As a result of the experimental manipulation, the total amount of aggressive play in the study group fell markedly, demonstrating that aggression inhibits aggressive play. A "play" mode is necessary and appropriate for the development of fighting, chasing, and antipredator skills, but is unnecessary and inappropriate for the development of grooming, copulation, and many other species-typical behavior patterns.

In conclusion, I essentially agree with the view that the behavior of young organisms can be understood as a developmental process. On the other hand, as Bekoff (1974) correctly points out, individual animals exhibit some behavior patterns in two distinct modes; the term "play" seems to be a reasonable designation for one of these modes, and the possibility that play serves some short-term (nondevelopmental) functions remains open. Two other possible objections to the "developmental" position were raised: first, that play does not have developmental significance at all, and second, that it is not designed to produce species-typical behavior, except as an incidental effect, but to produce atypical, novel behavior. Throughout most of this book I dispute the first objection, and in the following chapter I argue that the second is almost surely incorrect.

Chapter eight

Play, Learning, and Behavioral Innovation

Several writers have suggested recently that the function, or a function, of animal and/or human play is to generate innovative or novel behavior patterns (Fedigan 1972, Miller 1973, Fagen 1974, Sutton-Smith 1975, in press, Wilson 1975b). Similarly, Baldwin and Baldwin (1977) suggest that play functions to optimize arousal by providing organisms with novel stimuli.

Fedigan, for example, noting a correlation between behavioral plasticity and playfulness in "higher" animals, suggests that by playing, young animals innovate and thereby individualize their behavior, and do not simply learn what the adults of their species already have learned. Miller implies that although specific skills may be developed as an incidental result of their use in play, play is designed to produce novelty, not skill. Fagen suggests that an animal's progeny increase their behavioral variability by playing, and thus play is functionally analogous to chromosomal processes that produce phenotypically variable offspring.

Learning, Behavioral Flexibility, and the Development of Skill

Novelty theories of play appear to have their origins in two assumptions. The first is the assumption of structuralists, analyzed in detail in the last chapter, that the practice/developmental theory of play cannot account for the differences between play and similar non-play behavior. The second is the assumption that, because animals with substantial learning abilities are more flexible behaviorally than animals with lesser abilities, the function of learning is to permit animals to acquire behavior patterns not shared by conspecifics. In this chapter the latter assumption is examined: although the primary focus is on rhesus monkeys, this assumption can be questioned both with respect to simpler organisms, such as birds, and more complex organisms, such as humans.

Many discussions of the evolution of animal behavior imply that the only function of the ability to learn is to permit organisms to adapt to unpredictable or variable environmental conditions through behavioral flexibility. Williams (1966), for example, argues that obligate adaptations (such as "instinct") always are cheaper genetically than facultative adaptations (such as learning), and that whenever a structural or behavioral characteristic is universally adaptive in a population it can be expected to be obligate. Williams maintains that learning will be found to be important only where animals must be prepared to adapt to unpredictable conditions. Similarly, Alcock (1975) writes that learning abilities evolve where environmental variability is predictable.

Learning Complex Discriminations

The well known phenomenon of imprinting can be used to exemplify the inadequacy of these views. Soon after hatching, ducklings and goslings will follow a moving object if that object has certain, fairly general, properties. Subsequently, they will follow only this object, on which they are said to have been "imprinted" (Marler and Hamilton 1966). This learning ability is not an adaptation to a variable or unpredictable environment in which newly hatched birds are equally likely to encounter rubber balls, Konrad Lorenz, and parent birds; on the contrary, it is the general absence of rubber balls and Konrad Lorenz that made the evolution of imprinting possible. Because the environment in which birds hatch is stable and predictable, and the first appropriately moving object encountered is virtually certain to be a parent bird, imprinting rarely proves maladaptive. The ability to be imprinted on a fairly wide array of objects may be a genetically more economical solution to a complex problem of discrimination than is "instinct." Immelmann (1975:245) writes: "Obviously the amount of information that can be stored in the genome is rather small as compared with the possibility of information storage in the memory. . . .

Therefore, object preferences based on learning will, as a rule, include more details and will thus be more precise than those based on genetic factors."

The relative economy of learning is suggested also by sex differences in sexual imprinting. When male ducks are raised with birds of a different species, upon reaching maturity most attempt to mate only with a member of the species with which they were raised, and are said to have been sexually imprinted on that species. Females, on the other hand, are resistant to sexual imprinting and generally choose to mate with members of their own species even when they have been raised with members of a different species (Marler and Hamilton 1966). This sex difference does not indicate that a female's most adaptive mate choice is predictable but a male's is unpredictable: invariably it is adaptive for both females and males to mate with a conspecific of the opposite sex.

The explanation of this sex difference may be that in most duck species females are selected for crypticity, and therefore are inconspicuously colored, while the males are highly conspicuous; as a result females of many species resemble one another while the males are distinctive in appearance (Marler and Hamilton 1966). Because males are brightly and distinctively colored, they can be discriminated easily, and obligate recognition of appropriate sex partners may be genetically economical for females, but learning may be the more economical solution to the difficult discrimination task facing males (see Immelmann 1975). This interpretation is supported by data on a sexually monomorphic duck species, the Chilean teal *(Anas flavirostris),* in which both sexes are drab and inconspicuous: only in this species do females have the ability to be sexually imprinted (Marler and Hamilton 1966). In sexually monomorphic species of dove both males and females can be sexually imprinted (Brown 1975).

Learning Complex Motor Skills

Although animals in a wide array of environments develop species-typical behavior patterns, these patterns nevertheless may be learned. Just as the ability to learn may be a genetically economical strategy for coping with complex discrimination problems, as in the example of imprinting, learning abilities may represent adaptations to develop complex motor patterns, even when these patterns are universally adaptive in the population and are exhibited by adults in an invariant, species-typical form. .For example, some bird species must learn species-typical songs (Brown 1975). This ability may be an adaptation to produce complex songs, which may be more effective than simple songs in attracting females (Nottebohm 1972) or maintaining territories by repelling rivals (Brown 1975). Rhesus monkeys (review in Mitchell 1970) and chimpanzees (Rogers 1973) that are deprived of the opportunity for all social learning lack many species-typical behavior patterns and exhibit many aberrant patterns. When such animals are tested in social situations they exhibit elements of normal behavior, but these elements are neither coordinated, in the proper sequence, nor exhibited in appropriate contexts.

Detailed research on development of skills has been conducted primarily on humans, but much of the analysis seems applicable to nonhuman animals as well (see also chapter 7). The development of skillful performances can be considered under five headings: (1) intention; (2) feedback; (3) patterns of action mediating intention and feedback; (4) reinforcement; (5) complex patterns (after Bruner 1973).

Bruner (1970, 1973) suggests that in human infants intention precedes skill in the sense that ineffective, initial movements are adapted (or "preadapted") to achieve recognizable goals or end states. These species-typical movements, the results of human evolution, constitute the "launching stock" from which the infant constructs skilled action. Feedback is of three types: internal signals of intention ("feedforward": Bruner 1973); effector signals during the action (Fitts and Posner 1967, Bruner 1973); and signals of the results of the completed act (Fitts and Posner 1967, Bruner 1973). Through practice, the infant coordinates these three types of feedback, comparing what was intended with what was achieved, and makes appropriate corrections. Once the initial movements achieve their goals they are modified through reinforcement (Klopfer 1970, Bruner 1973): they become less variable, and their patterning comes to anticipate the requirements of the act (Bruner 1973). As the initial movements are mastered, and become automatic, they appear as components of more complex skills (Bruner 1970, 1973), and the infant monitors the overall plan of the activity rather than its individual components (see Bruner 1970, 1972, Connolly 1970, Kay 1970). Bruner (1973:4) makes clear that the infant constructs behavior but does not acquire responses; the environment shapes responses but does not construct behavior:

> What leads to the emergence of particular higher-order action programs is a puzzle many of us share. They plainly are not selected by a process of reinforcement from a "lexicon" of random or near-random response elements. The new pattern emerges with an adaptive, serially ordered structure that reflects some internal principle of organization that is triggered by the environment.

The most significant points in this brief review are: (1) the initial movements that form the raw materials for complex skills are species typical; (2) the ordering of movements into complex action patterns reflects an internal organization that is appropriate with respect to specific goals; (3) action patterns are evaluated and modified in accordance with built-in criteria of successful performance. This analysis was developed largely from the study of the development of human infants' responses to objects. Since human motor patterns are far more open than those of any other animal species, nonhuman animals can be expected to exhibit even more stereotyped action patterns, sequences of action patterns, and criteria of correct performance.

Rhesus Behavioral Development

The ability to learn, then, is not necessarily an adaptation to unpredictable environments, and not all widespread species adapt to variable environmental conditions through variable behavior; many microorganisms, for example, have simple, widely encountered requirements. But even members of behaviorally flexible species rarely adapt through innovative behavior. For example, on the basis of individual experience and observation of other animals, rhesus monkeys learn to avoid certain stimuli, but they escape from fear-producing stimuli (along learned routes) with species-typical patterns of locomotion. Similarly, a rhesus mother learns to identify her offspring, and behaves differently toward it than she does toward other young monkeys; with practice, she may become an increasingly competent mother, but she does not learn novel techniques of mothering.

Rhesus behavioral flexibility is based on learning to discriminate many subtle cues and contexts and to select from a species-typical repertoire precisely graded responses that are appropriate to the circumstances. Distributed widely through north and central India, rhesus monkeys are an extraordinarily adaptable species. They survive in towns, villages, roadsides, railway stations, temples, bazaars, and forests (Southwick et al. 1965), and frequencies of many of their behavior patterns vary markedly with the locale. Urban monkeys, for example, are far more aggressive than forest-living monkeys (Southwick et al. 1974). But the form of aggressive patterns—stereotyped agonistic signals and unstereotyped fighting—is not known to differ throughout their range.

Seay and Gottfried (1975) review research conducted at the University of Wisconsin Primate Laboratory on the development of rhesus behavior in environmental settings of varying degrees of impoverishment. They find that, except for conditions of almost total social isolation, rhesus monkeys develop species-typical behavior patterns (by laboratory standards) in a great variety of social and physical environments; the setting affects primarily the frequencies with which behaviors are manifested. Moreover, Seay and Gottfried imply that abnormal behaviors that do appear under these highly unnatural laboratory conditions are not adaptations:

> By virtue of its membership in a species, an organism is possessed of a gestalt of reflexes, neuromuscular structures, perceptual capacities, and learning dispositions, which determine the probability of specific aspects of behavioral development. Across many environments, almost identical behavioral repertoires develop in conspecific animals; only in extremely unfavorable environments will the behavioral repertoire of the species fail to appear. Furthermore, even the organism maturing in an environment inadequate to support species-typical behavior will *not* develop unique techniques for coping with that environment. Rather, his behavioral repertoire will consist of fragments of the behavior patterns which ensure individual and species survival for most of his species-mates (p. 10).

Painstaking analyses have not been made of the ontogeny of rhesus behavior, as they have of human infant behavior, but the patterns exhibited by monkeys of various ages suggest continual development and improvement of such species-typical activities as grooming, sexual patterns, locomotor patterns, and playfighting. Nonsystematic observation supports the view that the "launching stock" of rhesus motor patterns, the ordering of these raw materials in complex sequences of behavior, and the internal programs of criteria by which performances are evaluated and modified, are, except for sex differences, the same for all members of the species.

Photo 8.1a *Leaping over during a male infant playfight.*

Photo 8.1b *Leaping over during a male juvenile playfight.*

In the last chapter I argued that rhesus play can be explained as an adaptation to develop complex motor skills. The question of the development of novel behavior patterns through play can be discussed within the framework developed in that chapter. It is difficult to describe in words and still photographs the changes that occur in rhesus play with age, especially since the conditions of observation did not permit the gathering of systematic developmental data. The reader can get a general impression of the ontogeny of playfighting by comparing the two examples of "leaping over" illustrated in photo 8.1. The monkeys in photo 8.1a are male infants, those in photo 8.1b are male juveniles.

In the infant playfight, although the leaper does manage to clear the leapee, the leap is not powerful enough to be really effective, and the leaper appears to have only ineffectually touched the leapee's head with his right hand. The leapee rears, but ineffectively—in part because he is off balance and leaning to his right. The juvenile leaper, on the other hand, makes a powerful, coordinated leap, pivoting in mid-air (counterclockwise) to land facing the leapee. The leapee rears in a balanced, stable fashion. (For further description of infant playfighting, including some of the ways in which it differs from juvenile playfighting, see examples E and F in appendix 1.)

In one sense, rhesus playfighting becomes less variable and more economical with age. The frequency of "extraneous" steps taken by tottering infants declines as monkeys learn to maintain balance in many positions, and individual movements become smooth, accurate, and consequently less variable. In another sense, playfighting becomes more variable with age, as monkeys develop the strength and skill required to execute complex movement combinations. Both deletions and additions, however, appear to increase effectiveness in biting while not being bitten.

Bruner (1973:7–8) suggests that play functions both to mature components of complex activities and to try out various orders of components:

> Play, then, has the effect of maturing some modular routines for later incorporation in more encompassing programs of action. It also seems to "trial run" a range of possible routines for employing already established subroutines. Not *all* forms of activity need such exercise. [Human walking is cited as an example.] . . . whenever action involves the serial application of constituents to external stimuli with the objective of altering a state of the world, then exercise is particularly needed. For exercise to be highly flexible, play must precede it.

In rhesus sexual behavior, as in human walking, a relatively invariant order of components is adaptive, and this order becomes less variable, and more species-typical, with age. Rhesus copulatory techniques are adequate with respect to their goals, and it is difficult to imagine that the addition of novel sexual behaviors would be of significant benefit. There is no evidence that immature sexual activities are designed to produce sexually flexible adults, even though sexual patterns must be learned and immature patterns differ from adult patterns.

Effective fighting behavior, however, has different requirements and constraints than sexual behavior. If monkeys develop fighting skills by playfighting, a variable order of playfighting movements is adaptive and to be expected. Moreover, if monkeys evaluate tactics in play and retain those that meet built-in criteria of utility, playfighting can be expected to be even more variable than fighting. As outlined above, I identified some apparent goals of rhesus playfighting (face the partner, get on-top or behind, bite without being bitten) but these almost surely are outcomes of a much more detailed playfighting program.

During a fight, behavioral innovation is adaptive to the extent that it increases the likelihood of biting without being bitten; any other effect is dysfunctional. It is possible that monkeys develop idiosyncratic fighting techniques through play, but detailed ontogenetic analyses using motion picture film or other video equipment would be required to test this hypothesis. This is a very restricted kind of novelty, however, and does not seem to be what novelty theorists of play have in mind. My observations of rhesus playfighting suggest the tentative conclusion that species-typical anatomy and neural programs result in all monkeys learning the same, or very similar, tactics.

Other observers of mammalian play have reached similar conclusions. Rasa (1971) observed improved playfighting performance with age among elephant seal pups, younger animals being slower and less coordinated. Gentry (1974) notes that in the ontogeny of sea lion play, single motor patterns are combined into structured sequences; different kinds of bites are combined into adult-like fighting strategies, and other components drop out, making playfighting appear increasingly streamlined and stereotyped. Gentry (1974:402–3) concludes:

> We may find that the main determinant of the above changes will involve expediency to the individual, i.e., animals will retain movement patterns or pattern combinations that work best in a given situation and will abandon others.
>
> . . . we should view play experience as a vehicle by which the frequency, intensity, and combination of behavioral patterns are changed over time.

During playchasing, and during solitary locomotor play as well, rhesus monkeys do not systematically introduce novel patterns of locomotion or bizarre acrobatics. Rather, they exhibit ever-increasing competence in species-typical locomotor patterns; older animals run and climb faster, leap farther and more accurately, and fall more skillfully. With age, rhesus locomotion becomes progressively simplified, precise, coordinated, powerful, and graceful.

Ripley (1967) reaches a similar conclusion in her description of langur locomotor play and playchasing. For example, immature langurs often jump from the ground to a branch several times in succession, apparently attempting to maximize the economy and precision of the jump and reach the branch with no wasted energy. In leaping from one flexible support to another, langurs pump in place on the take-off branch and ride the rebound of the branch on which they land before moving away. Ripley (1967:161) writes: "In play leaps the langur may often take many swings at both the take-off and landing points. The ideal toward which practice tends, however, appears to be a minimum of effort and graceful coordination of leap with various types of support."

The Natural Habitat and Innovation

In a well known passage, Washburn et al. (1965) write:

> It has become clear that, although learning has great importance in the normal development of nearly all phases of primate behavior, it is not a generalized ability; animals are able to learn some things with great ease and other things only with the greatest difficulty. Learning is part of the adaptive pattern of a species and can be understood only when it is seen as the process of acquiring skills and attitudes that are of evolutionary significance to a species when living in the environment to which it is adapted.

In the course of its evolutionary history an animal species experiences and adapts to a limited range of environmental conditions and, as Washburn et al. (1965) make clear, learning constraints and predispositions must be understood as adaptations to the natural environment (more properly, to a range of natural environments [Kummer 1971].) Maladaptive learning may occur even in a natural environment (Baldwin and Baldwin 1977, and see chapter 10), but it is far more likely to occur in an artificial environment.

Reports of novel behavior almost invariably describe animals in captivity, although even under the extreme conditions encountered in zoos, novel motor patterns are rare (Morris 1964). Behavioral artifacts of captivity may demonstrate little about the structure and function of behavior in a natural setting. Since captivity artifacts are possible, their absence in natural environments may indicate that natural selection has opposed their production but, not being prescient, selection cannot constrain learning under conditions the species has never encountered.

Learning abilities that represent adaptations to coping with environmental variability can be expected to be useful across a wide range of conditions, including many artificial ones. An animal might, for example, learn to avoid a predator never before encountered within the species' range. Probably the cumulative results of such learning are responsible for most "cultural" differences among groups or populations of free-ranging nonhuman primates (see Kummer 1971 and Menzel, ed., 1973b). But learning abilities that represent adaptations to develop complex motor skills probably depend on the existence of certain features normally encountered in a natural habitat.

Ewer (1968) reviews a number of instances, in which captive animals developed new types of movement during play, and concludes: "These performances are certainly captivity artefacts . . . but their very unnaturalness serves to emphasize the experimental and inventive aspect of play" (p. 299). Although animals can be considered to "experiment" in play, play nonetheless may be designed to provide only a limited range of "conclusions": if experiments are conducted with the same materials and methods, under the same experimental conditions, using the same techniques for assessing the results, identical conclusions will be drawn. Monkeys playfighting on a flat surface probably have highly similar experiences and therefore learn the same things. Natural rhesus environments vary primarily in the nature of their terrains. Free-ranging groups or populations probably develop different responses in play to the extent that their physical environments differ: rhesus monkeys can learn to deal with a wide range of naturally occurring physical substrates. Captivity artifacts emphasize that the disposition to experiment in play renders an animal vulnerable to learning unnatural, and possibly maladaptive, behavior when the "experimental conditions" to which it is adapted are absent.

Behavioral Innovation among Japanese Monkeys

The development of new behaviors by Japanese macaques (*Macaca fuscata*) is cited by Frisch (1968), Fedigan (1972), Fagan (1974), and Wilson (1975b) with respect to behavioral flexibility, play, and innovation among young animals, although none of these writers specifies the precise significance of this evidence. Innovative behaviors reported among Japanese monkeys include:

(1) Acceptance of new foods: When provisioning of Japanese monkeys began, there was relatively rapid acceptance by monkeys of all age-sex classes of sweet potatoes, wheat, apples, peanuts, oranges, damsons, and soy beans; but all classes were relatively indifferent to

boiled rice, bread, biscuits, and candy. Initially, some monkeys of all classes would eat candy, but it was accepted most frequently by infants (Yamada 1957, Itani 1958, also see Azuma 1973).

(2) Give-me-some behavior: (This pattern, and all other innovative patterns, have been reported only at the Koshima Island colony.) A monkey, usually an adult, waiting for a human to feed it peanuts, sits with the lower arm raised, forearm held out, fingers flexed and pointing upward (Kawai 1965).

(3) Bathing behavior: Monkeys first entered the sea to obtain peanuts, their favorite food, thrown there by humans in order to tempt them into the water. Subsequently, two- and three-year-old monkeys began jumping into the sea from rocks and swimming around. Bathing is common among Japanese macaques, although it had not been previously observed in this group (Kawai 1965).

(4) Sweet potato washing: In 1953, a year after provisioning of the Koshima troop began, a sixteen-month-old female began washing sweet potatoes using typical macaque food-rubbing movements while holding the potato under water. Subsequently, this pattern was acquired most readily by one- to two-and-a-half-year-old monkeys (Kawai 1965).

(5) Wheat washing: Monkeys drop handfuls of wheat and sand into the water and then pick out and eat the floating wheat after the sand sinks to the bottom. This pattern was invented by a four-year-old female, the same monkey who had previously invented sweet potato washing, and it was acquired most readily by two- to four-year-old monkeys (Kawai 1965).

There are several points of interest in these reports with respect to play, innovation, and adaptation: (a) Each innovation is the direct result of human modification of the environment (Kawai 1965). (b) The ability to learn allows animals to acquire adaptive behavior and renders them vulnerable to acquiring maladaptive behavior. Monkeys normally learn what to eat by watching older animals (Stephenson 1973) and by sniffing and tasting bits of food that the older animals drop (Kummer 1971). Infants are flexible enough to accept candy, but I question the adaptive value of candy-eating. (c) Only two patterns were originated by immature animals: candy-eating and sweet potato washing. The most "difficult" invention, wheat washing (Kummer 1971), was invented by a sexually mature female (Itani et al. 1963).

Photo 8.2 *Although this three-year-old female is devouring the book, her scholarly abilities are largely illusory. She is unlikely to digest the material, or, in fact, to pass.*

(d) No pattern involved the development of genuinely species-atypical movement patterns. (e) No pattern is the product of activities generally described as "play."

In conclusion, young monkeys are both more flexible and more playful than older monkeys, but the available data on Japanese macaques do not support the view that a function of activities commonly described as "play" is behavioral innovation.

Innovation and Object Play

The rhesus monkeys I observed engaged in virtually no object play (although juveniles sometimes incorporated an object such as a leaf or a twig into playchases, the chasee being the monkey holding the object), and they engaged in little exploratory manipulation[1] of non-food objects; the objects most frequently explored were man-made artifacts that washed up on the island or were stolen from observers. The goal of much of this exploration seemed to be to test objects for possible utility as food (photo 8.2). Lorenz (1956:637) describes the adaptive significance of similar "exploratory play" among ravens: "By treating

1. Many writers emphasize that play and exploration are different categories of behavior which vary independently among animal species, and should not be confused (e.g., Marler and Hamilton 1966, Müller-Schwarze 1971, Bekoff 1974, Aldis 1975). Aldis points out that play is primarily an effector activity whereas exploration is primarily a receptor activity.

each new situation as if it were biologically relevant—first as a potential enemy, then as a prey—the Raven will discover sooner or later the relevant objects in very different habitats."

Laboratory-reared rhesus monkeys, however, are said not only to play with objects (Rosenblum 1961), but also to pass through a series of developmental stages of object play culminating in object-oriented aggression. Harlow (1969:335) writes: "Nonhuman primates frequently express this object-directed aggressive exploration or aggressive play by tearing physical objects to shreds with their teeth." Zoo-living animals of many species exhibit similar behavioral artifacts (Morris 1964, Glickman and Sroges 1966).

The abnormal interest exhibited by caged animals in objects may result in the acquisition of abnormal, object-related abilities. Jolly (1966b), for example, gave a mechanical puzzle to five caged groups of lemur. Four of these groups consisted of two to three animals in small cages; these animals opened the puzzle repeatedly. The fifth group lived in a large cage and consisted of two males and two females who had established social relations and engaged in a great deal of locomotor and social play. This group, Jolly suggests, approximates the wild lemur troops she observed in which there is frequent social and locomotor play and no interest in, or manipulation of, non-food objects. The lemurs in this fifth group did not touch the puzzle. Jolly suggests that the object manipulation exhibited by the other four groups is an effect, or byproduct, of abilities whose adaptive significance is social learning.

Unlike prosimians and monkeys, chimpanzees in the wild, as well as in captivity, manipulate and play with objects, and the tool-using skills of adult chimpanzees far exceed those of monkeys (Lawick-Goodall 1970). Chimpanzees apparently require early experience with objects, before the age at which complex object manipulation begins, if they are to become effective tool-users as adults (Menzel et al. 1970).

Kohler (1927) describes how captive chimpanzees began using a stick to jump with in play and subsequently used this invention to obtain incentives hung out of their reach. He concludes that "manipulations undertaken in the course of play can become of great practical utility" (p. 69). Menzel (1972, 1973a) describes how enclosure-living chimpanzees progressed from manipulation of poles to the use of poles during play to ladder-making. Chimpanzee groups of constantly changing composition established "play traditions" with novel objects (Menzel et al. 1972), and there is evidence among free-ranging chimpanzees for interpopulation variation in technological traditions (Lawick-Goodall 1973, Teleki 1974).

Lawick-Goodall (1968, 1970, 1971) describes dragging, throwing, hitting with, and manipulation of objects in the social and nonsocial play of free-ranging chimpanzees, and speculates that skilled use of objects by adults might develop out of naturally rewarded manipulation of tools. Free-ranging chimpanzees occasionally exhibit idiosyncratic, novel behavior patterns, and such patterns may be imitated and enjoy a brief vogue. But in all observed cases, the new habit disappeared within a few months: the diffusion of a new pattern through the group has not been witnessed at the Gombe Stream Reserve (Lawick-Goodall 1973).

While it is clear that chimpanzees have an "innate tendency to manipulate and play with objects" (Lawick-Goodall 1970:243) and that this tendency underlies their generalized ability to use objects in adaptively significant ways, it does not follow that the function of object play is the invention of technology. A rhesus monkey develops fighting skills by playfighting with animals as naïve as himself; the neural programs that control such learning apparently are sufficiently specific so that species-typical adaptive behavior develops anew in each generation through peer interaction. But the development of the adaptive use of objects among free-living chimpanzees apparently depends on observing and imitating skilled tool users and on practice (Lawick-Goodall 1973). Goodall (1976:88) writes that "in the wild, young champanzees do spend much time watching others intently, particularly their mothers. Often, after watching some activity such as a male charging display or a complex tool-using performance, an infant may then try to perform the same actions. Subsequently he may practice the behavior time and again."

Lawick-Goodall (1973:161) speculates that although most or all feeding and tool-using behaviors "are not re-discovered by each chimpanzee, but are passed down from one generation to the next through observational learning in a social context," almost all such behaviors could be invented anew by each individual. Teleki (1974), however, discovered that using a tool to fish for termites—a technique which young chimpanzees require years of practice to master—is an extraordinarily complex and difficult skill; although Teleki diligently observed and imitated adult chimpanzees, and practiced faithfully, he never was able to approach the adult chimpanzees' levels of skill. It is unlikely that an individual chimpanzee could invent the developed patterns of termite-fishing through play or in any other fashion.

Obviously, at some point the components of adaptive "cultural" patterns must have been invented by individual chimpanzees, but such inventions need not imply the existence of behavioral tendencies (such as play) specialized to produce them. In natural environments adaptive invention seems to be infrequent enough to justify the hypothesis that it is fortuitous. I am suggesting that plastic or generalized tendencies to manipulate and play with objects evolved as part of a behavioral complex that includes tendencies to observe and to imitate conspecifics. One might speculate that part of this complex is a resistance to learning behavior patterns that are not exhibited by conspecifics. Certainly the Japanese monkeys' rapid acceptance of a wide array of new foods contrasts markedly with the Gombe Stream Reserve chimpanzees' almost uniform refusal to eat new foods that they were offered by humans (Lawick-Goodall 1973). Although mango trees have been growing in their home range for at least 60 years, mangoes have not yet become part of the chimpanzee diet (Lawick-Goodall 1973).

Chimpanzees that were separated from their mothers shortly after birth and reared for two years in impoverished, monotonous, and asocial environments developed striking individual differences in behavior (Rogers 1973)—probably far greater differences than in similarly deprived rhesus monkeys. Subsequently the deprived chimpanzees were given social experience with more normally reared chimpanzees, and "A large part of their eventual socialization was the elimination of idiosyncratic behaviors and the learning of patterns more typical of the species" (Rogers 1973:191). Rogers concludes that culture can "exert a leveling effect on the developing individual and function to reduce individual variability, thereby producing a conforming individual who communicates and responds in highly stereotyped and predictable ways" (pp. 190–91).

That individual captive chimpanzees, living in an impoverished and artificially secure environment requiring few survival-related activities, may invent useful object skills does not indicate that adaptive invention can be expected to occur frequently in the wild. Just as the structure of the vertebrate eye implies an environment containing certain frequencies of electromagnetic radiation, the specific features of the chimpanzee brain responsible for highly plastic and generalized object play and manipulation probably imply an environment containing adult chimpanzees who exhibit technological traditions of proven adaptive value.

Innovation and Human Play

The word "play," according to Loizos (1966), is itself one of the main problems in the study of animal play. "Play," she maintains, is a human concept that means other than or opposed to work. Since animals do not work in the human sense, neither can they be said to play in the human sense.

Webster cites two antonyms for "work": "work" in the sense of physical or mental effort to do or to make something contrasts with "rest"; it is "work" in the sense of labor or toil that contrasts with "play." All animals "work" in the first sense of the word; the second sense of "work" may not be distinctively human but rather peculiar to animals (human or nonhuman) living in certain kinds of artificial environments. Organisms living in a natural habitat may not toil.

Large-brained hominids with advanced tool technologies have existed for more than one million years (Clark 1976). For over 99 percent of this period humans lived in small nomadic groups without domesticated plants or animals. The hunting and gathering way of life is the only stable, persistent adaptation humans have ever achieved (Lee and DeVore 1968). While opinion is not unanimous (see Wilson 1975b), most students believe that insufficient time has elapsed since the invention of agriculture 10,000 years ago for significant changes to have occurred in human gene pools, and humans can be said to be adapted to a hunting and gathering way of life. Therefore, the environments of living hunter/gatherer peoples are most likely to approximate the environments to which humans are adapted. Without considering any group of people to represent living fossils, we may assume that the characteristics shared by most or all living hunter/gatherers, such as small groups, low population densities, division of labor, infanticide, and nomadism, characterized our Pleistocene ancestors as well, and these peoples therefore provide the best available evidence for the adaptive significance of human structure, behavior, and psyche.

Hunter/gatherers seem to "work" less than agriculturalists in the sense that they devote less time to subsistence activities (Sahlins 1972). Indeed, the Hadza, an east African hunter/gatherer people, until recently refused to take up agriculture, although they were surrounded by agriculturalists, because it "would involve too much hard work" (Woodburn, quoted by Sahlins 1972:27).

Hamburg (1963) argues that natural selection favors animals that find emotional gratification in adaptive activities. Since "toil" implies a nongratifying activity, this meaning of "work"—with which "play" often is contrasted—may be a postagricultural artifact, the result of existence in circumstances to which humans are not adapted.

Sharp (1958) mentions that the Yir Yoront, hunter/gatherers of Australia's Cape York Peninsula, do not distinguish work from play, and Steadman's (1971) report on the Hewa of highland New Guinea, a previously uncontacted people who practice both hunting and gardening, also is suggestive. If a Hewa male is angry at his wife for not cooking his food he may say: " 'I was not sitting down and doing nothing, or hunting for wild pig or cassowary; I was building a garden fence (or cutting down trees, or working on the new house etc.).' Presumably if he had 'only' been hunting instead of 'working' it might be thought he had not done his share of the day's work and he might be expected to cook his own food" (Steadman 1971:44).

The contrast between agricultural "work" and hunting is phychological; it is not related to the relative amounts of required physical effort. Steadman points out that to an "objective observer," Hewa hunting is hard work:

In contrast to a western hunter to whom hunting is a pleasurable sport and whose protein intake does not depend on his hunting abilities, the Hewa would not hunt without expecting success. Their hunting is not a relaxed stroll through gentle countryside where a person may by chance come across an animal. On the contrary: it is an intensive disciplined effort in which a man uses his experience to actively seek game. A man concentrates on hunting almost the entire time he is away from his house. He does not speak and every couple of minutes he stops for ten seconds or so and listens carefully for any sound which might give him a clue to an animal's presence (p. 45).[2]

2. On the other hand, the Hewa apparently consider cooking to be "work," and this is a traditionally female activity even among hunter-gatherer peoples. Moreover, while millions of Western males find hunting a pleasurable sport, Western females rarely gather vegetable produce for sport, and huge tracts of land are not set aside for recreational food-gathering. Perhaps women's work is older than men's work.

Goodall (1976:92) speculates that "From time immemorial human children must have been carefully watching their elders and imitating their behavior," and ethnographic data on living hunter/gatherer peoples indicate that children's activities, including those labeled "play," are generally imitations of activities of older members of the group and function to develop the social and physical skills required in adult life. Silberbauer (1972:315–16) writes of the G/wi Bushmen of the Kalahari Desert:

> The children play together at games which are mostly imitations of adult activities. . . . Child lore of adult activities is more accurate than is that of European children, and G/wi children's games are an effective part of training for adulthood.
>
> Boys training in subsistence activities is mainly through playing games involving mock hunts, imitating older boys, and, around the fires at night, listening to the men's conversation about their day's hunting. A father begins to take his son out on training hunts at ten or eleven, although instruction in the making, care, and use of weapons starts much earlier than this. It takes a long time to become a hunter. . . .

Tindale (1972) describes some aspects of play among Pitjandjara children of Australia's Western Desert. By the time they are seven years old boys are throwing toy spears, and soon afterward they begin using a hooked stick as a spear-thrower. For targets, they roll a circular piece of eucalyptus bark along the ground like a wheel, pretending it is a kangaroo or a wallaby. When they are a little older they make toy spears out of reeds and play at spear fighting.

Balikci (1970) describes the enormous dexterity and speed with which Netsilik Eskimo men spear trout in the central basin of a stone weir. The fish are then laid on the ground and "Boys played with little leisters spearing the fish on the ground and closely imitating their fathers' gestures" (p. 35). Children also snare a gull and then play with it for hours, letting it fly and pulling it back, and throwing stones at it. In the summer, small boys play for many hours a day throwing rocks and chasing lemmings with sticks and stones.

Laughlin (1968) describes both the general exercises and the specific games played by Aleut boys that prepare them for hunting sea mammals from kayaks. He also emphasizes that, in addition to acquiring skills with weapons, to become successful adult hunters boys must acquire systematic knowledge of animal behavior, and hunters often capture animals to use in instructing children in the behavior of their future prey. Lack of adult hunting success frequently can be traced to specific inadequacies in youthful training as, for example, when a child has been raised by a grandmother or other nonhunting person.

Turnbull (1962:129–30) describes how, by imperceptible degrees, Pygmy children become adults:

> Like children everywhere, Pygmy children love to imitate their adult idols. This is the beginning of their schooling, for the adults will always encourage and help them. What else is there for them to learn except to grow into good adults? So a fond father will make a tiny bow for his son, and arrows of soft wood with blunt points. He may also give him a strip of a hunting net. A mother will delight herself and her daughter by weaving a miniature carrying basket. At an early age boys and girls are "playing house." They solemnly collect the sticks and leaves, and while the girl is building a miniature house the boy prowls around with his bow and arrow. He will eventually find a stray plaintain or an ear of corn which he will shoot at and proudly carry back. With equal solemnity it is cooked and eaten, and the two may even sleep the sleep of innocence in the hut they have made.
>
> They will also play at hunting, the boys stretching out their little bits of net while the girls beat the ground with bunches of leaves and drive some poor tired old frog in toward the boys. . . . And one day they find that the games they have been playing are not games any longer, but the real thing, for they have become adults. Their hunting is now real hunting; their tree climbing is in ernest search of inaccessible honey; their acrobatics on the swings are repeated almost daily, in other forms, in the pursuit of elusive game, or in avoiding the malicious forest buffalo.

There are several features of interest in these descriptions:

(1) While adult activities differ from children's activities, there is no obvious work–play dichotomy. Adults engage in adaptive behavior and children, through their play and non-play behaviors, learn how to be adults.

(2) Although adults often teach and assist children, playing at adult activities clearly is its own reward; as among nonhuman animals, play is pursued for hours without adult supervision or interference. Washburn and Lancaster (1968:300) write: "The whole youth of the hunter is dominated by practice and appreciation of the skills of the adult males, and the pleasure of the games motivates the practice that is necessary to develop the skills of weaponry."

(3) Like many students of nonhuman animal behavior, ethnographers often consider immature behaviors to be "play" if they mimic hunting or fighting. Among hunting and gathering peoples adult males are the hunters and fighters, and boys play at hunting and fight-

ing. Consequently, as in many playful mammals, immature males seem to play more frequently than immature females do (see also Sbrzesny 1976). While G/wi boys are playing hunting games, the girls are learning how to be G/wi women by going out with their mothers to gather vegetable produce. Although daughters undoubtedly differ from their mothers in knowledge and effectiveness, this kind of juvenile activity is not usually considered to be "play."

(4) Sutton-Smith (in press) remarks that children at play generally do not appear to be euphoric, as some writers imply, but "vividly involved." Pygmy children play house solemnly; this does not mean that they are glum or unhappy, for Turnbull later notes that the transition from childhood to adulthood may hardly be noticed because "their life is still full of fun and laughter" (p. 130). Solemnity suggests that children's activities are as significant to children as adult activities are to adults.

During the Pleistocene humans adapted to more varied environmental conditions than any other mammal. This adaptation was based on a genome that programmed relatively few species-typical behaviors; adult activities were culturally variable, adapted to the circumstances of life encountered in each region. Children were extraordinarily flexible because they had to acquire unpredictable behaviors but, although the genome could not predict specific adult activities, the tendency for children to observe adults, to imitate adults, and to want to be adults was adaptive universally.

Recently, Sutton-Smith (1975, in press) has suggested that the biological and cultural function of human play is "adaptive potentiation": "In those situations where innovative behavior is required, play potentiates novel responses. It brings novel responses into being, and these then are ready for later usage" (Sutton-Smith in press). This hypothesis is based on two kinds of evidence. First, laboratory experiments have shown that groups of children given the opportunity or training for play subsequently exhibit more novel or creative responses than control groups. Second, supposedly there is more play in complex and rapidly changing cultures, where novel or creative behavior might be useful, than there is in traditional cultures, where novelty would be of little value.[3]

3. Hamilton (1975:150) argues precisely the opposite, that civilization reduces the propensity for creativity.

The archeological record indicates that for most of the million years that large-brained human big-game hunters existed on earth cultural change was exceedingly slow: some tool traditions lasted hundreds of thousands of years (Clark 1976). Within the lifetime of an individual, cultural change must have been virtually imperceptible, and the opportunity for a child to adapt by inventing novel behaviors during play must have been negligible compared with its opportunity to adapt by learning the adult physical and social skills upon which its survival and reproduction depended. The ethnographic record on hunter/gatherers corroborates that the function of human play is not innovation but mastery of the cultural heritage.

Most of us no longer live by hunting and gathering. Research on play among children in complex technological societies is interesting, appropriate, and may suggest techniques of socialization that will allow *Homo sapiens* to survive, but it reveals little about the adaptive significance of play. Natural selection does not anticipate the future, nor does it act instantaneously; humans are not biologically adapted to technological civilization. Observations in more natural environments indicate that the function of play among human and nonhuman animals is the development and practice of species-typical or culture-typical behavior. Behaviors observed in artificial environments—laboratories, zoos, and modern industrial societies—do not necessarily reflect adaptation to those environments, nor do they necessarily reveal function.

Children living in technological societies rarely observe economically significant adult behavior, and most adult "work" may provide biologically inappropriate models for children—models whose imitation would provide little pleasure. Few adults would do the work that they do if circumstances did not compel them to, and frequently they work so that their children will not have to follow in their footsteps. Where children are isolated from adult activities, provided with no appropriate models to imitate, and encouraged, often forced, to perform activities unrelated either to their own inclinations or to the circumstances of adult life, it is not surprising that they exhibit novel behaviors in play; but this is not evidence that the adaptive function of play is to produce novelty, nor is it evidence that the novelty thus produced is adaptive.

During the last ten thousand years the circumstances of human life have changed very rapidly, by evolutionary standards, and it is possible that some of this change was potentiated by divorcing children's play from its adaptive role as preparation for adult life. Children who are not constrained by the contingencies of life under which most of human evolution occurred, and who produce novel behaviors in play, may become adults who are more capable of producing novelty. A small fraction of this novelty may become codified and widespread, part of an accelerating pattern of cultural change. In the short run, this process has led to increased human reproduction, but whether in the long run it is adaptive for humans to produce novel behavior wholesale remains to be seen. The prospects so far are not encouraging.

Play and Novelty: Conclusions

The function of the ability to learn is not only to permit organisms to adapt to unpredictable or variable environmental conditions through behavioral flexibility. Learning abilities may represent adaptations to make complex discriminations or to develop complex motor skills that are universally adaptive in a population and are exhibited in species-typical form among adults. Behaviorally flexible species very infrequently adapt by developing new motor patterns. Flexibility almost invariably is based on learning to discriminate cues and contexts and to select from a species-typical repertoire responses that are appropriate to the circumstances. Individual members of the few species, such as chimpanzees and humans, with relatively open motor patterns infrequently invent adaptive novel behaviors. Open motor patterns apparently are adaptations to learning culture-typical, rather than species-typical, behaviors. Adaptive function may not be revealed in artificial environments. If the present environment is known to be very different from those encountered in the evolutionary history of a species, it is more reasonable to assume that novel behaviors exhibited in this environment were opposed by natural selection than it is to assume that they are adaptations.

I agree with Bekoff (1975a) that more data are required to determine whether sequences of play behavior really are more variable than non-play behavior, but I disagree with the implication that sophisticated mathematical analyses of such data can prove or disprove novelty theories of play. These theories suffer not only from vague characterizations or descriptions of play but also from attempting to deduce function from "structuralist" contrasts between play and non-play behavior rather than from studies of the acquisition of skills and the ontogeny of behavior. Thus, novelty theorists allude to the relative "combinatorial freedom" of play, and speculate that some of these novel combinations may turn out to be useful: by beginning to playfight while mounting, are immature rhesus monkeys developing the potential, absent in non-playful species, of beginning a fight while copulating? Novelty theorists imply that the repetition in play is analogous to the variation-producing process of chromosomal duplication: is an infant rhesus monkey, jumping repeatedly at a branch just out of reach, developing a capability that may prove useful in adulthood should the need arise to jump repeatedly at a branch just out of reach?

Genuinely novel behaviors are observed occasionally during rhesus play, usually in intervals between playfights. For example, I have observed monkeys reach back with one hand and grasp a foot, and once, during a particularly manic play episode, I observed a monkey complete a standing back flip. But because they are so infrequent, play cannot be designed to produce such behaviors. If monkey nervous systems were constructed so that novelty per se was reinforcing, behavior might be expected to become increasingly varied and bizarre. But such tendencies are not evident; on the contrary, behavior comes increasingly to resemble species-typical adult norms.

Even if a rhesus monkey were to generate random movements full-time, it seems unlikely that it would hit upon an adaptive one. Even human artists and scientists who need to devote almost no time to the basic subsistence activities in which most humans have spent their lives, who live in a culture that cherishes novelty, and whose livelihood and reputation depend on the quality of their creativity, rarely are able to produce innovations of lasting merit.

Fagen (1974) proposes that play is a variation-generating biological mechanism analogous to chromosomal processes, including recombination: "Playful recombination of motor patterns and responses into new sequences could, like rearrangement of genetic material, tend to increase the phenotypic variability of an animal's offspring" (Fagen 1974:854). Chromosomal recombination during sexual reproduction clearly is an adaptation designed by natural selection to produce variability. Williams (1966:125) writes: "The machinery of sexual reproduction in higher animals and plants is unmistakably an evolved adaptation. It is complex, remarkably uniform, and clearly directed at the goal of producing with the genes of two parental individuals, offspring of diverse genotypes." But there is little evidence that play is so designed. A more appropriate analogy for behavioral innovation during play may be mutation. Mutations are inevitable and they are the basis of organic evolution. Yet natural selection always is for an (unachievable) mutation rate of zero (Williams 1966). Innovation may occur occasionally during play and serve, albeit extremely infrequently, as the basis for a new adaptive tradition: innovation may be an occasional effect of play without being its function.

Chapter Nine

Aggression and Play

Introduction: Functional Implications of Sex Differences in Aggressive Play

I have argued, on the basis of design, that the function of rhesus aggressive play is to develop skills useful in intraspecific aggression and in predator avoidance. Sex differences in rhesus aggressive play provide an independent, complementary method of assessing function, and therefore of testing this hypothesis.

Sex differences in rhesus aggressive play can be summarized as follows:

1. Males playfought, playchased, and initiated playfights 2½ to 3½ times more frequently than females.

2. Males playfought more frequently with males, and females with females, than expected if partners were chosen without respect to sex.

3. Male playfighting was much rougher (faster and more vigorous) than female playfighting. Insufficient motion-picture footage of female-female playfighting was obtained to quantify this observation (vigor might be estimated by determining rates of movement), but substantial sex-differences were apparent.

4. Regardless of the sex of the partner, males fled from playfights less frequently, and females more frequently, than expected if fleeing were independent of sex.

5. Regardless of the sex of the animal attempting to initiate the playfight, males refused playfighting initiations less frequently, and females more frequently, than expected if refusal to play were independent of sex.

6. Juvenile males achieved advantageous positions (behind and on-

top) far more frequently against females than females achieved these positions against males. Males achieved these positions more frequently against other males, and females less frequently against other females, than expected if achievement were independent of sex. In this sense females might be said not to try so hard as males to achieve favorable positions; there was more frequent passive holding during female-female playfights.

7. Although playfights terminated in aggression very infrequently within and between all age/sex classes, female-female playfights were more likely to end in aggression (and male-male playfights less likely to do so) than expected if aggressive termination were independent of age/sex class, despite more frequent occurrence of apparently painful stimuli—being dragged in the teeth of another monkey, or pulled out of a shrub and thrown to the ground—during male-male playfights.

8. Only males played with C Group's peripheral males.

9. Only males played with members of other social groups. In summary, males sought out playfighting more, rejected it less, played more frequently and harder, fled less, and played with more vigorous partners (central and peripheral C Group males and males from other groups) than females did. Males achieved advantageous positions against partners of either sex more frequently than females did, reflecting either greater male skill, greater female passivity, greater male tendency to seek these positions, or some combination of these factors.

More frequent and rougher play by male rhesus has been reported in laboratory studies (Rosenblum 1961, Hansen 1962, Harlow 1965, Hinde and Spencer-Booth 1967, Harlow and Harlow 1969, Suomi and Harlow 1971, Redican and Mitchell 1974), at Cayo Santiago (Altmann 1968) and among free-ranging Indian groups (Lindburg 1971). Immature males also mount and threaten more frequently than females do and, when raised without mothers in groups of peers, males outrank females in the dominance hierarchy (Rosenblum 1961, Harlow et al. 1966).

If pregnant rhesus females are injected with testosterone propionate during the middle trimester of gestation, they produce normal male offspring but their female offspring are physically masculinized pseudohermaphrodites. These pseudohermaphrodite females exhibit frequencies of play initiation, playfighting, playchasing, threat, and mounting that are intermediate between those of normal males and females

(Goy 1968, Goy and Resko 1972, Phoenix 1974). As adults, pseudohermaphrodite females exhibit higher levels of aggression than normal female controls (Eaton et al. 1973).

Several lines of evidence demonstrate that among immature animals typical male-female differences are not the result of direct hormonal action but of a central nervous system modified by prenatal testosterone so that normal males and pseudohermaphrodite females are predisposed to acquire male behavior patterns. The fetal testis secretes more androgen than the fetal ovary and the female placenta secretes more progesterone (which antagonizes androgen activity) then the male placenta (Resko 1974). Soon after birth, male plasma testosterone levels fall to nondetectable amounts, remaining low until puberty (Resko 1970), and males castrated at birth exhibit typical male behavior patterns as infants and juveniles (Goy 1968). Postnatal testosterone injections do not affect frequencies of aggressive play (Goy and Resko 1972), although females thus injected become more aggressive and replace males in the top positions in the dominance hierarchy (Joslyn 1973). Pseudohermaphrodite females are not masculinized completely either because testosterone is not injected throughout the gestation period (Goy and Resko 1972) or because of the high levels of progesterone in the fetal female circulatory system (Resko 1974) or for both reasons. Goldman et al. (1974) confirm the existence of a sex difference in the cortical development of rhesus monkeys.

As Goy (1968) points out, these experimental findings do not prove that experience is unimportant in the development of sex-typical behavior. On the contrary, in both sexes experience is crucial to the development of normal behavior. The evidence suggests, however, that individual experience acts on a brain already biased in a male or female direction.

Since natural selection acts at all stages of an organism's life cycle to maximize reproductive success (Williams 1966), the striking and pervasive differences in the play of immature rhesus males and females must reflect sex differences in reproductive strategies. Beer (1975:20) points out that one method of assessing function is the comparative approach: "By comparing cases in which the characteristic in question is present and cases in which it is not, one tries to find correlated circumstances that could account for the distribution of the characteristic in terms of survival value." Such comparisons typically are made between closely related species, but they also may be made within a single species. Thus, the hypothesis that playfighting functions to develop fighting skills through practice can be evaluated by examining the role of fighting in the life histories of rhesus males and females. I shall therefore review the literature on rhesus behavior pertaining to competition, aggression, fighting, dominance, and differential reproduction. The practice theory of aggressive play will be corroborated if success at fighting is shown to be a more important determinant of male than of female reproductive success.

Competition and Aggression

Human beings almost always draw a moral distinction between an individual's killing to promote his own interests and the same individual's killing for a real or supposed group interest (Durbin and Bowlby 1950). This distinction often impedes understanding of nonhuman-animal violence (and human violence as well). Perhaps because nonhuman animals are thought to be "natural" and hence to provide both insight into "human nature" and evidence for "desirable" or "ethical" behavior, patterns of animal aggression are often imagined to be in harmony with a human system of ethics and to promote more acceptable interests than the mere self-interests of the combatants. Nonhuman-primate aggression has been said to have such high-minded functions as maintaining the "fabric of primate society," and even such apparently meaningless functions as "sexual selection."

Competition does not invariably result in aggression, but the existence of aggression is evidence for competition. Because aggressive behavior entails expenditures of time and energy and exposure to risk, it could be favored by selection only in circumstances where success usually increased fitness by gaining access to scarce resources. Competition is not necessarily the proximate cause of all conflict, nor does the winner of a contest necessarily gain immediate benefits; ultimately, aggression must pay off or long ago the meek would have inherited the earth.

Competition and Food

That food shortages, or actual starvation, reduce the frequency of rhesus aggression (Southwick 1967, Loy 1970, Marsden 1972), sometimes is cited as evidence that aggression is not the result of self-interested competition. But several aspects of these reports suggest that alternate interpretations are possible. First, in each report of food deprivation the decline in agonistic behavior is a concomitant of (energy conserving) lethargy and a decline in *all* social behaviors. If the frequency of agonistic behaviors during food shortages is compared to some other social behaviors during the deprivation, rather than to preshortage baselines, the frequency of agonistic behaviors seems high. Thus, in two experiments Southwick (1967) found declines in the frequency of agonistic behavior when a captive group's food supply was reduced by 50 percent, although only one of two declines was statistically significant; but the frequencies of sexual and play behaviors dropped to zero during food reduction, and Loy (1970) provides similar, though less extreme, data.

Second, in Loy's (1970) and Marsden's (1972) reports the little available food was dispersed widely; there were no concentrations of food to be competed for, and monkeys wandered about lethargically searching for anything that might prove edible. This behavior probably represents the adaptive response to food shortages in a natural habitat. Loy (1970: 268–69) writes:

> The significant decrease in number of fights per hour is no doubt connected to the fact that the amount of food provided in the feeders went from almost a normal level to no food at all very rapidly. Therefore chow was not an incentive for inter- or intragroup fights. Also, the monkeys were widely scattered as they foraged, and there were few squabbles over choice items of vegetation. If a small amount of chow had continued to be provided, a rise in the number of fights per hour might have been expected to occur.

Third, in Southwick's (1967) experiment the relative infrequency of agonism did not reflect equitable food distribution, but monopolization of resources by dominant adult animals. Southwick (1967:195–96) writes:

> During these food shortages, the level of food intake of each monkey was directly related to its position in the dominance hierarchy. The highest ranking animals had first access to the food, and apparently took as much as they wanted. The mid-ranking animals then consumed the remaining food, with the result that the lowest-ranking subadults had very little to eat. They ate the final scraps that had been handled, partially eaten, and thrown away by the higher ranking animals. It was obvious that the lowest half of the dominance hierarchy did not get enough to eat and was under rather severe starvation. The two lowest ranking subadults almost died apparently from starvation, and they had

to be removed and hand fed for two weeks to restore their health. Both had lost 35% of their normal weight.

The ten juveniles in Southwick's group certainly could not have succeeded in obtaining by fighting the food monpolized by the seven adults. The juveniles' choice, in these highly unnatural circumstances, was between slow starvation, if the food reduction continued, and a quick, violent defeat. To the extent that rhesus living in natural environments ever face such decisions, the first strategy probably holds more promise.

In well-fed captive rhesus groups, dominant animals regularly monopolize food supplies until they have eaten or drunk their fill (Richards 1974), and in the Puerto Rican colonies most intergroup violence results from competition over concentrations of monkey chow at feeding stations (Gabow 1973, Drickamer 1975a). Intragroup aggression also is higher in feeding than in nonfeeding contexts (Kaufmann 1967, Drickamer 1975b). Southwick (1967) reports that concentrating the group's normal food supply increased aggression, and Southwick et al. (1974, 1976) report a two- to six-fold increase in aggression when free-ranging rhesus were being fed by villagers. They also note that more aggression resulted from competition over large pieces of food, such as bananas and chapatis, than over small pieces, such as rice and gram nuts.

The evidence with respect to food, then, supports the view that aggressive and pacific behaviors are competitive tactics, adapted to a range of exigencies and opportunities. Hungry or starving monkeys husband their resources and do not waste time and energy fighting when fighting is unlikely to gain access to food, as is the case when physical disparities are great or when available food is dispersed widely, but even well-fed monkeys may fight over concentrated food resources, and the greater the potential payoff the more frequently monkeys risk violence in competition for it.

Conventional Competition

Giving advice to upwardly mobile princes, Machiavelli wrote that men "will revenge themselves for slight wrongs, while for grave ones they cannot. The injury therefore that you do to a man should be such that you need not fear his revenge." According to benevolent views of nature, nonlethal competition among animals is to be expected, but since natural selection, like Machiavelli's ideal prince, operates upon the principle of expediency, the apparent infrequency of killing requires explanation.

1. By harming a conspecific with which it shares genes, an animal reduces part of its own genetic fitness, and selection therefore reduces the severity of conflict among closely related animals (Hamilton 1964, Maynard Smith 1972, Eberhard 1975) and among animals that can recognize the existence of shared genes independent of kinship (Hamilton 1975). An animal is expected to love its neighbor as itself as a direct function of the number of genes they have in common.

2. Selection reduces the severity of conflict among animals that profit from each other's existence through reciprocal exchange of benefits (Trivers 1971).

3. Unlike princes, nonhuman animals do their own killing, and the disparity in power between two contesting animals rarely will be as great as it is between princes and their victims. Selection simultaneously favors gaining scarce resources and minimizing risk, resulting in complex and subtle competitive interactions and in the evolution of stereotyped agonistic signals.

Using game theory and computer simulation, Maynard Smith (1972) and Maynard Smith and Price (1973) demonstrate that selection at the level of the individual organism can favor the evolution of stereotyped agonistic signals. They examine various strategies of conflict, assigning arbitrary, but apparently reasonable, payoffs in terms of reproductive success for: (1) the advantage of winning compared with the disadvantage of losing; (2) the disadvantage of being injured; (3) the disadvantage of wasting time and energy in the contest. They make the simplifying assumptions that: (a) there are only two kinds of competitive tactics, "conventional" tactics (such as stereotyped agonistic signals, displays, or benign fighting techniques) which are unlikely to cause injury, and "dangerous" tactics which are likely to seriously injure the opponent; (b) the contestants have no memory of past conflicts; (c) the contestants are equal in fighting prowess.

Since the optimal competitive strategy depends on the strategies other members of the population adopt, the authors ask whether there are evolutionarily stable strategies such that if they are adopted by most members of a population there is no mutant strategy that will give superior reproductive fitness. They find certain "limited war" strategies, involving primarily but not exclusively "conventional" tactics, to be evolutionarily stable and superior to the unstable strategies of "hawk," in which an animal always attacks with "dangerous" tactics, retreating only if injured, and "mouse," in which an animal employs only "conventional" tactics. Among species capable of inflicting physical injury the evolution of wholly symbolic conflict is not possible because a mutant that employed physical attack would have a reproductive advantage (Maynard Smith and Price 1973). Machiavelli observed that "there are two ways of carrying on a contest; the one by law, and the other by force. The first is practiced by men, and the other by animals; and as the first is often insufficient, it becomes necessary to resort to the second."

In a real animal population severe fighting can be expected to be even less frequent than the Maynard Smith/Price model predicts because: (1) frequently there are more than two kinds of competitive tactics; (2) the results of past conflicts do influence present decisions; (3) animals are not equal in prowess, and selection favors the ability to detect inequality, which allows the probable loser to avoid the conflict.

Dominance, Fighting, and Reproductive Success Among Rhesus Monkeys

The Concept of Dominance

Graded agonistic signals and the ability to remember outcomes of past conflicts and to assess the probability of success in competitive interactions frequently result in hierarchical, or dominance, relationships. In the study of free-ranging rhesus monkeys, dominance has proved to be a persistent and useful concept. It represents a natural category, recognized both by human observers and by monkeys.

In its original formulation, "dominance" referred to unidirectional agonistic relations between fowl: chicken A would peck chicken B if B did not get out of A's way fast enough, but B did not peck A. A was said to be dominant to B, and B subordinate to A (for histories of the dominance concept see Gottier 1972 and Wilson 1975b). Early studies of chickens and laboratory groups of rhesus monkeys showed that a male's rank in the dominance hierarchy correlated highly with his sexual access to females (Gottier 1972). Wilson (1975b) reviews the substantial body of evidence that in natural habitats high-ranking animals of many species are more fit than low-ranking animals because they have priority of access to space, food, mates, or nesting sites and shelters.

Recently, the concept of dominance has been criticized on several grounds. Perhaps the major criticism has been that dominance frequently is measured not by the direction of agonistic signals but by priority of access to commodities. In a given group of animals, dominance ranks based on priority of access to various kinds of commodities do not invariably correlate with each other (but see Farres and Haude 1976) nor do they invariably correlate with rank order based on agonistic interactions (Gartlan 1968, Syme 1974). Although many studies do show very high positive correlations between rank orders based on agonistic interactions and those based on priority of access to many commodities (e.g., Richards 1974), it is probably best to restrict "dominance" to the direction of agonistic signals and then determine empirically what other factors can be predicted by the order thus obtained.

In almost all field studies of rhesus monkeys, dominance heirarchies have been based on agonistic interactions. The great majority of such interactions consist of sterotyped signals, not fighting; the dominant animal emits threat signals (intention to attack), the subordinate emits submissive signals (intention to retreat). These relationships are relatively stable and, at any given time, the monkeys in a social group can be ranked in a linear hierarchy of dominance; triangular and other nonlinear relationships are rare or nonexistent.

The current debate about the utility of the concept of "dominance hierarchy" results in part from its reification. A dominance hierarchy is an abstraction, not an entity; the result of a series of compromises made by the members of a social group, not the cause of anything. Although it is the consequence of functional behavior, a dominance hierarchy has no function (see Williams 1966 and Alexander 1974).

Gartlan (1968) and Rowell (1972, 1974) criticize the frequently stated view that dominance hierarchies function to control aggression, maintaining that hierarchies cannot possibly have this function since they are most evident in the most aggressive species and in the most aggression-producing circumstances, such as captivity.[1]

1. Someone who believed a dominance hierarchy to be a functional organization might liken this argument to the claim that the function of firemen cannot be to extinguish fires because they are reliably associated with fires.

But a hierarchy does not function: rather, it is defined by ritualized, unidirectional aggression and/or submission. If the members of a group never exhibit agonistic behavior, a dominance hierarchy cannot be said to exist, and if fighting is unrestrained (as in Jolly's [1966a] study of mating in *Lemur catta*) there will be winners and losers, but not dominance and subordinance. In her studies of captive primates, Rowell (1966, 1972, 1974) found that the hierarchy is "maintained" primarily by subordinates: dominant animals move about freely, while subordinate animals behave cautiously, avoiding behaviors that might prove provocative to their superiors. Rowell (1966:437) writes: "the hierarchy is maintained, or expressed, chiefly by subordinate activities, and . . . it is the lower ranking animals which do most to perpetuate rank distinctions." Richards (1974), and others, have found that dominant animals frequently threaten subordinates without apparent provocation, but the important point is that the existence of submissive behavior is the *sine qua non* of dominance hierarchy. It should be no surprise that pre-emptive subordinance is most frequently observed where the danger is greatest, as in captivity. As Poole (1973:410) has stated: "Fear of an opponent combined with powers of recognition represent the key factors in the maintenance of rank order."

Dominance and Reproductive Success

Data from laboratories (Bernstein and Sharpe 1966, Gottier 1972, Duvall et al. 1976), from the Puerto Rican island colonies (Carpenter 1942a, Altmann 1962a, Koford 1963a, Conaway and Koford 1965, Kaufmann 1965), and from India (Southwick et al. 1965, 1967, Neville 1968a, Lindburg 1967, 1971, 1975) indicate that, on the average, dominant rhesus males are reproductively more successful than lower-ranking males, although the correlation between rank and reproductive success is neither perfect nor evidenced in every case.

In an established laboratory group containing 8 sexually mature males, Duvall et al. (1976) determined paternity eliminations for 29 offspring of 26 females on the basis of polymorphisms in serum proteins, red cell enzymes, and leucocyte antigens. Reproductive success was not correlated with rank for the first year but was for the second. Continuing this work, Duvall (personal communication) found that in smaller groups, containing two or three adult males, the alpha (first-ranking) male sired all offspring, but these data have been collected for only one year. In a larger group into which four adult males and several females were introduced, all four males produced offspring the first year and the correlation between rank and reproductive success was low; the second year it was high and significant.

Kaufmann (1965) found that in one Cayo Santiago group the highest-ranking male was first to become active in the breeding season, the only male to form exclusive consort relationships with individual females, and the most active breeder by far. Kaufmann found a high correlation between male rank and proportion of mating activities performed, number of copulations, and number of estrous females associated with per day. In comparing his data with data obtained on the same group in previous breeding seasons by Conaway and Koford (1965), Kaufmann showed consistent changes in mating activity paralleling changes in male rank. He found dramatic increases in mating activity when a male became alpha, and the mating activities of other males closely followed rank changes.

Lindburg (1975) found that during one breeding season, alpha males of forest-living groups in India performed 52.6 percent of all observed copulations. In two groups, the alpha males mated for 54 percent and 60 percent of the days on which they were observed while all other males mated for 4 percent and 31 percent of the days observed. Alpha males were associated with 61 percent of all females at some time during their estrous periods, and when only one female in the group was in estrus she was accompanied by the alpha male on 61.5 percent of the observations. Moreover, alpha males were more likely than other males to copulate during the phase of the estrous period in which ovulation is most likely.

Loy (1971), however, found a nonsignificant relationship between male rank and frequency of copulation in a free-ranging group containing 12 breeding males on Cayo Santiago, although high- and mid-ranking males mated much more frequently than low-ranking males. Factors which may partly account for Loy's findings are: (1) the alpha male, an initially active breeder, left the group about two weeks after the occurrence of the first fertile mating; (2) the beta male suffered a 2–3 inch slash wound on his scrotum, and did not mate for 24 days following this wound;[2] (3) the fifth-ranking male was a castrate. (Cas-

2. Loy (1971) notes that such wounds do not invariably affect mating, and may not have caused the lack of mating in this case.

Table 9.1 Male Rank and "Effective Copulation"

Male Rank[a]	Mean Age Female Partner[a]	Probability of Female Giving Birth[b]	Probability of Infant Surviving to 6 Months[b]	Percent Effective Copulation[c]
High (N=4)	5.0	.729 (5 year-old females)	.62 (5 year-old females)	45.2
Mid (N=4)	4.1	.689 (4 year-old females)	.53 (4 year-old females)	36.5
Low (N=4)	2.8	.136 (3 year-old females)	.50 (3 year-old females)	6.8

[a] Data from Loy (1971)
[b] Data from Drickamer (1974a)
[c] An "effective copulation" is a copulation with a female who will produce an offspring that survives to six months of age, which equals the probability that a female will give birth times the probability of an infant surviving to six months of age. For the purposes of this table it is assumed that high-ranking males mate only with 5-year-old females, mid-ranking males mate only with 4-year-old females, and low-ranking males mate only with 3-year-old females.

tration does not necessarily end mating activity, but Wilson and Vessey [1968] show that it tends to reduce it.)

Loy (1971) also found, as did Conaway and Koford (1965), that higher-ranking males tend to mate with older females: the mean age of female partners was for high-ranking males 5.0 years, for mid-ranking males 4.1 years, and for low-ranking males 2.8 years. This may have significant implications for relative rates of male reproductive success. Drickamer (1974a), in reviewing 10 years of reproductive data from the La Parguera colony, has shown a strong positive correlation between female age and fertility: older females are more likely than younger females to become pregnant, and the infants of older females are more likely to survive to six months of age than are the infants of younger females. Loy's (1971) and Drickamer's (1974a) data can be combined to demonstrate the effect of age of the female partner on male reproductive success. Even if all the males in a group were to copulate an equal number of times, the frequency of "effective copulation" nonetheless would be directly related to rank (table 9.1). (An "effective copulation" is defined as a copulation with a female who will produce an offspring that survives to six months of age.) In free-ranging forest groups, Lindburg (1975) found that in nearly every case in which males persisted in rejecting a female's sexual solicitation, the females were the youngest in the population.

Low-ranking rhesus males may adopt "behavioral subterfuges" (Crook 1971) in order to increase their mating activity. Kaufmann (1965:508) describes an "opportunistic" male "who spent much of his time hurrying furtively about, with frequent glances over his shoulder, as if looking for an estrous female."[3]

The proximate basis for the correlation between male rank and reproductive success in not clear. Loy (1971) speculates that "character or personality" traits can overshadow the effects of dominance. Bernstein (personal communication), on the basis of many years' experience with captive groups of rhesus monkeys, notes that some males seem to be natural "lovers," independent of rank. These observations, and the fact that rhesus monkeys do not rape, point to a female role in determining mating activities. Sexual solicitation is not sex-specific, and female solicitation is most frequent near the time of ovulation (Czaja and Bierlert 1975). Lindburg (1975) found that in 78 percent of the estrous periods he observed, the female solicited a male at some point during estrus, and he speculates that the higher rate of mating activities of alpha males may result from female choice. Males

3. At La Parguera, Drickamer (1974b) found a strong correlation between male rank and mating activities, but also noted that high-ranking males are more likely to be observed than are the furtive, peripheral, low-ranking males (see chapter 2). When the observed frequencies of mating activity were adjusted for observability, the positive correlation between male rank and mating success disappeared, and Drickamer concludes that high-ranking males are not more reproductively successful than low-ranking males.

Kaufmann (1965:508) also notes that "This tendency of some low-ranking males to conduct part of their mating activity furtively and in concealment is a source of error which exaggerates the apparent difference in activity between high and low-ranking males," but adds, "I do not believe that this error endangers the validity of the stated relationship between rank and breeding success."

When classes of monkey are not equally likely to be observed, a straightforward adjustment of the data for observability is not necessarily justified. Low-ranking males are secretive, furtive, and spatially peripheral to the main group because they avoid high-ranking males, who are associated spatially with females. It cannot be assumed that when low-ranking males are out of sight of the observer they are as likely to be mating as when they are in sight. To illustrate this point, consider Loy's (1971) data on mating in F group on Cayo Santiago. Loy observed that 95% of the matings of F group females were with F group males, and 5% were with males of other groups. If Loy had adjusted these data to take into account the relative frequencies with which F group males and non-F group males were observed, presumably he would have concluded that F group females usually mate with males of other social groups. In fact, it is possible that Loy did underestimate the frequency of intergroup matings, but clearly it would have been absurd to adjust for observability of males. Thus, Drickamer's interpretation may be correct, but it is also conceivable that, if they become much more visible when mating than at other times, the mating success of low-ranking males is overestimated. Studies that focus on peripheral males or employ rigorous sampling techniques may clarify this problem.

occasionally are observed to attack the female member of a consort pair when the male member is lower-ranking than the attacker (Carpenter 1942a, Lindburg 1971, personal observations). Among free-ranging Indian rhesus Neville (cited in Agar and Mitchell 1975) reports that the alpha male could suppress the sexual activity of any female in the group and that females rarely rejected an extremely dominant, aggressive, and feared male.

In summary, most studies find a strong but imperfect correlation between male rank and reproductive success. Drickamer's (1974a) analysis of ten years of reproductive data for the La Parguera colony reveals a correlation between female rank and reproductive success as well: 10 percent more high-ranking females than low-ranking females gave birth each year; daughters of high-ranking females gave birth for the first time at a younger age than did daughters of low-ranking females; among older monkeys, the infants of high-ranking females were more likely to survive their first year of life than were the infants of low-ranking females.

Fighting and Dominance

Southwick (1972) reports that of 15,574 aggressive interactions (threats, chases, one-sided attacks, and mutual fighting) in ten Indian rhesus groups in urban, rural, and forest locations, only .4 percent were mutual fighting. In four groups, Southwick et al. (1974) report that aggressive interactions in non-feeding situations varied from a low of .231/hour/monkey to a high of .397/hour/monkey; the frequency of fights ranged from .0014/hour/monkey to .0016/hour/monkey (my calculations). Although fighting is infrequent relative to other forms of aggressive interaction, if all monkeys are equally likely to fight, and if fights occur at a constant rate, each monkey will fight every 26 to 30 days. Since infants and juveniles rarely fight, some monkeys evidently fight more frequently than these figures indicate.

Male, but not female, rank in the dominance hierarchy is known to change as a result of fighting, and thus the outcome of fights may indirectly affect male reproductive success. Although at any given time rhesus monkeys are ranked in a linear hierarchy, female rank is stable and predictable while male rank is unstable and unpredictable (Missakian 1972, Sade 1972). Rhesus begin aggressive encounters as old infants or young juveniles, and within each age class monkeys are ranked linearly in the same order as their mothers. By removing and introducing animals, Marsden (1968b) disrupted the hierarchy of a captive rhesus group and found that offspring rose or fell in rank as their mothers did. As a female matures, she becomes dominant to all females subordinate to her mother and consequently comes to rank just below her mother in the adult hierarchy; males, however, may gain or lose rank at puberty (see Koford 1963b, Sade 1967, 1972, Vessey 1971, Missakian 1972).

Kaufmann (1967:75) reports that the alpha male of a group on Cayo Santiago "began to show signs of weakening authority in July, 1963, when he received a neck wound. By September, 1963, he had slipped to third place. . . ." Neville (1968b) reports that the alpha male of a free-ranging Indian group was deposed following a series of male-male aggressive encounters. Shortly after the La Parguera colony was established, an alpha male apparently was killed and replaced by another adult male. The replacing male was wounded on the arms and shoulders, but was still able to mount three high-ranking females in succession (Vandenbergh 1967). Even nonlethal fights that do not result in rank changes can, of course, affect reproductive success. Evidence has been cited above for a second-ranking male ceasing to mate for 24 days following a slash wound in his scrotum (Loy 1971). Conaway and Koford (1965) report that an alpha male decreased his mating activity after suffering a severe cut on his foot, although he did not loose rank. (The male died a week later, but by the time his carcass was discovered it was so decomposed that the cause of death could not be determined.)

Fighting and Socionomic Sex Ratios

Writing of the tendency of wild primate troops to avoid one another, Washburn and Hamburg (1968) note that the field worker is more likely to observe the results of intergroup aggression than the aggression itself; this is true of aggressive behavior in general. For example, the frequency of serious fighting seems much higher if based on wounds than if based on observations of fighting (Lindburg 1971). Southwick (1972:4) writes: "The slashing canine teeth of adult males may produce serious flesh wounds, and quite commonly rhesus monkeys are seen in India with gaping wounds, particularly around the thighs, shoulders, ears and face." Boelkins and Wilson (1972) report that most rhesus fighting on Cayo Santiago takes place at dusk or later, when observation is not possible. I encountered the same conditions in my field work on La Cueva: with the beginning of the breeding season, adults began to be wounded, often severely, but I never observed a fight that led to wounding.

Another way in which the field worker observes the results of aggression rather than aggression itself is in the socionomic sex ratio. In five accurately censused forest-living rhesus groups, Lindburg (1971) observed a ratio of adult females to adult plus subadult males of 2.3:1, and similar data were obtained on three other, less easily censused, forest-living groups. Drickamer (1974a), analyzing ten years of survivorship data for the La Parguera colony, found that males and females were equally likely to survive to 48 months of age, but after 48 months, the number of surviving males declined with each age interval, while all females who survived 48 months were still alive at the end of the study. (No female between four and eight years of age died.) By eight years of age, 26 percent of the original group of males, but 60 percent of the original group of females, remained alive. In a year-long study of aggressive behavior at La Parguera, Drickamer (1975b) found that adult males were the most aggressive, the most aggressed against, and the most frequently wounded class of monkey, and that most adult male aggression was directed at other adult males (also see Koford 1966 and Wilson and Boelkins 1970).

It is therefore misleading to consider the differential mating activities of males in a social group, or the correlations between male rank and mating activities, to be an accurate measure of differential reproduction or of the intensity of male-male competition. The results are already biased, as the only males observed to mate or not mate, to be dominant or subordinate, are those that remain alive. All available evidence indicates that the male-female differences in survivorship data results from the higher frequency and intensity of male-male fighting.

Fighting and Xenophobia

Rhesus monkey groups are highly xenophobic, a trait which can be considered under three headings: intergroup interactions; change in group membership; and experimental studies.

Intergroup Interaction

Rhesus groups are ranked in a linear hierarchy which generally correlates with group size, and avoidance patterns tend to reduce the frequency of intergroup conflict. Intergroup rank has been thought to result from the activities of high-ranking males (Carpenter 1942b), peripheral and subadult males (Marsden 1968a, Vessey 1968, Boelkins and Wilson 1972), adult females (Vandenbergh 1967, Drickamer 1975a), or some combination of the above (Gabow 1973). But regardless of which class determines rank, it is clear that aggression occurs frequently during intergroup contacts and that most serious intergroup fighting involves adult males.

Peripheral males are most frequently involved in intergroup aggression both in India (Southwick et al. 1965, Lindburg 1971) and in the Puerto Rican island colonies (Marsden 1968a, Vessey 1968, Boelkins and Wilson 1972, Gabow 1973). Most of these interactions consist of threats and chases, not attacks or mutual fighting. Vessey (1968) reports that mutual fighting occurred in only 2 percent of the intergroup encounters he observed in the La Parguera colony, and that all fights were between adult males. In a more recent study of the same colony, Drickamer (1975a) found that mutual fighting occurred in 19 percent of intergroup interactions. Adult males arrived first in the zone occupied by another group: "They would threaten, then chase and attack adults and juveniles of the defending group, usually precipitating the appearance of the adult male leader(s) of the defending group who returned the threats and then led the troop in a hasty retreat" (p. 28). This increase in the frequency of intergroup fighting at La Parguera probably results from increasing population density; although aggression occurred in 36.6 percent of all intergroup encounters among low-density, forest-living rhesus groups, serious intergroup fighting was not observed (Lindburg 1971). On Cayo Santiago, four-year-old males were most frequently involved in both aggressive and nonaggressive intergroup interactions (Hausfater 1972). The most frequent participants in the less intense intergroup aggressive interactions were adult females and two- to five-year-old males. Adult males were involved only in the most intense intergroup violence, so although females were wounded more frequently than males, males received more severe wounds and more wounds on anterior parts of the body.

Change in Group Membership

Female rhesus monkeys rarely change groups but males, without regard to status, leave their natal group and attempt to join other groups (Altmann 1962a, Koford 1963a, 1965, 1966, Conaway and Koford 1965, Lindburg 1967, 1969, 1971, Neville 1968b, Boelkins and Wilson 1972, Sade 1972, Drickamer and Vessey 1973). Summarizing ten years of data on F Group on Cayo Santiago, Sade (1972) reports that females form the stable core of the group and males an unstable adjunct to that core; with one exception, no male remained a member of F Group for more than four years. In the La Parguera colony, Drickamer and Vessey (1973) report that by seven years of age all males had left their natal groups, the mean age of depature being four years. Rank in a new group is not correlated with rank in the old group: males initially are peripheral to the group they are attempting to join, ranking at the bottom of its hierarchy. Many males shifted groups several times, always remaining low in rank, but a few were able to penetrate the hierarchy of their new groups, often remaining with the group indefinitely.

Drickamer and Vessey suggest that body size and length of tenure in a new group interact to determine male rank. They believe that bonds with the group's females, formation of coalitions with other males, and fighting ability are of secondary importance in determining rank, "but might greatly influence how long a male remains in a group" (p. 367). Lindburg (1969) reports that among free-ranging forest groups in India, the mobility of males is a frequent source of conflict:

> Male shifting is accomplished only after a transition period during which groups show their intolerance of the intrusion. . . . Actual fighting between males in such situations was observed only once, but the occurrence of a number of severe wounds in adults of both sexes during transition periods suggests it may have been frequent (p. 1177).

Male fighting ability may increase the likelihood of penetrating a new group, of rising to high rank, and of remaining a group member. Since females rarely change rank or leave their natal groups, their fighting skills appear to be of lesser adaptive significance. Neville (1968b) reports that an alpha male ran toward an adult female who was copulating with a non-group male and chased her back to the group, and Altmann (1962a) makes similar observations. At the La

Parguera colony, a male moving from the periphery to become the new alpha male attacked and seriously wounded several adult females (Vessy 1971); Lindburg (quoted above) reports that females, as well as males, were wounded as a consequence of male mobility. But the existence of male attacks on females is not evidence for the importance of female fighting ability: although adult females may, in certain circumstances, outrank adult males, females lack the body size and weapons required to hold their own with an adult male in combat.

Experimental Studies

Although females of many primate species may engage in more agonistic interactions than males do, the female is not more deadly than the male: males are far more likely than females to engage in mutual fighting, and the physical consequences of male-male aggression are usually much more serious (Bernstein 1970, Bernstein and Gordon 1974). In the laboratory, Angermeier et al. (1968) found that of 27 pairings of adult female rhesus, four resulted in fights; of 27 pairings of adult male rhesus, all resulted in fights.

In many vertebrate species, newly established groups exhibit high levels of aggression, which subside with the emergence of dominance orders (Gottier 1972). Bernstein et al. (1974a), summarizing their studies of group formation among captive rhesus, report that in the hour following introduction all social interaction may be aggressive. Initial responses include slashing with canines, but this rapidly is replaced by nipping with incisors, threats, and submission, as social relations become established. Mutual fighting is much more characteristic of males than of females. As killings and serious woundings occurred infrequently in the formation of new rhesus groups, Bernstein et al. (1974a) suggest that mutual fighting is controlled, or ritualized. Perhaps the degree of "control" exercised is in part a function of confidence, or lack of fear, since rhesus introduced to established groups may be killed.

In a series of field experiments in India, Southwick (1972) and Southwick et al. (1974) report consistent xenophobia: all non-infant rhesus monkeys introduced to established free-ranging groups were attacked and driven away or killed. Flight or cowering by intruders led to increased threats, chases, and attacks.

Bernstein et al. (1974b) report substantial sex differences in behavior observed when monkeys were introduced to established, captive rhesus groups. (1) Males were more aggressive and were more frequently aggressed against. Male members of the host group sometimes suffered serious slash wounds, but host group females never did: males used incisors against females and canines against males. This sex difference is not a result of greater female submissiveness; on the contrary, "Male subjects persisted in exhibiting higher levels of submission than did females over time, but they also received much more intensive and prolonged attack" (p. 229). (2) The most intense aggression by far was observed when males were introduced to all-male groups: "The eight males individually introduced to an all-male group for the first time received much more aggression from host animals than was recorded in any other introduction. In fact, one male was killed, and only by virtue of active experimenter interference were four other animals able to survive" (p. 226). (3) Males introduced to all-female groups were not attacked; females in heterosexual groups did attack male intruders, but inflicted little damage. In summary, host groups containing males responded to intruders with more intense aggression, and intense responses were specific to male intruders.

Aggression may also result from removing and subsequently reintroducing rhesus monkeys to a social group. Vessey (1971) reports that the removal and reintroduction of free-ranging rhesus monkeys at the La Parguera colony often resulted in serious fighting and wounding. Some alpha males were able to reestablish themselves when released, but two others did not attempt to rejoin their groups, and became solitary. One alpha male joined a new group at the bottom of its hierarchy after being attacked and driven off when he attempted to rejoin his original group.

Among captive rhesus groups, short-term removal and reintroduction of males produced no social changes, but males reintroduced after periods ranging from a few weeks to a year generally took positions at the bottom of the hierarchy without challenge (Bernstein et al. 1974b). In two instances males attempted to reassert themselves after a long absence: one formerly number-three male was killed in the consequent fighting; in the second case, a formerly low-ranking male was able to regain his old position by fighting and defeating the few males he had outranked. Bernstein et al. (1974b:231) conclude: "In a small group with only a few adult males, a newly arrived male may thus effectively join a group with high initial status if he can inflict a few quick injuries to the resident males. It is only when the sheer number of resident adult males being challenged is so great that the subject cannot hope to injure any significant number of opponents that vigorous aggressive defense on the part of a new male is clearly ill adapted to his ready integration into a group.''

Fighting and Sexual Competition among Rhesus Monkeys

Fieldworkers report little overt or obvious fighting among rhesus males over access to sexually receptive females (Conaway and Koford 1965, Kaufmann 1965, Lindburg 1975). Nevertheless, there is substantial evidence that most male fighting ultimately is the result of sexual competition. Both in the Puerto Rican island colonies and in Indian populations, male-male aggression and fighting is much more frequent during the mating than during the nonmating season (Kaufmann 1965, 1967, Southwick et al. 1965, Lindburg 1971, Vessey 1973, Drickamer 1975b). Lindburg (1971:63) writes: ''The highest incidence of aggressive episodes occurred in November, at the peak of the mating season. The tensions associated with sexual activity were clearly the principal factors contributing to aggressive encounters at this season.''

On Cayo Santiago, Wilson and Boelkins (1970) found that males, but not females, were wounded more frequently during the mating season, and at La Parguera, Vandenbergh and Vessey (1968) report that males were wounded 4.5 times as frequently during the mating season as during the nonmating season. For two of the four years of Vandenbergh and Vessey's study, females also were wounded more frequently during the mating season, but in all years the seasonal variation in female wounds was much smaller than was the variation in male wounds. Drickamer (1975b) found that adult males were wounded 3.5 times (and adult females 1.4 times) as frequently during the mating season as during the nonmating season at La Parguera. Wilson and Boelkins (1970) report that 86.6 percent of male deaths occurred during the five-month mating season on Cayo Santiago; females died more frequently during the nonmating season, but the difference was not statistically significant. In India, serious aggression is observed far more frequently among urban groups than it is among forest groups that more closely approximate a natural habitat (Southwick 1972). In a sample of 115 monkeys in a low-density forest environment, Lindburg (1971) observed 93 woundings; only eight were "severe," but two led to death, both during the mating season. Lindburg, investigating a severe quarrel, found a mature adult male in prime condition lying helpless on the ground, surrounded by four other males who threatened, slapped, and poked him for 15 minutes. After the male died, Lindburg counted four severe, and 27 superficial, cuts and puncture wounds on the carcass. The second death caused by wounding was an adult female, the first in her group to become sexually receptive in the mating season; Lindburg did not witness the actual attack.

Male mobility and group change clearly is related to puberty and to the mating season (Lindburg 1967, 1969, Boelkins and Wilson 1972, Sade 1972, Drickamer and Vessey 1973). Because males regularly copulated with females in a new group, Lindburg (1969) posits a sexual motive for group change. Neville (1968b) observed adult and subadult males following free-ranging Indian groups during the breeding season, attempting to copulate with the group's females. The adult males, especially the alpha male, attempted to drive off these intruders or to break up courtships. Drickamer and Vessey (1973:365) speculate: "As the young males mature they may either be chased from the group or voluntarily leave it, perhaps because they cannot gain access to sexually receptive females." This speculation is supported by their observation that most males move to a group with a higher female/male ratio than their old group.

Although males become sexually mature and potent at three years of age, Drickamer's (1974a) data indicate that males do not begin to suffer a higher mortality rate than females until four years of age. The explanation may be that three-year-old males are relatively ineffective breeders. In Loy's (1971) study of mating in F Group on Cayo Santiago, the five three-year-old males averaged 12.6 copulations during the mating season with female partners whose mean age was 2.8 years. Drickamer's (1974a) data (see table 9.1) reveal that only 6.8 percent of three-year-old females produce an offspring that survives to six months of age. If three-year-old males copulated only with three-year-old females, their observed "effective copulations" would be

.96/monkey/mating season. For comparison, the single four-year-old F Group male was observed to copulate 31 times with partners whose mean age was 4.4 years; if this represents 19 four- and 12 five-year-old female partners, this male then was observed to engage in 12.4 "effective copulations," or approximately 13 times the mean for three-year-old males. At four years of age males begin to mate effectively and, for the first time, their mortality rate exceeds that of females.

Variation in male rhesus testosterone production provides additional evidence that male-male aggression results from sexual competition. Testosterone is implicated in high levels of aggression in males of many mammal species (Beach, ed., 1965), and among free-ranging rhesus monkeys male testosterone levels are much higher during the mating season—when male aggression, woundings, and deaths are most frequent—than during the nonmating season (Vandenbergh 1965, Gordon et al. 1976). Captive rhesus males show a two- to three-fold increase in testosterone levels when exposed to sexually receptive females (Rose et al. 1972, Bernstein et al. 1974c). During the nonmating season at La Parguera, sexually quiescent males became sexually active when exposed to females that had been artificially brought into estrus with estradiol benzoate (Vandenbergh 1969).

In a more recent study at La Parguera during the nonmating season, two free-ranging rhesus females were captured, brought into estrus with estradiol benzoate, and then allowed to rejoin their group. Of the nine adult males in the group, the three most dominant were first to exhibit reddening of the sexual skin, indicating testosterone production of mating-season levels, and were the only males observed to copulate with the estrous females (Vandenbergh and Drickamer 1974). Among a captive group of 34 adult male rhesus monkeys, Rose et al. (1971) found a positive correlation between rank and testosterone level. Bernstein et al. (1974c) report that testosterone levels among captive rhesus males rose after winning fights, despite injuries sustained, and fell after losing fights. Moreover, a rise in rank increased testosterone levels, and a fall in rank lowered testosterone levels, independent of fighting, as demonstrated by removal and reintroduction experiments (Bernstein et al. 1974c) and by group-formation experiments (Rose et al. 1975).

Restraints on Fighting

Restraints on fighting can be understood as the results of individual competitive strategies. The lowered testosterone level of rhesus males following defeat or loss of status probably is an adaptation to avoid further conflict when success is improbable. Bernstein et al. (1974c) showed that defeat is a more powerful determinant of testosterone levels than is exposure to receptive females, since defeated males exhibited lowered testosterone levels in the presence of females. The dysfunctional effect of high testosterone levels in circumstances where aggression is unlikely to be successful is suggested by experiments in which low-ranking rhesus males were injected with testosterone. They did not rise in rank, but did exhibit a higher frequency of wounds, apparently resulting from subtle, testosterone-induced behavioral changes detected by high-ranking monkeys (Bernstein et al. 1974c).

Winners may not press an attack because even a beaten and submissive animal can prove dangerous if its life is threatened and it has nothing to lose; a winner runs increasing risk as it increases the level of violence. Maynard Smith and Price (1973) predict, within the limits of their model, that animals employing an evolutionarily stable competitive strategy will respond to escalated attack by escalating in return. Bernstein and Gordon (1974) report that defeated rhesus males passively accepted incisor bites, but abruptly wheeled and slashed with their canines when the victor employed his own canines. (This was revealed in analysis of motion picture film.)[4]

The expression of aggression is in part a result of individual learning. In the laboratory, mice, rats, chickens, and rhesus monkeys are likely to fight if they have experienced success in previous fights and to be

4. Poole (1973) observed a level of polecat fighting typical of cagemates, termed "companion fighting," that was intermediate in intensity between playfighting and the uninhibited fighting characteristic of strangers. He notes, however, that "In both uninhibited and companion fighting a high intensity attack is more likely to lead to an agonistic response than a low intensity one. Thus the higher the level of intensity of attack the less likely is the opponent to ignore it and the more likely it is that a fight will result" (Poole 1973:409). The relation between intensity of attack and retaliation appears to be reciprocal: the higher the intensity of attack the greater the likelihood of retaliation; retaliation increases the likelihood of intense attack. Fox (1969:255) notes that among wolves, with increasing intensity of aggression, "orientation of attack progresses from muzzle-oriented biting to the shoulder hackles and finally to the throat, at each stage the bite being inhibited, but the intensity of the bite and of head-shaking increases if the adversary, when once seized, does not remain passive but instead retaliates."

submissive if they have experienced failure (Gottier 1972). Selection favors animals that can predict probable victory and defeat, and there is evidence that members of several vertebrate species learn from agonistic experiences to detect cues, such as body size, that are relevant to winning or losing and to apply this knowledge to new situations (Gottier 1972).

Among social species, one result of the evolution of conventional competitive tactics and individual learning is the formation of dominance hierarchies. Alcock (1975:301–2) writes:

> Subordinate individuals do not persist in accepting their status, giving up food, mates, and space to others, because they are altruistic and intend to sacrifice themselves for the benefit of the group. They do so because of the realities of the situation in which they find themselves. They do not contest their low status because they have in their contacts with others judged that they are incapable of physically defeating the higher-ranking members of the group. They remain in the group because of the benefits this brings (protection from predators, increased probability of finding or capturing food, etc.). By conserving their resources, by not wasting them in a constant struggle to improve their status, subordinate animals have a better chance of living to compete for higher status (and all that goes with it) another day when the odds in their favor are improved.

Potentially violent rhesus monkeys are able to lead a fundamentally social existence because most agonistic interactions consist of ritualized threat and submission between animals with established positions in a linear hierarchy. Kaufmann (1967:97) writes that "in large, tightly organized groups such as those of rhesus monkeys, there is a definite advantage in a well-defined rank system which is expressed chiefly through harmless signals. . . . Such a system might depend on selection (increased survival) for monkeys which, regardless of their rank, achieve the highest degree of social integration." Moreover, the frequency and severity of fighting over rank is expected to be minimized among close relatives (Eberhard 1975).

Delgado (1967) reports that the nature of the agonistic behavior induced in rhesus monkeys by radiostimulation of the nucleus posterior ventralis of the thalamus and central grey was largely a function of prior social experience. When stimulated, the alpha male attacked subordinates, but not indiscriminately; for example, he never attacked a female with whom he had established friendly relations. When the two lowest-ranking males were stimulated in the same parts of the brain they were attacked more than usual by the dominant male, and became even more submissive. Dominance traditions can be very strong: Southwick and Siddiqi (1967) describe a dying alpha male, severely wounded by dogs, who remained dominant to a peripheral male and kept this male away from the group with weak threats.

A rhesus male's reproductive success may depend in part on his ability to form cooperative aggressive alliances with other males, and this ability may constitute another restraint on the expression of violence. Aggressive alliances have been reported both in captivity (Bernstein et al. 1974a) and among free-ranging rhesus (Altmann 1962a, Lindburg 1971). In newly formed captive groups alliances were established extremely quickly and sometimes endured for years; they were, however, situation-specific, and long-standing alliances between males dissolved immediately when they were forced to join another social group or when a female was introduced into a group of males (Bernstein et al. 1974a). Boelkins and Wilson (1972) report that one way a young male became accepted by a new group was by forming an association with one of its males. This association was demonstrated by frequent mutual grooming, and by "the member male acting in support of the new male in aggressive encounters with other main group or subgroup animals" (p. 135). Four-year-old males attempting to penetrate the central male hierarchy tended to join in a common defense against older males (Kaufmann 1967).

Fighting and Group Security among Rhesus Monkeys

Dominant male, but not female, rhesus are reported to exhibit violence in two additional contexts: protecting the group from external threat, and policing internal quarrels. Group-protective behavior by dominant males, especially alphas, has been reported among captive groups (Bernstein 1964, 1976, Bernstein and Sharpe 1966, Southwick 1967), in the Puerto Rican colonies (Vandenbergh 1967, Marsden 1968a), and in forest-living Indian groups (Lindburg 1967, 1971, in press). Bernstein and Sharpe (1966) report that when the alpha male of a captive group was locked in a small cage, a group member pursued by human handlers would crouch next to the cage, suggesting that it recognized the alpha's protective behavior. Lindburg

(1971, in press) reports bluff charges by dominant males against humans and dogs that menaced the group.

In captive groups (Bernstein and Sharpe 1966), in the Puerto Rican colonies (Koford 1963a, Conaway and Koford 1965, Kaufmann 1965, 1967, Vessey 1971), and in India (Lindburg 1969, 1971, Neville 1968b) dominant males are reported to terminate intragroup fighting by threatening, chasing, or attacking group members involved in disturbances. Kaufmann (1967) reports that of 98 intragroup fights broken up, high-ranking central males broke up 91. Males rising to the alpha position are reported to exhibit sudden and dramatic increases in the frequency with which they terminate intragroup disturbances (Conaway and Koford 1965, Vessey 1971).

Sex Differences in Fighting and Playfighting: Conclusions

Male-female differences in the frequency and severity of fighting can be understood as differing reproductive strategies. An animal can be said to be successful in obtaining food to the extent that it satisfies certain absolute nutritional requirements, regardless of the feeding success of other animals; but it can be said to be reproductively successful only relative to the reproductive rates of the other members of the population: in this sense, reproductive competition is inevitable (Williams 1966) and "promiscuous intercourse in a state of nature is extremely improbable" (Darwin 1871:362).

Like most animal species, rhesus monkeys exhibit a marked sex difference in "parental investment," defined as: "any investment by the parent in an individual offspring that increases the offspring's chance of surviving (and hence reproductive success) at the cost of the parent's ability to invest in other offspring" (Trivers 1972:139). Although male rhesus exhibit occasional infant care (Breuggeman 1973), they invest very little in each offspring, while female parental investment is substantial. These sex differences in patterns of parental investment result in corresponding sex differences in patterns of sexual competition. A male's reproductive success is limited mostly by the number of females he can fertilize, while a female's reproductive success is limited mostly by the quality of care she gives to her offspring. The number of males with whom a female copulates is irrelevant to her reproductive success. Kaufmann (1965) reports that the three most sexually active females in one Cayo Santiago group averaged three times as many estrous periods, 15 times as many days of estrous activity, and three times as many male partners as the three least active females; and yet each of the six females gave birth to one offspring during each of the three years of the study.

Hausfater (1975) argues that to conclusively demonstrate differential reproduction, one must ascertain reproductive success for many animals over their entire lifetimes. Nevertheless, among rhesus monkeys the data relating male mating activities and rank, and the striking sex differences in survivorship data, provide convincing evidence that male reproductive success is highly variable: some males sire many offspring at the expense of other males who sire few or none. But all females are limited to one or no offspring each year. Thus, "At every moment in its game of life the masculine sex is playing for higher stakes" (Williams 1975:138). The most reproductively successful males are those that gamble and win, and sexual selection favors calculated risk-taking in male-male competition. The resulting selection for male structures, behaviors, and dispositions that are useful in male-male competition results in the marked sexual dimorphism of rhesus monkeys, in the greater frequency of serious fighting and wounding among males, and in socionomic sex ratios that markedly favor females. Washburn (cited in Tiger 1975) argues that the female represents the basic size of the species, adaptation to diet, etc., and that male anatomy should be regarded as a deviation from the female norm. Apart from differences in the reproductive organs, sexual dimorphism is a result of "the anatomy of bluff and fighting (collectively, aggression). Contrary to our cultural biases, very little anatomy is directly concerned with sex, and a great deal with the ability to fight. . . . This view of the male-female differences allows one to see behavioral-structural patterns so that the relations of play, hormones, muscles, teeth, callosities, hair, etc., *all* become understandable" (p. 121).

Since available evidence indicates that the male-female difference in survival results from the higher frequency and intensity of male-male fighting, and since invariably it is more adaptive to survive a fight than to succumb, male survival and reproduction depend more than do female survival and reproduction on successful fighting. The development of fighting skills may increase a male's reproductive success by increasing the probability that he will: (1) avoid being killed or wounded; (2) eliminate competitors by killing or wounding them; (3) succeed in joining a social group; (4) succeed in remaining in a social group; (5) defeat rivals and achieve high rank, and avoid being defeated and losing rank, which result, on the average, in more frequent copulation, more frequent copulation with older, more fertile females, and more frequent copulation in the fertile phase of the female's estrous cycle.

Although invariably it is more advantageous to win than to lose fights once they have begun, victories may be Pyrrhic, and it is also advantageous for combatants to minimize the injuries they sustain and to terminate the fight quickly. Rhesus monkeys are relatively long-lived animals, and if a loser survives he will have future reproductive opportunities. Male reproductive success, more than female reproductive success, probably depends upon skillful control and management of aggression. This may include the ability: (1) to estimate the likelihood of defeating strangers, to choose the most propitious time for challenging known animals (Brown 1975), and to avoid fighting when the risks outweigh the probable benefits; (2) to participate in dominance hierarchies; (3) to form aggressive alliances with other males; (4) to use behavioral subterfuges to obtain access to estrous females; (5) to detect probable loss quickly during a fight in order to submit or flee, thereby sustaining minimum injury. Furthermore, if rhesus fighting is restrained in some circumstances—among kin, for example—the ability to regulate precisely the intensity of fighting would be adaptive.

A female has little to gain by competing for males: when she is in estrus there is rarely or never a shortage of applicants. Rather, selection favors females that choose to mate with males who give signs of fitness (Williams 1966, Trivers 1972). While Drickamer (1974a) demonstrates a reproductive advantage for high-ranking rhesus females, the benefits of high rank appear to be relatively slight compared with benefits accruing to high-ranking males. Moreover, female-female fighting can be very risky: Nash (1974) reports that a female baboon delivered a dead infant 12 days after a severe fight with two other females. Thus, for rhesus females the potential benefits of fighting rarely outweigh the risks, and females seldom engage in severe fights or change rank.

Crook (1972) suggests that "social selection" might favor males with abilities to maintain a secure and stable environment in which females can forage and rear their young. By protecting the group from external threat, high-ranking males protect their genetic investment in animals they are likely to have sired (Bernstein 1976). Group protection can be considered to constitute male parental investment, but unlike most female parental investment, it depends upon skills in violence and augments selection for sex-differences in structure and behavior. By threatening or attacking group members engaged in fights, an alpha male may both protect infants and juveniles he is likely to have sired and preserve the established social order. It is to be expected that the status quo will be maintained most vigorously by individuals who profit most from it.

In many respects rhesus males and females are similar: they travel the same distances over the same terrain, they sleep in the same trees, eat the same foods, are menaced by the same predators, live in social groups, recognize dominance relationships, affiliate with and groom other monkeys, and communicate with very similar repertoires of signals. They differ, of course, in copulatory behaviors and in that females become mothers and exhibit a variety of patterns of infant care. Other male-female differences in life histories—in group change, stability of rank orders, frequency of serious fights and wounds, socionomic sex ratios and survivorship data, variability in reproductive success, group protection and policing—uniformly support the view that fighting success is more important in determining male than female reproductive success. There is no evidence that rhesus aggressive patterns have been shaped by selection to achieve any other goal than individual reproductive success.

That playfighting among immature rhesus and fighting among mature rhesus are primarily male activities supports the evidence of design, that playfighting functions, at least in part, to develop fighting skills. Washburn and Hamburg (1968:473) write of baboons:

> The aggressive actions are practiced and brought to a high level of skill in play. . . . the whole practiced, skillful, aggressive complex is present before the canine teeth erupt. The really dangerous weapon is not present until the male monkey is a fully adult, experienced member of the social group. As the canine teeth erupt, the temporal muscles more than double in size, and the male changes from a roughly playing juvenile to an adult that can inflict a very serious wound, even death, with a single bite.

Fighting skills include the ability to bite without being bitten, but may also include the ability to detect inequalities. Even if males did not become proficient in biting without being bitten, but did learn to discern quickly when they were outclassed in a fight, allowing them to flee or submit and thereby minimize injury, playfighting experience would provide major benefit. That intergroup play is solely a male activity (this study, Marsden 1968a, Vessey 1968, Hausfater 1972) may be related to male group change: intergroup play may facilitate a male's integration into a new group. Inhibition of aggressive responses to painful stimuli is requisite to the existence of sustained, vigorous playfighting: that the much rougher male-male play is less likely to result in aggression than the more passive female-female play provides further evidence of the importance of playfighting to male reproductive success.

Comparative data on sex differences in play support the practice hypothesis. More frequent or vigorous male than female play is reported in many primate species including common langurs (Jay 1965, Sugiyama 1965), Nilgiri langurs (Poirier 1970), vervets (Lancaster 1971), Sykes's monkeys (Dolan 1976), squirrel monkeys (Baldwin 1969), baboons (Owens 1975a, 1975b), and humans (Aldis 1975). Aldis (1975) summarizes evidence on several mammalian species relating sex differences in playfighting to sex differences in adult aggressive patterns and to sexual dimorphism. Poole and Fish (1976) report that male rats (*Rattus norvegicus*) playfight more frequently than females do, but both sexes use the same behavior patterns. They relate this finding to the evidence that male rats are generally more aggressive than females and that there are no sex differences in the form of agonistic behavior patterns. (They deny, however, that this is evidence that play is practice fighting.) Gentry (1974) attributes his finding that male sea lion pups are five times as likely as female pups to bite during play to the extreme sex differences in the structure and behavior of adult sea lions, and Owens (1975b) suggests that the striking sex differences in immature baboon playfighting result from selection for adult male fighting success. Qualitative, rather than quantitative, sex differences are reported in the play of two mammalian species. Among elephant seal pups immature males playfight with the motor patterns of adult male fighting while female pups playfight with motor patterns characteristic of adult female aggression (Rasa 1971). Linsdale and

Tomich (1953) report that mule deer (*Odocoileus hemionus columbinaus*) of both sexes engage in locomotor play, which they suggest provides practice in antipredator behaviors; but butting with the head, which mimics adult male breeding season contests, is observed only between immature males.

Chapter ten

Speculations on Play, Sports, and War

In chapter 8 it was argued that human play, like the play of nonhuman animals, functions to practice and perfect adult activities. But proximate and ultimate causation of human behavior is so complex that, insofar as they induce a false sense of simplicity, analogies with nonhuman animals may mislead more frequently than they enlighten, and the controversies surrounding the use of animal-behavior studies and evolutionary theory in understanding human behavior are at present unresolvable. This chapter attempts to show that the relationships among play, sports, and war are far more complex than they have sometimes been made to appear.

The playfighting of children on playgrounds is in many ways, such as wrestling for superior position and typical sex differences, similar to the playfighting of nonhuman animals (Aldis 1975). As fighting among human children has not been studied, Aldis was unable to ascertain the relationship between children's fighting and playfighting, but certainly most serious adult human violence is not rehearsed in the playfights Aldis describes, since in all human societies serious adult violence is characterized by the use of weapons.

Boys in Western societies play with toy guns, and Tindale (1972:260) describes Pitjandjara boys playing at spear fighting, using reeds for spears, "courting attack so that they can divert the spear with a touch of their spear-thrower or elude it by a quick move to one side or the other." But even if childhood practice with toy guns or spears produces adults who are skilled in the use of real weapons, among preliterate, as well as literate, peoples the social processes that make possible sustained, cooperative human combat appear to be learned through instruction as well as practice. Among the fierce and warlike Yanomamö of southern Venezuela, for example, boys regularly play at club fights and other forms of adult combat (Chagnon 1968). But Chagnon also notes:

> Yanomamö boys, like all boys, fear pain and personal danger. They must be forced to tolerate it and learn to accept ferocity as a way of life. During one feast the adult men of two allied villages agreed to satisfy their grievances in a chest-pounding duel. They also took this opportunity to educate their small sons in the art of fighting and forced all the young boys from eight to fifteen years old to duck-waddle around the village periphery and fight each other. The boys were reluctant and tried to run away, afraid they would be hurt. Their parents dragged them back by force and insisted that they hit each other. The first few blows brought tears to their eyes, but as the fight progressed, fears turned to anger and rage, and they ended up enthusiastically pounding each other as hard as they could, bawling, screaming, and rolling in the dirt while their fathers cheered them on and admired their ferocity (pp. 130–31).

The relationships between adult human violence and children's play are clearly far more complex than those between fighting and playfighting among nonhuman animals.

"The Battle of Waterloo was won in the playing fields of Eton" expresses a popular conviction that human military skills are developed in certain kinds of play. In the present context three questions seem pertinent: (1) Is the epigram true? (2) Is the kind of play that occurs in the fields of Eton homologous with human and/or animal playfighting? (3) Are battles such as Waterloo homologous with individual human and/or animal fighting? Some writers imply, perhaps not intentionally, that the relationship between human play and war is as direct as that between animal playfighting and fighting. Wilson (1975b:165), for example, begins a paragraph: "The question before us then is to what extent animal play is also serious business." He distinguishes the structuralist from the functionalist approach to play, and concludes: "For the functionalist, the wars of England were indeed won on the playing fields of Eton." Just as nonhuman primates develop fighting skills in play, so, according to Washburn and Hamburg (1968), throughout human history the aggressive behavior of young males "was learned in play, was socially approved, and was personally gratifying" (p. 474). Washburn (1966:11) writes: "The basis for the majority of contemporary sports was the preparation for war, and the purpose of the sports was to render the individuals taking part in them physically and psychologically tough, so that they would be capable of and would enjoy the physical destruction of other human beings." Ghiselin (1974) (who, it will be recalled, does not believe that animal play serves developmental functions) distinguishes between unstructured, unsupervised human play and competitive games: "Little boys playing soldier are not practicing to slaughter their fellow men, but furthering peaceful life within their own society. The way to make a killer out of a child is to put him into a genuinely competitive situation—such as Little League baseball" (p. 261). The cross-cultural association of warfare and combative sports (Sipes 1973) also suggests that sports and war are related, but the precise nature of the relationship is not revealed.

The history of football in England (Dunning 1963) suggests that speculations about functional relationships between sports and war should be made with caution. Although football has been played in England since at least the twelfth century, before 1840 matches were loosely organized and rough: they were frequently accompanied by serious injury and death. Far from being considered by authorities to be a crucible of manliness, character, and discipline, football was regarded as a public nuisance and a danger to life, property, and public order. Furthermore, England's rulers disliked football because it took time away from archery practice, an activity they valued and encouraged owing to its utility in the waging of war. In 1365 Edward III issued the following order to the Sheriffs of the City of London:

> To the Sherriffes of London. Order to cause proclamation to be made that every able bodied man of the said city on feast days when he has leisure shall in his sports use bows and arrows or pellets and bolts . . . forbidding them under pain of imprisonment to meddle in the hurling of stones, loggats and quoits, handball, football, or other vain games of no value; as the people of the realme, nobel and simple, used heretofore to practise the said art in their sports when by God's help came forth honour to the kingdom and advantage to the King in his actions of war; and now the said art is almost wholly disused and the people indulge in the games aforesaid and in other dishonest, unthrifty or idle games, whereby the realme is likely to be without archers (Dunning 1963:838).

In the opinion of England's rulers from Edward III to Victoria, football not only did not prepare players for war but actually obstructed such preparation. Although it was outlawed, however, football could not be suppressed with the existing means of social control. Neither authority nor patriotism was, apparently, sufficient to cause football players to set England's interests above what they perceived to be their own.

In the nineteenth century, urbanization—which drastically reduced open spaces—and the development of more effective police systems led to the decline of traditional football, except in rural areas and in the public schools. In the 1840s, as a result of the masters' increasing power over their pupils in the public schools, football was "civilized": rules were written, and football became an instrument to further the masters' educational aims. It was during this period that the epigram "The Battle of Waterloo was won in the playing fields of Eton" first appeared (Longford 1969).[1] Since the old, brutal style of football persisted for at least 500 years despite legal sanction and the likelihood of serious injury, many men must have enjoyed it. Dunning gives no clues as to the satisfactions this sport provided, nor does he speculate about the effects of football on the reproductive success of the players; but if the benefits for the individuals involved are unclear, any benefits for the community, England, or the ecosystem are more obscure still.

It has only recently become apparent that while natural selection may operate at the level of the group or population, selection at these levels is almost always negligible compared with selection at the level of the individual organism (Williams 1966, Alexander 1975). Accordingly, a reasonable first approach to ultimate explanations of human behavior is to ask how behavior functions in maximizing the reproduc-

1. This epigram generally is attributed to the Duke of Wellington, but it is highly unlikely that he ever said or believed anything of the kind (Longford 1969). Wellington left Eton in 1794 after spending three unhappy and unsuccessful years there and never returned unless he had to. In 1855, three years after Wellington's death, the French writer and parliamentarian Count de Montalembert visited Eton in search of material for a book, and subsequently wrote: ". . . one understands the Duke of Wellington's *mot* when, revisiting during his declining years the beauteous scenes where he had been educated, remembering the games of his youth, and finding the same precocious vigour in the descendants of his comrades, he said aloud: *'C'est ici qu' a été gagnée la bataille de Waterloo'* " (Longford 1969:16). Longford notes first, that none of Wellington's visits to Eton seem appropriate for such a remark, second, that the epigram is more Napoleonic than Wellingtonian, and third, that there is no mention of "playing fields" and hence no justification for inferring a reference to the beneficial effects of organized games on military prowess. Sir Edward Creasy subsequently carried the legend further, writing that as Wellington passed the playing fields at Eton he remarked, "There grows the stuff that won Waterloo" (Longford 1969). The famous epigram itself, combining Montalembert's original *mot* and Creasy's "playing fields" embellishment, appeared for the first time in English in a book by Sir William Fraser (1889).

tive success of individual humans. Such a view necessarily emphasizes human "selfishness," although selfishness in the evolutionary/adaptive sense of contributing to reproductive success obviously overlaps only partially with the usual connotations of this word. Wilson (1975b) argues that the central problem of sociobiology is to explain the evolution of altruism ("self-destructive behavior performed for the benefit of others"); the solution has been to take the altruism out of altruism. Activity of an individual animal that appears to reduce its personal fitness and to augment the fitness of another animal has been explained in two ways: (1) the beneficiary and the altruist share genes, so that the net effect of the altruistic act is to increase the representation of the altruist's genes in the next generation (Hamilton 1964, Alexander 1974, Eberhard 1975); (2) the beneficiary and the altruist have established a long-term arrangement in which altruistic acts are reciprocated, to their mutual benefit (Trivers 1971, Alexander 1975). The central question in a functional approach to human behavior is: to what extent does the complexity of human affairs conceal the adaptiveness of the behavior of individual humans, and to what extent is human behavior, in fact, not adaptive? With respect to functional interpretations of play, sports, and war, both points of view may be of value.

Human Behavior as Adaptation

The behavior of individual humans probably is more adaptive than Western intellectual traditions of human nature dispose us to believe. Adaptiveness may be obscured because : (1) Selection may favor individuals who conceal their "selfish" motives from others. Whether or not behavior is altruistic, it is often advantageous to make it appear to be so (Trivers 1971, Alexander 1974, 1975).[2] (2) Humans operate

2. Alexander (1974, 1975) also argues that selection favors individuals who are ignorant of the "selfish" effects of their own behavior since the sincere belief in one's own altruism makes one's deceptive performances more believable. Semantic difficulties aside, I find this argument unconvincing. Our ape-like ancestors must have been far less self-conscious and insightful than we are, but not less selfish. Human self-consciousness and insight evolved along with unprecedented "altruism" (in the sense that human concern with kin and with reciprocal exchange of benefits among non-kin is unmatched among vertebrates) as well as unprecedented chicanery. One might as easily argue that self-insight is in part an adaptation—imperfect, as are all adaptations—to detect other people's trickery and deceit by becoming aware of one's own propensities, and to assess other people's vulnerabilities by analogy with one's own.

within a framework of social constraints and opportunities of unprecedented complexity.

The Battle of Waterloo, for example, was a distinctly human event—made possible by human intelligence, language, planning, cooperation, weapons, teaching, and perhaps play—in which about 50,000 boys and men were wounded or killed. This fact alone, however, is not evidence for maladaptive behavior. An interpretation of the Battle of Waterloo from the standpoint of individual adaptation and self-interest might take into account conscription and the penalties for avoiding it, the benefits of military life as compared with the alternative of poverty for many of the enlisted men, the high desertion rate at Waterloo despite severe penalties, and the tangible rewards for survivors who demonstrate "valor" in battle. Such an interpretation also would take into account that all strategies have their attendant risks, and that failures do not necessarily indicate the existence of pathological or altruistic behavior; lions sometimes catch and kill fleeing gazelle without endangering the principle that flight is an adaptive antipredator device for gazelles. The extreme violence and cruelty documented in the human historical record probably result in part from human cooperation, which frequently produces inequalities between rivals unprecedented among nonhuman animals, and in part from the intelligence by which humans create and recognize circumstances in which killing can be pursued with great gain or little risk to the killers. Indeed, selection for skills in cooperative violence may have played an important role in the evolution of human intelligence (Alexander 1971, 1974, 1975, Bigelow 1973, Alcock 1975, Hamilton 1975).

Human Behavior as Nonadaptive

Considerations of self-interest notwithstanding, in postagricultural societies, at least, a great deal of human behavior simply cannot be accounted for as individual adaptation. The events at Waterloo, for example, probably resulted in part from individuals systematically exhibiting maladaptive behavior, taking risks that were not in their own reproductive interests. In one early-afternoon battle the British repelled a French assault, but, flushed with success, the cavalry units of Lord Edward Somerset and Sir William Ponsonby charged to the French front, where they were devastated. Ponsonby was killed, as were 2500

English horsemen, one third of the number taking part, most of them after the real business of the charge was over (*Encyclopaedia Britannica*). Fraser (1889:198–99) describes this apparently maladaptive behavior in terms that suggest the participants' motives: "The British Cavalry on that day performed deeds of valour, and prowess that will forever live in history. . . . This unhappily in several instances led to the almost entire destruction of these fine Regiments."

Durbin and Bowlby (1950) maintain that adult human aggression differs from the aggression of children and nonhuman animals in two respects—adult human aggression is normally a group activity, and it is normally rationalized: " A moral distinction is always made between the individual killing for himself and the same individual killing for some real or supposed group interest. . . . Men will die like flies for theories and exterminate each other with every instrument of destruction for abstractions" (pp. 12–13). To compare the behavior of humans with the behavior of nonhuman animals it may prove fruitful to determine who, if anyone, benefits from acts of human violence that are not adaptive for the actors, and how such morals, theories, and abstractions develop.

Among nonhuman animals the form and frequency of play are determined by the players themselves, and no individual is compelled to play. One can then assume that, on the average, such play is adaptive and increases the player's reproductive success. A great deal of human play—especially, perhaps, in simple societies—also is controlled by the individual players, but humans influence each other's behavior in subtle, profound, and unprecedented ways: humans are the only animals that actively teach each other (Barnett 1968), and only humans play in teams (Alexander 1975). When the nature of play is substantially influenced by individuals other than the players, and especially when it is influenced by nonrelatives, one cannot assume that the learning occurring in play is adaptive for the players. The more plastic an organism's behavior is, the more varied are the maladaptive, as well as the adaptive, behaviors it can learn. The more teachable an organism is, the more fully it can profit from the experiences of its ancestors and associates and the more it risks being exploited by its ancestors and associates. The more an animal "goes in for ethicizing" (Waddington 1960) the more it can acquire traditions of social wisdom that are too complex or subtle to be learned through individual experience and the more it can acquire worthless and destructive superstitions. The more cooperatively interdependent the members of a group become, the greater is their collective power, the more fulsome are the opportunities for individuals to manipulate one another for their own ends, and "the more scope there is for the inconspicuous idler" (Hamilton 1975:145).

Five general processes or circumstances individually or in combination may be responsible for systematic, maladaptive human behavior.

1. Because humans are so plastic behaviorally, and the influences on human behavior so numerous and complex, some human behavior and traditions may occur randomly with respect both to individual and group fitness as incidental, yet unavoidable, byproducts of flexibility. Wilson (1975b) refers to this phenomenon as "tradition drift."

2. Natural selection is not prescient and does not anticipate the future: organisms are adapted to past conditions, not the present or future. Cultural activities can change the circumstances of human life so rapidly it is likely that some formerly adaptive human traditions and genes outlive their utility. As suggested in chapter 8, humans are probably adapted to the nomadic hunting and gathering way of life of our Pleistocene ancestors, in which events like Waterloo could not have existed. Thus, while Alexander (1975) pursuasively argues that evolutionary theory and ultimate causation provide a theoretical approach to behavior that is not even remotely equalled in generality and usefulness by any other theory, to the extent that humans are not adapted to postagricultural and postindustrial environments, human behavior can not be expected to be explicable in terms of ultimate causation.

3. Alexander (1974:376) argues that because humans are, and possibly always have been, composed of competing and hostile groups which may, as a result of culture, differ greatly in reproductive and competitive abilities, and because "human groups are uniquely able to plan and act as units, to look ahead and purposely carry out actions designed to sustain the group and improve its competitive position," significant group selection may have occurred in the course of human evolution. If so, this might account for human propensities to exhibit occasional group-adaptive self-sacrifice. But this hypothesis is of limited explanatory value, since Alexander (1975) also suggests that during human evolution selection never lost its potency at the level of the individual.

4. Traditional beliefs may spread by a process of "cultural" group

selection, so that in certain circumstances human groups in which boys are taught, perhaps through sports, that self-sacrifice is valorous expand and flourish at the expense of groups in which boys are taught discretion. Keegan (1976:192) suggests that football was, in fact, responsible for the British victory at Waterloo, that the French were "beaten not by wiser generalship or better tactics or superior patriotism but by the coolness and endurance, the pursuit of excellence and of intangible objectives for their own sake which are learnt in game-playing—that game-playing which was already becoming the most important activity of the English gentleman's life." While Dunning's history (1963) indicates that Keegan may have misjudged the nature of English football at the beginning of the 19th century, the general point may be nonetheless correct. Southwick (1972) and others have suggested that subordinate male rhesus monkeys may function as "soldiers," exhibiting aggressive behavior detrimental to their own interests but beneficial to group survival. Although some defensive behavior by peripheral males might be favored by selection if the risks were low and the benefits to the males' kin were high (Eberhard 1975), little theoretical or factual support exists for significant "altruistic" violence among nonhuman primates. Among nonhuman animals, patterns similar to human warfare are developed most clearly in the social insects, apparently because the extremely high degree of genetic interrelatedness among members of a group permits selection for the "altruistic" behaviors that may make "war" possible (Maynard Smith 1972).

Among humans, "cultural" group selection would not be subject to the difficulties that make genetic group selection improbable, and self-sacrifice rare among nonhuman animals, since the elimination of self-sacrificing humans would not necessarily diminish the tradition-based propensity for group-adaptive self-sacrifice. Although natural selection favors individuals who are resistant to learning traditions that reduce their total genetic fitness, because human genotypes make possible a wide range of eventual behavior and because culture can change so much more rapidly than gene pools, the potential for the cultural evolution of group-adaptive self-sacrifice always is present. Also, it may be "difficult" selection to favor genes that make humans resistant to learning certain traditions without at the same time reducing adaptive flexibility.

5. Humans generally communicate to promote their own interests

(Goffman 1969). Person A (or group A) may structure communication to B (or group B) so that B comes to believe that it is in his interest (e.g., valorous) to exhibit behavior whose ultimate effect is to benefit A at B's expense. Hamilton (1975:135) writes: ". . . as language becomes more sophisticated there is also more opportunity to pervert its use for selfish ends: fluency is an aid to persuasive lying as well as to conveying complex truths that are socially useful." If traditional beliefs, values, laws, morality, and religion are the cumulative outcomes of communication among individual humans, this process might correspond with the Marxian view that morality is the product of social conflict and must be understood as competing sets of social partisan demands (Venable 1966). Had Edward III effectively controlled the socialization of English children—and hence their hearts and minds—archery, not football, might have flourished despite primitive means of social control.

As argued above, while selection favors individuals who recognize self-interest and resist being exploited, human genotypes make possible a wide range of eventual behavior. Since behavioral changes precede and lead evolution (Manning 1975, Wilson 1975b) the genetic evolution of resistance to exploitation inevitably must lag behind the cultural evolution of chicanery.

In summary, human wars and animal fighting probably have the same ultimate goals, the acquisition of commodities—food, space, mates—that promote reproductive success: the basic, if not always the immediate, cause of all conflict is Malthusian (Lack 1969). But the circumstances surrounding warfare and preparation for warfare differ in important respects from those that surround animal fighting and play-fighting, and comparisons must be made cautiously. Human behavioral plasticity provides unprecedented opportunities for learning maladaptive behavior. This may occur as the inevitable byproduct of plasticity, as the result of group-adaptive cultural evolution, or as the result of manipulation and exploitation of some individuals or groups by other individuals or groups. These circumstances, of course, constitute part of the environment in which natural selection occurs, and selection favors individuals who resist learning traditions that do not promote their own reproductive interests. But such selection can occur only to the extent that individuals are not simultaneously rendered resistant to learning traditions that are in their interests. Since cultures can change so much more rapidly than gene pools, tradition drift, cultural selection, and exploitation are inevitable features of human existence.

I do not mean to imply that all nonhuman-animal learning is adaptive and all human learning is problematical. A male rhesus monkey who, by chance, had only female playmates during his formative years could conceivably develop a dysfunctional, exaggerated estimate of his fighting skills. Similarly, it is obvious that humans evolved behavioral plasticity and cultural capabilities because throughout most of human evolution most learning was adaptive.

The line of reasoning pursued here is relevant to ultimate explanations of all human behavior, but it may be especially relevant to considerations of human warfare: there is some question, at least in my mind, whether many events of war could occur at all if individuals consistently acted only in their own interests.

Whether maladaptive human behavior is considered to be "altruistic" or pathological seems largely a question of definition and of the level of focus. The important point is that the student of human behavior must ask not only whether an individual's behavior is adaptive but also, adaptive for whom?

Chapter eleven

Other Considerations, Summary, and Conclusions

On the basis of my observations of playfighting and playchasing among free-ranging rhesus monkeys and of analysis of filmed playfights I have argued that aggressive play has a recognizable design. During playchases monkeys exhibit locomotor patterns typical of intraspecific aggression and probably of predator avoidance. During playfights monkeys attempt to bite without being bitten, a goal which is achieved in part by gaining positions favorable for biting and avoiding positions that increase susceptibility to being bitten. On the basis of this design, I suggest that the practice and perfection of skills in predator avoidance and aggression is an adaptive function of aggressive play, in the rigorous sense that aggressive play was shaped by natural selection for these purposes. Brief reviews of the literature indicate that most mammalian play has a similar design, supporting a practice/developmental functional theory of play.

The marked sex differences in rhesus aggressive play have been considered to constitute a natural experiment, providing evidence about adaptive function independent of the evidence of design. Since playfighting was far more frequent and intense among immature males than among immature females, and since fighting success has been shown to be a far more important determinant of male than of female reproductive success, I conclude that sex differences in play support the evidence of design—that playfighting functions to develop fighting skills.

The practice theory—although it is by no means universally, or even widely, accepted—is one of the oldest and most persistent explanations for the existence of play. In fact, it has been said that the adaptive significance of extended immaturity is to provide opportunity for learning, in large part through play.

For example, Groos (1898:xx) writes: "perhaps the very existence of youth is due in part to the necessity for play; the animal does not play because he is young, he has a period of youth because he must play." Washburn and Hamburg (1965b:618) make a similar point: "Prolonged youth would have no advantage unless the inner drive to activity led to knowledge and skills. Merely to grow slowly would be a liability, unless in that time adults were developed that were more likely to survive." On the other hand, Ghiselin (1974) maintains that there is no evidence that the opportunity to learn is the function of extended immaturity.

Ewer (1968) suggests that for play to exist an animal must have: (1) a period of immaturity; (2) a certain minimal learning capacity; (3) a "requirement for quick movement, accurately oriented in relation to the variable external world, with failure of a first attempt carrying a heavy penalty" (p. 301). If extended immaturity is requisite for play to exist, then a correlation between youth and play is to be expected, and does not necessarily prove that youth functions to provide play opportunity. If youth existed for some other reason, selection would favor animals who made most effective use of immaturity, and animals that maximized skills in species-typical activities through play would have a selective advantage.

Since most play is aggressive play, and since an animal is skilled or unskilled in aggressive behavior only relative to its competitors, the lack of play during lean years, when immature animals must spend most available time and energy foraging (Hall 1963, Loy 1970, Baldwin and Baldwin 1976, 1977), can be expected to have little effect on reproductive efficiency as long as competing animals suffer similar degrees of play deprivation. If the adaptive significance of most play is the development of competitive skills and not, as is frequently suggested, "socialization," the absence of severe behavioral and social deficits among nonplaying squirrel monkeys (Baldwin and Baldwin 1973, 1974, 1977) is not surprising. Perhaps analysis of evolutionary convergences and divergences in both play and extended immaturity will shed light on their relationship.

It remains an open question whether play serves functions in addition to the development of skills, but several lines of evidence suggest that all animal play cannot be explained as practice. First, adults of several species have been observed to play: for example, female Steller sea lions (Farentinos 1971), female lions (Schaller 1972), male bonnet macaques (Simonds 1965), and common marmosets (*Calithrix jacchus jacchus*) of both sexes (Stevenson and Poole 1976). Adult play generally is reported to be more inhibited than the play of younger animals (chapter 7), and adults usually play with juveniles rather than with other adults. Moreover, adult play is observed infrequently and sporadically: four of eleven adult male bonnet macaques were not observed to play (Simonds 1965). Thus adult play seems to have little potential for improvement of skills. Second, the variability in frequency of female rhesus play was higher than the variability of male play even though the male variability probably was overestimated (see chapter 4). All males played frequently, a few females played as frequently as some males, but many females played infrequently. Some females may play more frequently than is required to achieve adaptive levels of proficiency. Third, some playfights and playchases are so nonvigorous it is hard to imagine that they could have significant impact on development of skills. (This is true especially of some female-female and juvenile-infant play.) Fourth, it was my impression that monkeys were able to use play for a variety of purposes. A two-year-old female initiated play with her mother "in order to" touch the infant that her mother held (chapter 4). Similarly, juvenile females sometimes seemed to initiate playfights with infants "in order to" hold and carry them, and actually playfought with the infants only enough to retain their interest. Occasionally it seemed that play was used by a larger monkey to bully or intimidate a smaller one, and in these circumstances the primary goal of the smaller monkey apparently was to be allowed to leave.

While rhesus motor patterns are relatively fixed and species-typical, the expression of these patterns is highly variable and is based on substantial skills in social perception. As Welker (1971) remarks, like humans, animals may have a variety of motives for their behavior. Whether play can be said to serve functions in addition to practice, or whether these "uses" of play are better regarded as incidental effects, like the snow-tramping of Williams's fox, probably cannot be determined at present and may be unanswerable. Surely most functions begin their career as effects.

I have suggested that practice theories of play have been rejected for two quite opposite reasons: (1) Play patterns are said to be so similar to the serious patterns they mimic that play cannot improve performances of the serious patterns. (2) Play patterns are said to be so dissimilar to the serious patterns they mimic that the primary function of play cannot be to practice these serious patterns.

The first criticism fails to consider the nature of proficiency and the development of skill. A review of behavioral changes that occur with practice indicates that there are many ways in which play could improve the performance of motor skills. The second criticism is met by considering in turn each feature in which play is said to contrast with similar behavior seen in other contexts. These features not only are in harmony with the practice theory but, in addition, many are predicted by it. I also suggested that the theory that play functions to develop novel, rather than skillful, behavior probably is incorrect with respect to both human and nonhuman animals, although play occasionally may have such an effect.

That the practice theory of play continues as a minority position probably has several additional explanations. One might point to the infrequent use of motion picture film in the study of animal behavior; ethology's preoccupation with the form of motor patterns and, until recently, with relatively simple animals; American psychology's preoccupation with laboratory animals and the learning of tasks with no clear adaptive significance; the belief that quantification is the *sine qua non* of science (see Aldis 1975). But I believe there are also more profound reasons. Gould (1975) recently pointed out that not a single one of Darwin's contemporaries unambiguously accepted natural selection; they accepted the fact of evolution, but not its mechanism. And according to several biologists (Williams 1966, Alexander 1974, Ghiselin 1974, Hamilton 1975), Darwin's insights have not informed much twentieth-century biological thought. In large part, this may result from

> the radical departure from the Western intellectual tradition that was implicit in Darwin's new cosmology. A world populated by organisms striving to no end but rather playing ridiculous sexual games, a world in which the brain is an extension of the gonads, and where killing one's brother is a virtue, so long as it furthers one's mother's reproductive success, simply cannot be reconciled with the old way of thinking. Darwin may be considered the Newton of biology. . . . (Ghiselin 1973:968).

Williams (1966:255) speculates that "biology would have been able to mature more rapidly in a culture not dominated by Judeo-Christian theology and the Romantic tradition. It might have been well served by the First Holy Truth [attributed to the Buddha] from the Sermon at Benares: 'Birth is painful, old age is painful, sickness is painful, death is painful.' . . ." Williams suggests that much misunderstanding in biology results from attempts "to find not only an order in Nature but a moral order. . . . There is a rather steady production of books and essays that attempt to show that Nature is, in the long run and on the average, benevolent and acceptable to some unquestionable ethical and moral point of view. By implication, she must be an appropriate guide for devising ethical systems and for judging human behavior" (pp. 254–55).

The list in chapter 1 of the functions attributed to animal play is striking by virtue of the diversity of functions and the frequency with which they reflect an essentially harmonious view of nature-as-system. One retains the impression that an organism's primary goal is to be cooperative and affiliative, to become an integrated unit of a larger functional entity. How social interaction and communication can develop in species that do not play is rarely considered, nor is the reason why harmonious goals are pursued with motor patterns that generally mimic the most intensely competitive activities of which a species is capable. This approach to aggressive play appears to be consistent with a broader treatment often accorded animal aggression. For example, published reviews of aggressive behavior among nonhuman primates seem invariably to assume, without explanation or justification, that behavior is adapted to promote more encompassing and public-spirited interests than individual reproductive success. Perhaps to many students of animal behavior it is particulary unacceptable that play, a behavior which lacks obvious immediate benefit and, more than any other social behavior, seems to lie outside the materialistic logic of Darwinism, should be, not only a comprehensible part of that logic, but the origin of skill in tooth and claw.

Examples of Aggressive Play: B–G

Example B

A: 2 year old male (G2)
B: 2 year old male (H4)
Time from A's look at B to A's flight: approximately 1.2 seconds
Location: bare ground under a low shrub

A	B
Stands under shrub, about 1½ feet from B, facing straight ahead (about 90 degrees to the left of B).	Sits next to the trunk of the shrub, looking at A.
Takes 2 steps forward, looks to right at B's face and steps left with left foot.	
Plants feet, bending at knees, twisting upper body to face B, play-face.	Rears, leans forward raising hands off ground, reaching toward A with his left hand. Play-face.
Rears, reaches toward B with his right hand, apparently parrying B's reach.	
Leaps off hind feet, rising about 1 foot in the air directly over B, right hand pushing B's left	Falls forward onto his right hand, pivoting left off this hand.

A	B
shoulder.	
Flips legs over his head and simultaneously twists 180 degrees, so he is facing B as he lands on his hind feet.	Plants feet, pivots (mostly off left foot) to the left 180 degrees so he faces A as A lands. He steps toward A, bipedally, reaching toward him with his right hand.
Rears, twists to right off hind feet 180 degrees, facing away from B, leaps away and flees.	
	Takes about 2 steps after A, stops and stands.

Notes to Example B

1. Monkeys frequently look at partner's face at beginning of interaction (B:2; A:6–7).
2. Monkeys rear to facilitate reaching, grasping, and mobility (B:10–12; A:15—16).
3. Play-faces given at beginning of interaction (A:12; B:13).
4. Reach is parried (A:15–18).
5. Hand on ground used as a pivot (B:20–22).
6. Leaper's hand touches leapee during leap over (A:20–24).
7. Leap over includes 180 degree twist or pivot so leaper lands facing leapee (A: 26–30).
8. Monkeys move to face partner (A:26–30; B:26—29).
9. Monkey orients away from partner before flight (A:33–36).
10. Smaller monkey flees (A:33–36).
11. Fleeing monkey followed briefly (B:37–38).

Example C

A: 2 year old male (H1)
B: 3 year old female (C0)
Time from beginning of A's leap to end of contact: approximately 4 seconds
Location: dock

A	B
Approaches dock, walking on mangrove roots, looking at B.	Sits on dock, back to A.
Leaps onto dock, reaching	Turns head and upper body

toward B with right hand, play-face.	to right, looking at A's face, play-face.
Grasps B on right side with right hand, stepping bipedally toward a position behind her. Lands on left hand, twisting 90 degrees off this hand, facing B	Rears onto hind feet, left hand on dock, steps with hind feet, pivoting 180 degrees to the right off her left hand, facing A who has stepped behind her, her rotational momentum is halted by planting her hind legs wide apart, bending at knees, after she faces A.
Squats, facing B, looking at her face.	Squats, almost sitting, facing A, looking at his face.
Hands come off dock, bipedal leap toward and over B's head, presses with right hand on B's left shoulder as he goes over.	Forequarters pushed down by A as he goes over, then bobs back up, hands come off the dock, twists head up and to the left as A goes over, bites at his right flank but apparently does not make contact.
Leap carries him directly over B, both hands and feet touching her back as he goes over, lands first on left hand, then pivots 180 degrees on this hand as his feet come to the ground, so he is *behind* B, facing her back as he lands.	
Reaches toward B's head with right hand, but misses as B falls forward.	Falls forward, play-face, right hand comes to dock, then left hand to dock, turning slightly to the right, weight largely on left hand, steps forward with left foot (foot now in front of left hand) weight largely on left foot,

A	B
	twists to right, reaching behind her toward A with right hand.
Rears to bipedal stand, grasping B's right hip with right hand, her left hip with left hand. Steps with left foot to the left, then steps left with right foot, as B twists to the right, staying behind her. Falls forward, turning head to right, with the side of his mouth placed on B's lower back.	
	Reaches back with right hand, grasps A's right hand (which is grasping her) and left hand grasps the edge of the dock.
Steps left again with left foot, mouth moves down B's back and he bites at the top of her right leg.	
	Steps forward with right foot, grasping edge of dock with it, twists to right off this foot (toward A) right hand releasing grip on A and arching over his head.
Steps left with left foot, then left with right foot, keeping behind B.	
	Steps to right with left foot, crossing right foot, begins to spring away from A, steps to right with right foot, continuing the spring and simultaneously twisting left, away from A. Springs off dock into mangroves, power coming from hind legs. (May be

Sits. (3rd monkey dives into him and they wrestle.)	avoiding approach of 3rd monkey.)

Notes to Example C

1. Play initiated with a partner who is not looking at the initiator (A:5–7).
2. Monkeys frequently look at partner's face at beginning of interaction (B:5–7, 21–22; A:21–22).
3. Play-faces given at beginning of interaction (A:7; B:7) and here they last through most of the interaction.
4. Rearing to a bipedal position facilitates reaching, grasping, and mobility (A:9–12, 55; B:10–13).
5. Monkey in the behind position, or moving to the behind position, grasps and thereby controls the in-front monkey (A:9–10, 55–58).
6. Monkey moves to stay behind partner (A:9–12, 24–42, 58–62, 73–76, 84–86).
7. A hand on the ground used as a pivot (B:10–13; A:12–14, 37–40).
8. Unless fleeing, monkey in in-front position attempts to face partner (B:10–15, 77–82). Monkeys move to face partner (B:5–7; A:13–14).
9. Body movement halted planting widespread feet, bending at knees (B:15–19).
10. Monkey leaping directly over partner presses the partner with a hand (A:24–28).
11. A sitting or squatting monkey being leaped over raises head, attempting to bite the leaper (B:27–32).
12. Leap over accompanied by 180 degree twist so leaper faces partner when landing (A:34–42).
13. Monkey in behind position bites but cannot be bitten (A:62–66, 73–76).
14. Monkey in the in-front position uses own hand to pull away grasping hand of behind partner (B:67–69).
15. Monkey orients away from partner before flight (B:87–92). Female flees.
16. Monkey flees to cover (B:92–94).

Example D

A: 1 year old female (L3)

B: 2 year old female (G1)

Time from start of A's leap to end of contact: approximately 1.5 seconds

Location: open ground

A	B
Crouches on ground, approximately 1′ from B, facing B.	Stands on ground, posterior toward A.
Leaps at B, play-face, feet leaving ground, reaching toward B, grasps B, right hand on right hip, left hand on left hip, bites B's lower	

	A	B
10	back.	
11		Sits, pivots to right to
12		face A.
13	Leans and falls to her left,	
14	away from B.	
15		Reaching with right hand,
16		grasps A's right shoulder.
17	Leaps, all 4 feet, away from	
18	B, her right side facing B,	Rears onto hind feet, steps
19	B's right hand holding her	bipedally after A, eyelid
20	shoulder. Turns upper body	flash, continuing to hold A's
21	to left, pivoting off right	shoulder.
22	foot, steps bipedally away	
23	from B, forequarters held	
24	slightly off ground by B.	
25		
26	Completes turn to left, runs	Runs after A, right hand releases
27	quadrupedally away from B.	grip, reaches and grasps A's
28		left flank with her left hand,
29		head moves to A's right side,
30		mouth opens, bites A's right hip.
31		
32	Leaps away, runs into	
33	mangroves.	
34		Sits.

Notes to Example D

1. Play initiated with a partner not looking at initiator (A:5–7).
2. Play-face by initiating monkey (A:5). B does not give play-face (relaxed open mouth) until she bites at the end of the interaction (B:30).
3. Grasping with hands used to control partner when biting partner (A:6–9; B:27–30).
4. Monkey moves to face partner unless about to flee (B:11–12).
5. Monkey orients away from partner before flight (A:17–26)). Smaller monkey flees.
6. Rearing facilitates reaching, grasping, and mobility (B:18–22; A:20–23).
7. When caught, fleeing monkey is bitten (B:26–30).
8. Monkey flees to cover (A:32–33).

Example E

A: infant male, approximately ½lb. heavier than B
B: infant male
Time from beginning of B's approach to A's flight: about 14 seconds
Location: bare ground

A	B
Sits on ground.	Approaches A at a gamboling run, play-face when about 9″ from A.
Rears onto hind feet.	
	Reaches toward A with right hand, twisting head to right, mouth moving into A's belly.
(Standing bipedally as B dives into him.) Falls across B's back, bites near base of tail.	
	Collapses to ground under A's weight.
Stands bipedally, anterior to B, leaning over B, holding B with hands (*on-top*).	
	Twists onto back, facing A, pushing at A's face with feet.
Steps with left foot as B rolls and twists under him. Bipedal leap to B's left side, lands about 6″ away from B, arms waving to keep balance.	
	Rolls to left, facing A.
Leans toward B, reaching toward him with both hands, but B is too far away. (Still standing bipedally, legs flexed.)	
	Play-face, watching A's face, rolls left onto belly. Pushes upper body off ground with arms, pivoting 90 degrees to right, so head is pointed toward A, pushes off ground with feet, face moving toward A's neck, bites A on neck.
Reaches with right hand behind B, grasps hair on back of B's neck.	
	Rears onto hind feet, reaches with left hand behind A and grasps the hair of A's upper

A	B
	back. Steps left with left foot.
Pulls right with right hand (which is grasping back of B's neck), bites B's now-exposed neck on the right side and simultaneously is pushed to a sitting position by B.	
	Steps bipedally, to keep balance, rearing to full bipedal stand, legs fully extended and bending forward at the waist, mouth is pulled away from A's neck by A's right hand.
(Inferred, out of sight: grasps B's right side with left hand, pulls down.) Inner right arm simultaneously pushes left against side of B's neck in same direction left hand is pulling.	
	Is thrown to the ground, falling to his own right.
Does not immediately pursue advantage. Turns head to right, then back to face B. Wide play-face.	
	Rolls onto belly and begins to rise, hindquarters pushed off the ground by almost fully extended hind legs, but head still near ground.
Leans forward, face moving toward exposed back of B's neck, bites back of B's neck.	
	Falls to his left, catching himself first with his left hand, then with his right. Falls to a sitting position.
From sitting position with hands on ground, leans toward B, then springs off hind legs, reaching toward B with both hands. Feet come	

slightly off ground in this leap.	
	Twists upper torso to right, facing A, reaches up and grasps A's torso with right hand.
Leap slightly overshoots B, so that A's belly hits B in the face, knocking him over. Steps bipedally forward as legs hit the ground, then, leaning forward, places right hand on the ground.	
	Knocked backward by force of A's leap, rolls onto back, simultaneously curling (bringing knees up to the chest), then extends legs and pushes A's face with feet and pushes A's torso with hands.
(On-top.) Pivots left off right hand, moving in direction of leap to position anterior to B. Twists upper body to left, moving around B's head and moves toward B from B's right side. Steps on B's face with left hind foot as he moves to B's right.	
	Rolls onto right side, facing A.
Moves face inside B's arms and bites B's upper chest.	
	Brings left arm toward midline of his body, between his chest and A's teeth.
Raises head until free of B's left arm, rearing onto hind feet, play-face, looking at B's belly, steps back to position anterior to B losing balance slightly and beginning to fall backward, waving arms to keep balance, head directly over B's head, standing bipedally.	

A	B
	Rolls onto back, facing A's face, arms waving.
Arms waving, leans forward and to the right, twisting head to the left, moving face toward B's belly from B's right. Legs fully extended, hindquarters raised.	
	Reaches with left hand toward A's head but misses it, rolling back to right side, continuing to face A who is now on the right.
Continues to fall forward, mouth moving toward B's lower belly.	
	Reaches toward A's head with left hand.
Turns head to left, bites B's inner left forearm.	
	Left arm moves down to side, away from A's mouth.
Turns head to right, moves face, with open mouth, to B's chest, bites. (Standing bipedally over B.)	
	Curls left arm, catching A's face in the crook of the arm and dislodging A's face from his chest.
Raises head until free of B's left arm, bites B's left wrist, then moves face back toward B's belly and bites belly.	
	Curls, bringing knees up toward chest, catches toes of left foot in A's right orbit and extends leg.
Head pushed back, bite broken by B's left foot. Mouth open wide.	
	Leg moves back to normal position.
(Still standing bipedally	

on B's right.) Moves face back to B's lower belly.	
	Reaches behind A's head with left hand.
Raises head slightly, stepping bipedally farther to B's right.	
	Grasps A's left ear with left hand, pulls down.
Turns head to left and bites B's left forearm.	
	Retracts left arm, away from A's teeth.
Leans slightly away from B, head about 4'' from B's belly, stepping right with right foot.	
	Rolls-twists on back keeping directly under A, facing A, legs waving.
Steps to right, mouth moving toward B's belly.	
	Curls, pushes A's face away with left foot before face makes contact.
Head pushed back by B's left foot.	
Jumps bipedally to the left, moving face toward B's belly from B's left side.	Pushes at A's head with right foot, but foot misses head, grasping at A with hands.
Steps back, apparently slightly losing balance from momentum of bipedal jump.	
	Legs curling and waving slightly, moves feet toward A's head.
Steps back, away from B's feet, feet do not reach his head.	
Takes one bipedal step	

A	B
backward (apparently for balance), leans forward, falling toward B's belly, bites.	
	Left hand comes up as A's face approaches, hand comes between A's teeth and his belly. Curls, bringing feet near A's face.
Steps with right foot to B's right side, but falls backward slightly.	
	Rolls to right, facing A, pushes A's face with left hand.
Bipedal leap backward, away from B. Falls backward in direction of leap, catching himself with right hand on the ground.	
	Rolls completely onto right side, facing A.
Runs off.	
	Rises and sits, looking after A.

Notes to Example E

1. Approach at a gambol (B:1).
2. Play-face at beginning of interaction (B:2).
3. Monkeys rear to reach, grasp, and for mobility (A:4; B:42).
4. Rotation (movement in transverse plane) occurs during approach and bite, and may bring teeth into biting position (B:5–7).
5. On-top position achieved twice by larger infant (A:16, 109) and never by the smaller. Larger maintains on-top position through most of interaction.
6. Monkey moves to face partner unless fleeing (B:17–18, 25, 32–35, 91–92, 118, 134–35, 143–45, 195–96, 235, 242–43).
7. Monkey watches partner's face (B:31).
8. On-bottom monkey rises when not prevented by the on-top monkey (B:32–38, 72–76).
9. Bites often aimed at neck (B:37–38, A:48–50, 77–79) or ventral torso (A: 119–20, 156–57, 165–67, 178–79, 224–26).
10. A neck bite is broken by reaching behind the biter, grasping the hair and skin on the back of the neck or upper back, or, occasionally, grasping an ear, and pulling the biter's teeth away (A:39–48; B:42–44, 180–86).
11. Grappling bipedal monkey moves to throw partner (A:59–65).
12. Larger monkey (A) scores one "semi-behind" when he bites the back of B's neck as B is face down before him (A:77–79).

13. On-bottom monkey curls ventrally, extends legs, pushing partner's face away with his feet (B:103–7, 168–71, 200–202, 215–17, 230–31).
14. On-bottom monkey pushes on-top with his hands (B:180, 235–36) or arm (B: 159–62).
15. Hand flat on ground is used as a pivot (A:109–10).
16. On-top monkey scores all torso bites while the animals are in an on-top, on-bottom position (A:119–20, 157, 167, 179, 226).
17. Monkey being bitten brings arm between body and partner's teeth (B:121–23).
18. Defensively used limbs often are bitten (A:151–52, 163–65, 187–88).
19. When a defensively used limb is bitten, usually it is retracted (B:153–54, 189–90).
20. Larger infant flees (A:244). ("Winner" of interaction may flee.)
21. Because the monkeys in this interaction are infants, many moves are clumsy or ineffective compared with juveniles' moves, as the following examples indicate. A juvenile, dived into from the front, generally rears and then leaps over the diver, or holds the diver face down with his hands and bites the back of the neck, or grapples. Here, A simply fell forward as B dived into him and bit B at the base of the tail (A:9–11). Several of the leaps were imprecise. A leaped to B's side (a movement frequently seen in on-top juveniles who move to bite from the side and not directly over on-bottom's face), but A's leap carried him out of reach of B (A:21–28). A also overshot his target on another leap (A:84–97); a juvenile would have kept its head low, moving its face into the partner's belly or neck. A lost his balance when leaping to B's side (A:206–14), and there was a good deal of arm waving for balance; arm waving is infrequent in juvenile playfighting. B collapsed under A's weight (B:12–13). This was not seen in juvenile play. A stepped on B's face (A: 115–17). Juveniles were not observed to do this. The infants lost their balance during bipedal stepping (A:127–31, 211–14, 222–24). Some grasping and pushing was misaimed and ineffective (B:208–9, 215–17). An apparently extraneous movement occurred (A:69–70).

Example F

A: infant male, approximately ½ lb. heavier than B

B: infant male

Time from beginning of B's spring to A's following B: approximately 5.5 seconds

Location: mostly bare mangrove branch, some leaves on its end, about 4′ above rocky ground

	A	B
1	Standing on top of mangrove	
2	branch, gripping it with	
3	all 4 limbs, holding a man-	
4	grove leaf in his mouth.	
5	Facing away from B.	
6		Climbs small metal signpost,
7		about 3′ high, springs up

	A	B
8		toward A, grasping branch
9		behind A with hands.
10	Turns upper body left,	
11	looking at B, pivots off	
12	hands, swinging hind-	
13	quarters around, com-	
14	pleting 90 degree pivot,	
15	body at right angles to	
16	B, looking at B's face.	
17		Steps on branch with hind
18		feet, reaches with hands
19		toward A. (Out of sight:
20		grasps A with hands.)
21		
22	Falls under branch.	Falls under branch.
23		
24	(Branch bending low under	weight of monkeys.)
25		
26	Releases hand grips on	
27	branch and grasps B's back	
28	with both hands, hanging	
29	by feet only.	Hangs below branch by left
30		hand only, reaches up,
31		grasps branch with right hand,
32		back now turned to A. Curls
33		lower body up and grasps
34		branch with both feet, now
35		hanging below branch with
36		all 4 limbs.
37	Pulls self toward B with	
38	his hands and, curling upward,	
39	bites B on the back, and	
40	pulls B down with his hands.	
41		Is dislodged from branch,
42		falls feet first to ground.
43		
44	Continues to hold B	
45	with hands and branch	
46	with feet as B falls	
47	below him, maintaining	
48	biting contact with B's	
49	back.	
50		Lands on left side.
51	When B is on ground below	

him he releases grip on branch and on B and drops next to B, landing on his hands and twisting his hind-quarters as he lands so he is on his hind feet facing B's right side holding B with his hands (*on-top*).	
Steps forward on hind feet and bites B's right side.	
	Twists and rolls to right, to face A, first onto his back, then onto his right side, moving open mouth toward A, reaching toward him with hands.
Leaps back bipedally and sits.	
	Rears onto hind legs, play-face, pivots to left and leaps away from A, running into mangroves.
Leaping off hind feet, follows B. (More wrestling ensues.)	

Notes to Example F

1. Monkeys move to face their partner unless they are fleeing (A:10–16, 51–58; B:62–65).
2. Hand used as a pivot (A:10–14, 54–58).
3. Monkey looks at partner's face (A:16).
4. Wrestling in trees results in monkeys falling under the branch, grasping it from below (A:22; B:22).
5. During social play in trees many movements are oriented to branches rather than the partner (e.g., B:29–36). Here B's back is turned to A as B attempts to regrasp the branch above him.
6. Grasping with hands is used to control the partner being bitten (A:37–39, 44–49, 58–61).
7. Monkey dislodges partner by pulling partner, breaking his hold on the branch, and letting him fall to the ground (A:40).
8. When a monkey being bitten moves, or is moved, the biter moves to keep his face in contact with the bitee (A:44–49).
9. The larger infant dominates the interaction. He dislodges the smaller from the branch (A:40), scores all the bites and the only on-top (A:59). The smaller infant flees (B:70–73).

10. Rearing to a bipedal position facilitates reaching, grasping, and mobility (A:60–61; B:70).
11. Monkey orients away from partner before flight (B:70–73).
12. Monkey flees to cover (B:72–73).
13. Fleeing monkey is followed (A:75–76).

Example G

A: 3 year old male (C4)
B: 2 year old male (G2)
Time from beginning of A's stagger to A's look into mangroves: approximately 11 seconds
Location: dock

A	B
(Has just chased a 3rd juvenile off dock.)	
Standing position.	Sits on dock about 5′ from A, looking at A.
Staggers toward B. Hindquarters are elevated, legs completely extended, head is lowered to within an inch of the dock, arms are bent. Direction of travel is toward B, but steps first with left hand wide to the left, then with the right hand wide to the right, lurching back and forth. Swings left hind foot all the way forward and places it in front of his left hand, so body almost with left side facing B.	Stands facing A. Takes 2 steps toward A.
Looks at B's face, walks sideways toward B, play-face, eyelid flash.	
	When A is about 6″ away, pivots to the left off hind feet, 180 degrees, takes 2 steps away from A, lowers forequarters and tucks

	right arm to chest, lowers right shoulder to the dock and rolls onto the shoulder and over onto his back, then sits up.
Walks toward B, stops about 1′ away.	
	Stands quadrupedally, head toward A.
(Nonplay: brings fingers of right hand to nose, sniffs.)	
	Sits facing A.
Places right hand back on dock. Turns head to left, looking at B, lowers forequarters, body at 90 degree angle to B, forearms almost resting on dock, left side facing B, right side of head brought to within 1″ of dock, hindquarters raised with legs almost fully extended. Continues to look at B's face. (Head-down position.)	
	Two steps toward A, stops and stands quadrupedally, looking at A's face.
Pivots to right off hind feet, hands coming off dock, looking over his shoulder at B as he turns. Just before head is completely turned away makes clear play-face. 180 degree turn completed, runs down dock away from B.	
	Immediately runs after A.
Gamboling about 8′, plants hind feet at about the same time, turns upper body to left, stepping bipedally with hind feet, looking back	

	A	B
75	over shoulder at B, wide	
76	play-face. Several small	
77	steps with all four feet	
78	complete a 180 degree pivot	
79	to left, faces B, eyelid	
80	flash.	
81		Stops, crouches, half turns
82		to right, away from A.
83	Leaps bipedally at B,	
84	legs fully extended, feet	
85	almost coming off dock, arms	
86	raised to level of head,	
87	mouth open very wide, falls	
88	forward, reaching toward B,	
89	stepping forward bipedally.	
90		Continues 180 degree turn to
91		right, runs back up the dock
92		4 steps, left shoulder to
93		dock, rolls onto the shoulder,
94		then onto the back.
95	Stops 2′ from B, looks into	
96	mangrove.	

Notes to Example G

1. Certain movements are regularly seen to precede and accompany play but not to precede or accompany other rhesus activities, such as the stagger (A:6–23). Here, a play-face accompanies this movement. B responds with approach (B:7–8). Similar movements include shoulder roll onto back (B:27–33, 92–94) and gamboling (A:70).
2. Play-face given near beginning of interaction (A:23).
3. Frequent looking at partner's face (A:22, 55; B:59).
4. Head-down position functions as invitation (A:45–56) and is followed by B's approach (B:57–59). If one form of invitation does not succeed, another may be used; here, A looks over his shoulder and runs away (A:60–68), which elicits chasing (B:69).
5. Play-face given as A moves away from B (A:64–66).
6. After invitation succeeds in eliciting playchasing, chasee turns and chases (A:70–78).

Calculation of Expected Values

Calculations of expected values (E) for play interactions if interactions are only a function of degree of playfulness of a class:

Age-Sex Class	*No. Monkeys in Class*	*Participation in Play for Class*
A	n_A	N_A
B	n_B	N_B
C	n_C	N_C
Total	n	N (=2x no. of interactions)

$P_A \equiv \frac{N_A}{N} \times \frac{1}{n_A}$ = Probability that a given monkey of class A will engage in a play interaction involving his class.

$n_A n_B$ = no. of possible pairings of monkeys from classes A and B.

$n_A n_B P_A P_B N = n_A n_B \frac{N_A}{n_A N} \frac{N_B}{n_B N} N$ = Expected no. of interactions between classes A and B = $\frac{N_A N_B}{N}$

$\frac{n_A(n_A-1)}{2}$ = no. of combinations of monkey within class A.

$\frac{n_A(n_A-1)}{2} P_A \frac{N_A}{(n_A-1)N} N$ = Expected no. of interactions between members of class A = $\frac{N_A^2}{2N}$

References

Agar, E. and G. Mitchell 1975. "Behavior of Free-Ranging Adult Rhesus Macaques: A Review." In G. H. Bourne, ed., *The Rhesus Monkey,* vol. 1: 323–42. New York: Academic Press.

Alcock, J. 1975. *Animal Behavior: An Evolutionary Approach.* Sunderland, Massachusetts: Sinauer Associates.

Aldis, O. 1975. *Play Fighting.* New York: Academic Press.

Alexander, R. D. 1971. "The Search for an Evolutionary Philosophy of Man." *Proceedings of the Royal Society of Victoria* 84:99–120.

—— 1974. "The Evolution of Social Behavior." *Annual Review of Ecology and Systematics* 5:325–83.

—— 1975. "The Search for a General Theory of Behavior." *Behavioral Science* 20:77–100.

Altmann, S. A. 1962a. "A Field Study of the Sociobiology of Rhesus Monkeys, *Macaca mulatta.*" *Ann. of the N.Y. Acad. of Sci.* 102:338–435.

—— 1962b. "Social Behavior of Anthropoid Primates: Analysis of Recent Concepts." In E. L. Bliss, ed., *Roots of Behavior,* pp. 277–85. New York: Harper & Brothers.

—— 1967. "The Structure of Primate Social Communication." In S. A. Altmann, ed., *Social Communication among Primates,* pp. 325–62. Chicago: The University of Chicago Press.

—— 1968. "Sociobiology of Rhesus Monkeys III: The Basic Communication Network." *Behaviour* 32:2–32.

Altmann, S. A. and J. Altmann 1970. *Baboon Ecology.* Chicago: University of Chicago Press.

Angermeier, W. F., J. B. Phelps, S. Murray, and J. Howanstine 1968. "Dominance in Monkeys: Sex Differences." *Psychon. Sci.* 12:344.

Angst, W. 1975. "Basic Data and Concepts on the Social Organization of *Macaca fascicularis.*" In L. A. Rosenblum, ed., *Primate Behavior: Developments in Field and Laboratory Research,* vol. 4:325–88. New York: Academic Press.

Azuma, S. 1973. "Acquisition and Propogation of Food Habits in a Troop of Japanese Monkeys." In C. R. Carpenter, ed., *Behavioral Regulators of Behavior in Primates,* pp. 284–92. Lewisburg, Pennslyvania: Bucknell University Press.

Baldwin, J.D. 1969. "The Ontogeny of Social Behaviour of Squirrel Monkeys (*Saimiri sciureus*) in a Seminatural Environment." *Folia primat.* 11:35–79.

Baldwin, J. D. and J. I. Baldwin 1973. "The Role of Play in Social Organization: Comparative Observations on Squirrel Monkeys (*Saimiri*)." *Primates* 14:369–81.

—— 1974. "Exploration and Social Play in Squirrel Monkeys (*Saimiri*)." *American Zoologist* 14:303–15.

—— 1976. "Effects of Food Ecology on Social Play: A Laboratory Simulation." *Z. Tierpsychol.* 40:1–14.

—— 1977. "The Role of Learning Phenomena in the Ontogeny of Exploration and Play." In S. Chevalier-Skolnikoff and F. E. Poirier, eds., *Primate Bio-Social Development: Biological, Social, and Ecological Determinants.* New York: Garland.

Baldwin, L. and G. Teleki 1976. "Patterns of Gibbon Behavior on Hall's Island, Bermuda." *Gibbon and Siamang* 4:21–105.

Balikci, A. 1970. *The Netsilik Eskimo.* Garden City, New York: The Natural History Press.

Barnett, S. A. 1968. "The 'Instinct to Teach.' " *Nature* 220:747–49.

Bateson, G. 1955. "A Theory of Play and Fantasy." *Psychiatric Research Report* 2:39–51.

Beach, F. A. 1945. "Current Concepts of Play in Animals." *Amer. Nat.* 79:523–41.

——, ed. 1965. *Sex and Behavior.* New York: Wiley and Sons.

Beer, C. G. 1975. "Multiple Functions and Gull Displays." In G. Baerends, C. Beer, and A. Manning, eds., *Function and Evolution in Behaviour,* pp. 16–54. Oxford: Clarendon Press.

Bekoff, M. 1972. "The Development of Social Interaction, Play, and Metacommunication in Mammals: An Ethological Perspective." *Quart. Rev. Biol.* 47:412–34.

—— 1974. "Social Play and Play-Soliciting by Infant Canids." *American Zoologist* 14:323–40.

—— 1975a, "Animal Play and Behavioral Diversity." *Amer. Nat.* 109:601–3.

—— 1975b. "The Communication of Play Intention: Are Play Signals Functional?" *Semiotica* 15:231–40.

—— 1976a. "Animal Play: Problems and Perspectives." In P. P. G. Bateson and P. H. Klopfer, eds., *Perspectives in Ethology,* vol. 2:165–88. New York: Plenum.

—— 1976b. "The Social Deprivation Paradigm: Who's Being Deprived of What?" *Developmental Psychobiology* 9:497–98.

—— (in press). "A Sequence Analysis of Social Interaction in Infant Canids: Social Play and Aggression."

Bernstein, I. S. 1964. "Role of the Dominant Male Rhesus Monkey in Response to External Challenges to the Group." *Journal of Comparative and Physiological Psychology* 57:404–6.

—— 1970. "Primate Status Hierarchies." In L. A. Rosenblum, ed., *Primate Behavior: Developments in Field and Laboratory Research* 1:71–109. New York: Academic Press.

—— 1976. "Dominance, Aggression and Reproduction in Primate Societies." *J. Theor. Biol.* 60:459–72.

Bernstein, I. S. and T. P. Gordon 1974. "The Function of Aggression in Primate Societies." *American Scientist* 62:304–11.

Bernstein, I. S., and W. A. Draper 1964. "The Behaviour of Juvenile Rhesus Monkeys in Groups." *Anim. Behav.* 12:84–91.

Bernstein, I. S., T. P. Gordon and R. M. Rose 1974a. "Aggression and Social Controls in Rhesus Monkey (*Macaca mulatta*) Groups Revealed in Group Formation Studies." *Folia primat.* 21:81–107.

—— 1974b. "Factors Influencing the Expression of Aggression During Introductions to Rhesus Monkey Groups." In R. L. Holloway, ed., *Primate Aggression, Territoriality, and Xenophobia*, pp. 211–40. New York: Academic Press.

—— 1974c. "Behavioral and Environmental Events Influencing Primate Testosterone Levels." *Journal of Human Evolution* 3:517–25.

Bernstein, I. S. and W. A. Mason 1963. "Activity Patterns of Rhesus Monkeys in a Social Group." *Anim. Behav.* 11:455–60.

Bernstein, I. S. and L. G. Sharpe 1966. "Social Roles in a Rhesus Monkey Group." *Behaviour* 26:91–104.

Bertrand, M. 1969. *The Behavioral Repertoire of the Stumptail Macaque. Bibliotheca Primatologica* No. 11. Basel: S. Karger.

Bigelow, R. 1973. "The Evolution of Cooperation, Aggression, and Self-Control." In J. K. Cole and D. D. Jensen, eds., *Nebraska Symposium on Motivation 1972,* pp. 1–57. Lincoln: University of Nebraska Press.

Boelkins, R. C. and A. P. Wilson 1972. "Intergroup Social Dynamics of the Cayo Santiago Rhesus (*Macaca mulatta*) with Special Reference to Changes in Group Membership by Males." *Primates* 13:125–39.

Bourliere, F., D. Hunkeler and M. Bertrand 1970. "Ecology and Behavior of Lowe's Guenon (*Cercopithecus campbelli lowei*) in the Ivory Coast." In J. R. Napier and P. H. Napier, eds., *Old World Monkeys,* pp. 297–350. New York: Academic Press.

Breuggeman, J. A. 1973. "Parental Care in a Group of Free-Ranging Rhesus Monkeys (*Macaca mulatta*)." *Folia primat.* 20:178–210.

Brown, J. L. 1975. *The Evolution of Behavior.* New York: W. W. Norton & Co.

Brownlee, A. 1954. "Play in Domestic Cattle in Britain: An Analysis of Its Nature." *Brit. Vet. Journ.* 110:48–68.

Bruner, J. S. 1970. "The Growth and Structure of Skill." In K. Connolly, ed., *Mechanisms of Motor Skill Development,* pp. 63–94. New York: Academic Press.

—— 1972. "Nature and Uses of Immaturity." *American Psychologist* 27:687–708.

—— 1973. "Organization of Early Skilled Action." *Child Development* 44:1–11.

Carpenter, C. R. 1934. *A Field Study of the Behavior and Social Relations of Howling Monkeys. Comp. Psych. Monog.* 10(2).

—— 1942a. "Sexual Behavior of Free-Ranging Rhesus Monkeys." *Journal of Comp. Psych.* 33:113–62.

—— 1942b. "Societies of Monkeys and Apes." *Biol. Symposia* 8:177–204.

—— 1964. "An Observational Study of Two Captive Mountain Gorillas." In C. R. Carpenter, *Naturalistic Behavior of Nonhuman Primates,* pp. 106–121. University Park: The Pennsylvania State University Press.

Chagnon, N. A. 1968. "Yanomamö Social Organization and Warfare." In M. Fried, M. Harris and R. Murphy, eds., *War: The Anthropology of Armed Conflict and Aggression,* pp. 109–59. Garden City, N.Y.: the Natural History Press.

Chance, M. and C. Jolly 1970. *Social Groups of Monkeys, Apes and Men.* London: Jonathan Cape.

Chepko, B. D. 1971. "A Preliminary Study of the Effects of Play Deprivation on Young Goats." *Z. Tierpsychol.* 28:517–26.

Clark, J. D. 1976. "The African Origins of Man the Toolmaker." In G. Ll. Isaac and E. R. McCown, eds., *Human Origins: Louis Leakey and the East African Evidence,* pp. 1–53. Menlo Park, Calif.: W. A. Benjamin.

Conaway, C. H. and C. B. Koford 1965. "Estrous Cycles and Mating Behavior in a Free-Ranging Band of Rhesus Monkeys." *Journal of Mammalogy* 45:577–88.

Connolly, K. 1970. "Skill Development: Problems and Plans." In K. Connolly, ed., *Mechanisms of Motor Skill Development,* pp. 3–21. New York: Academic Press.

Crook, J. H. 1971. "Sources of Cooperation in Animals and Man." In J. F. Eisenberg and W. S. Dillon, eds., *Man and Beast: Comparative Social Behavior,* pp. 235–60. Washington, D.C.: Smithsonian Institution Press.

—— 1972. "Sexual Selection, Dimorphism, and Social Organization in the Primates." In B. Campbell, ed., *Sexual Selection and the Descent of Man 1871–1971,* pp. 231–81. Chicago: Aldine.

Czaja, J. A. and C. Bielert 1975. "Female Rhesus Sexual Behavior and Distance to a Male Partner: Relation to Stage of the Menstrual Cycle." *Archives of Sexual Behavior* 4:583–97.

Darwin, C. 1871. *The Descent of Man and Selection in Relation to Sex.* London: John Murray.

Delgado, J. M. R. 1967. "Social Rank and Radio-Stimulated Aggressiveness in Monkeys." *J. of Nerv. and Ment. Dis.* 114:383–90.

Dolan, K. J. 1976. "Metacommunication in the Play of a Captive Group of Syke's Monkeys." Paper presented at the 45th annual meeting of the American Association of Physical Anthropologists, April 14–17, St. Louis, Missouri.

Dolhinow, P. 1971. "At Play in the Fields." *Natural History* (Dec.), pp. 66–71.

Dolhinow, P. J. and N. Bishop 1970. "The Development of Motor Skills and Social Relationships among Primates through Play." *Minnesota Symposia on Child Psychology* 4:141–98.

Drickamer, L. C. 1974a. "A Ten-Year Summary of Reproductive Data for Free-Ranging *Macaca mulatta.*" *Folia primat.* 21:61–80.

—— 1974b. "Social Rank, Observability, and Sexual Behaviour of Rhesus Monkeys (*Macaca mulatta*)." *J. Reprod. Fert.* 37:117–20.

—— 1975a. "Patterns of Space Utilization and Group Interactions among Free-Ranging *Macaca mulatta.*" *Primates* 16:23–33.

—— 1975b. "Quantitative Observation of Behavior in Free-Ranging *Macaca mulatta:* Methodology and Aggression." *Behaviour* 55:209–36.

Drickamer, L. C. and S. H. Vessey 1973. "Group Changing in Free-Ranging Male Rhesus Monkeys." *Primates* 14:359–68.

DuMond, F. V. 1968. "The Squirrel Monkey in a Seminatural Environment." In L. A. Rosenblum and R. W. Cooper, eds., *The Squirrel Monkey,* pp. 88–145. New York: Academic Press.

Dunning, E. G. 1963. "Football in Its Early Stages." *History Today* 13:838–47.

Durbin, E. F. M. and J. Bowlby 1950. *Personal Aggressiveness and War.* New York: Columbia University Press.

Duvall, S. W., I. S. Bernstein, and T. P. Gordon 1976. "Paternity and Status in a Rhesus Monkey Group." *Journal of Reproduction and Fertility* 47:25–31.

Eaton, G. G., R. W. Goy and C. H. Phoenix 1973. "Effects of Testosterone Treatment in Adulthood on Sexual Behaviour of Female Pseudohermaphrodite Rhesus Monkeys." *Nature New Biology* 242:119–20.

Eberhard, M. J. W. 1975. "The Evolution of Social Behavior by Kin Selection." *The Quarterly Review of Biology* 50:1–33.

Ewer, R. F. 1966. "Juvenile Behaviour in the African Ground Squirrel, *Xerus erythropus* (E. Geoff.)." *Z. Tierpsychol.* 23:190–216.

—— 1968. *Ethology of Mammals.* New York: Plenum Press.

Fady, J. C. 1969. "Les jeux sociaux: le compagnon de jeux chez les jeunes. Observations chez *Macaca irus.*" *Folia primat.* 11:134–43.

Fagen, R. 1974. "Selective and Evolutionary Aspects of Animal Play." *Amer. Nat.* 108:850–58.

Farentinos, R. C. 1971. "Some Observations on the Play Behavior of the Steller Sea Lion (*Eumetopias jubata*)." *Z. Tierpsychol.* 28:428–38.

Farres, A. G. and R. H. Haude 1976. "Dominance Testing in Rhesus Monkeys: Comparison of Competitive Avoidance, and Competitive Drinking Procedures." *Psychological Reports* 38:127–34.

Fedigan, L. 1972. "Social and Solitary Play in a Colony of Vervet Monkeys (*Cercopithecus aethiops*)." *Primates* 13:347–64.

Fisler, G. F. 1967. "Nonbreeding Activities of Three Adult Males in a Band of Free-Ranging Rhesus Monkeys." *J. Mamm.* 48:70–78.

Fitts, P. M. and M. I. Posner 1967. *Human Performance.* Belmont, California: Brooks/Cole.

Fleishman, E. A. 1966. "Human Abilities and the Acquisition of Skill." In A. Bilodeau, ed., *Acquisition of Skill,* pp. 147–67. New York: Academic Press.

Fox, M. W. 1969. "The Anatomy of Aggression and Its Ritualization in Cani-

dae: A Developmental and Comparative Study." *Behaviour* 35:242–58.
—— 1971. *Behaviour of Wolves, Dogs and Related Canids.* New York: Harper and Row.
Fraser, W. 1889. *Words on Wellington.* London: George Routledge & Sons.
Frisch, J. E. 1968. "Individual Behavior and Intertroop Variability in Japanese Macaques." In C. Jay, ed., *Primates: Studies in Adaptation and Variability,* pp. 243–52. New York: Holt, Rinehart and Winston.
Gabow, S. L. 1973. "Dominance Order Reversal between Two Groups of Free-Ranging Rhesus Monkeys." *Primates* 14:215–23.
Gartlan, J. S. 1968. "Structure and Function in Primate Society." *Folia primat.* 8:89–120.
Gentry, R. L. 1974. "The Development of Social Behavior through Play in the Steller Sea Lion." *American Zoologist* 14:391–403.
Ghiselin, M. T. 1973. "Darwin and Evolutionary Psychology." *Science* 179:964–68.
—— 1974. *The Economy of Nature and the Evolution of Sex.* Berkeley: University of California Press.
Glickman, S. E. and R. W. Sroges 1966. "Curiosity in Zoo Animals." *Behaviour* 26:151–88.
Goffman, E. 1969. *Strategic Interaction.* Philadelphia: University of Pennsylvania Press.
Goldman, P. S., H. T. Crawford, L. P. Stokes, T. W. Galkin, and H. E. Rosvold 1974. "Sex-Dependent Behavioral Effects of Cerebral Cortical Lesions in the Developing Rhesus Monkey." *Science* 186:540–42.
Goodall, J. 1965. "Chimpanzees of the Gombe Stream Reserve." In I. DeVore, ed., *Primate Behavior: Field Studies of Monkeys and Apes,* pp. 425–73. New York: Holt, Rinehart and Winston.
—— 1976. "Continuities between Chimpanzee and Human Behavior." In G. Ll. Isaac and E. R. McCown, eds., *Human Origins: Louis Leakey and the East African Evidence,* pp. 81–95. Menlo Park, Calif.: W. A. Benjamin.
Gordon, T. P., R. M. Rose, and I. S. Bernstein 1976. "Seasonal Rhythm in Plasma Testosterone Levels in the Rhesus Monkey (*Macaca mulatta*): A Three Year Study." *Hormones and Behavior* 7:229–43.
Gottier, R. F. 1972. "Factors Affecting Agonistic Behavior in Several Subhuman Species." *Genetic Psychology Monographs* 86:177–218.
Gould, S. J. 1975. "Darwin's 'Big Book.' " *Science* 188:824–26.
Goy, R. W. 1968. "Organizing Effects of Androgen on the Behaviour of Rhesus Monkeys." In R. P. Michael, ed., *Endocrinology and Human Behaviour,* pp. 12–31. London: Oxford University Press.
Goy, R. W. and J. A. Resko 1972. "Gonadal Hormones and Behavior of Normal and Pseudohermaphroditic Nonhuman Female Primates." *Recent Progress in Hormone Research* 28:707–33.
Groos, K. 1898. *The Play of Animals.* New York: D. Appleton.
Hall, K. R. L. 1963. "Variations on the Ecology of the Chacma Baboon (*P. ursinus*)." *Symp. Zool. Soc. Lond.* 10:1–28.

—— 1965. "Behavior and Ecology of the Wild Patas Monkey, *Erythrocebus patas,* in Uganda." *Journ. Zool.* 148:15–87.

Hall, K. R. L. and I. DeVore 1965. "Baboon Social Behavior." In DeVore, ed., *Primate Behavior,* pp. 53–110. New York: Holt, Rinehart and Winston.

Hamburg, D. A. 1963. "Emotions in the Perspective of Human Evolution." In P. H. Knapp, ed., *Expression of the Emotions in Man,* pp. 300–317. New York: International Universities Press.

Hamilton, W. D. 1964. "The Genetical Evolution of Social Behavior." *J. theoret. Biol.* 7:1–52.

—— 1975. "Innate Social Aptitudes of Man: An Approach from Evolutionary Genetics." In Robin Fox, ed., *Biosocial Anthropology,* pp. 133–55. New York: John Wiley & Sons.

Hansen, E. W. 1962. *The Development of Maternal and Infant Behavior in the Rhesus Monkey.* Ph.D. thesis, University of Wisconsin.

—— 1966. "The Development of Maternal and Infant Behavior in the Rhesus Monkey." *Behaviour* 27:107–49.

Harlow, H. F. 1969. "Age-Mate or Peer Affectional System." *Advances in the Study of Behavior* 2:333–83. New York: Academic Press.

Harlow, H. F. and M. K. Harlow 1965. "The Affectional Systems." In A. Schrier, H. Harlow and F. Stollnitz, eds., *Behavior of Nonhuman Primates* vol. 2:287–334. New York: Academic Press.

—— 1969. "Effects of Various Mother-Infant Relationships on Rhesus Monkey Behaviors." In B. M. Foss, ed., *Determinants of Infant Behavior* IV, pp. 15–36. London: Methuen.

Harlow, H. F., W. D. Joslyn, M. G. Senko, and A. Dopp 1966. "Behavioral Aspects of Reproduction in Primates." *J. Anim. Sci.* 25:49–67.

Hausfater, G. 1972. "Intergroup Behavior of Free-Ranging Rhesus Monkeys (*Macaca mulatta*)." *Folia primat.* 18:78–107.

—— 1975. *Dominance and Reproduction in Baboons* (*Papio cynocephalus*). Basel: S. Karger.

Henry, J. D. and S. M. Herrero 1974. "Social Play in the American Black Bear: Its Similarity to Canid Social Play and an Examination of Its Identifying Characteristics." *American Zoologist* 14:371–89.

Hinde, R. A. 1966. *Animal Behaviour.* New York: McGraw Hill.

—— 1971. "Development of Social Behavior." In A. M. Schrier and F. Stollnitz, eds., *Behavior of Nonhuman Primates* 3:1–68. New York: Academic Press.

—— 1975. "The Concept of Function." In G. Bearends, C. Beer, and A. Manning, eds., *Function and Evolution in Behaviour,* pp. 3–15. Oxford: Clarendon Press.

Hinde, R. A. and T. E. Rowell 1962. "Communication by Postures and Facial Expressions in the Rhesus Monkey (*Macaca mulatta*)." *Proc. Zool. Soc. Lond.* 138:1–21.

Hinde, R. A., T. E. Rowell and Y. Spencer-Booth 1964. "Behaviour of Socially Living Rhesus Monkeys in Their First Six Months." *Proc. Zool. Soc. Lond.* 143:609–49.

Hinde, R. A. and Y. Spencer-Booth 1967. "The Behaviour of Socially Living Rhesus Monkeys in Their First Two and a Half Years." *Anim. Behav.* 15:169–96.

Hooff, J. A. R. A. M. van 1967. "The Facial Displays of the Catarrhine Monkeys and Apes." In D. Morris, ed., *Primate Ethology,* pp. 7–68. London: Morrison and Gibb.

—— 1972. "A Comparative Approach to the Phylogeny of Laughter and Smiling." In R. A. Hinde, ed., *Non-Verbal Communication,* pp. 209–41. Cambridge: Cambridge University Press.

Horwich, R. H. 1974. "Development of Behaviors in a Male Spectacled Langur (*Presbytis obscurus*)." *Primates* 15:151–78.

Immelmann, K. 1975. "The Evolutionary Significance of Early Experience." In G. Baerends, C. Beer, and A. Manning, eds., *Function and Evolution in Behaviour,* pp. 243–53. Oxford: Clarendon.

Itani, J. 1958. "On the Acquisition and Propagation of a New Food Habit in the Natural Group of the Japanese Monkey at Takasaki-Yama." *Primates* 1:84–98.

Itani, J., K. Tokuda, Y. Furuya, K. Kano, and Y. Shin 1963. "The Social Construction of Natural Troops of Japanese Monkeys in Takasakiyama." *Primates* 4:1–42.

Jay, P. 1965. "The Common Langur of North India." In I. DeVore, ed., *Primate Behavior,* pp. 197–249. New York: Holt, Rinehart and Winston.

Jolly, A. 1966a. *Lemur Behavior: A Madagascar Field Study.* Chicago: University of Chicago Press.

—— 1966b. "Lemur Social Behavior and Primate Intelligence." *Science* 153:501–6.

—— 1972. *The Evolution of Primate Behavior.* New York: Macmillan.

Joslyn, W. D. 1973. "Androgen-Induced Social Dominance in Infant Female Rhesus Monkeys." *J. Child Psychiat.* 14:137–45.

Kaufmann, J. H. 1965. "A Three-Year Study of Mating Behavior in a Free-Ranging Band of Rhesus Monkeys." *Ecology* 46:500–12.

—— 1967. "Social Relations of Adult Males in a Free-Ranging Band of Rhesus Monkeys." In S. A. Altmann, ed., *Social Communication among Primates,* pp. 73–98. Chicago: University of Chicago Press.

Kawai, M. 1965. "Newly-Acquired Pre-cultural Behavior of the Natural Troop of Japanese Monkeys on Koshima Islet." *Primates* 6:1–30.

Kay, H. 1970. "Analyzing Motor Skill Performance." In K. Connolly, ed., *Mechanisms of Motor Skill Development,* pp. 139–59. New York: Academic Press.

Keegan, J. 1976. *The Face of Battle.* New York: The Viking Press.

Klopfer, P. H. 1970. "Sensory Physiology and Esthetics." *American Scientist* 58:399–403.

Koford, C. B. 1963a. "Group Relations in an Island Colony of Rhesus Monkeys." In C. H. Southwick, ed., *Primate Social Behavior,* pp. 136–52. New York: Van Nostrand.

—— 1963b. "Rank of Mothers and Sons in Bands of Rhesus Monkeys." *Science* 141:356–57.

—— 1965. "Population Dynamics of Rhesus Monkeys on Cayo Santiago." In I. DeVore, ed., *Primate Behavior*, pp. 160–74. New York: Holt, Rinehart and Winston.

—— 1966. "Changes in the Cayo Santiago Rhesus Monkey Population, 1960–1964." *Tulane Studies in Zoology* 13:1–7.

Kohler, W. 1927. *The Mentality of Apes*, 2nd ed. London: Routledge and Kegan Paul.

Kruuk, H. 1975. "Functional Aspects of Social Hunting by Carnivores." In G. Baerends, C. Beer, and A. Manning, eds., *Function and Evolution in Behaviour*, pp. 119–41. Oxford: Clarendon Press.

Kummer, H. 1968. *Social Organization of Hamadryas Baboons. Biblioteca Primatologica* No. 6. Basel: S. Karger.

—— 1971. *Primate Societies*. Chicago: Aldine.

Lack, D. 1969. "Of Birds and Men." *New Scientist* 16:121–22.

Lancaster, J. B. 1971. "Play-Mothering: The Relations between Juvenile Females and Young Infants among Free-Ranging Vervet Monkeys (*Cercopithecus aethiops*)." *Folia primat.* 15:161–82.

Laughlin, W. S. 1968. "Hunting: An Integrating Biobehavior System and Its Evolutionary Importance." In Richard B. Lee and Irven DeVore, eds., *Man the Hunter*, pp. 304–320. Chicago: Aldine.

Lawick-Goodall, J. van 1968. *The Behavior of Free-Living Chimpanzees in the Gombe Stream Reserve. Animal Behaviour Monographs* 1(3).

—— 1970. "Tool-Using in Primates and Other Vertebrates." In D. S. Lehrman, R. A. Hinde and E. Shaw, eds., *Advances in the Study of Behavior* 3:195–249. New York: Academic Press.

—— 1971. *In the Shadow of Man*. Boston: Houghton Mifflin.

—— 1973. "Cultural Elements of a Chimpanzee Community." In E. W. Menzel, Jr., ed., *Precultural Primate Behavior*, pp. 144–84. New York: S. Karger.

Lazar, J. and G. D. Beckhorn 1974. "Social Play or the Development of Social Behavior In Ferrets (*Mustela putorius*)?" *American Zoologist* 14:405–14.

Lee, R. B. and I. DeVore 1968. "Problems in the Study of Hunters and Gatherers." In R. B. Lee and I. DeVore, eds., *Man the Hunter*, pp.3–12. Chicago: Aldine.

Leyhausen, P. 1973. "On the Function of the Relative Hierarchy of Moods." In K. Lorenz and P. Leyhausen, *Motivation of Human and Animal Behavior: An Ethological View*, pp. 144–247. New York: D. Van Nostrand (paper originally published 1965).

Lindburg, D. G. 1967. *A Field Study of the Reproductive Behavior of the Rhesus Monkey* (*Macaca mulatta*). Ph.D. thesis, University of California, Berkeley.

—— 1969. "Rhesus Monkeys: Mating Season Mobility of Adult Males." *Science* 166:1176–78.

—— 1971. "The Rhesus Monkey in North India: An Ecological and Behavioral Study." In L. A. Rosenblum, ed., *Primate Behavior* 2:2–106. New York: Academic Press.

—— 1975. "Mate Selection in the Rhesus Monkey, *Macaca mulatta.*" Paper presented at a symposium entitled "Sociobiology of the Genus *Macaca,*" American Association of Physical Anthropologists, Denver, Colorado, April 12.

—— (in press). "Feeding Behaviour and Diet of Rhesus Monkeys (*Macaca mulatta*) in a Siwalik Forest in North India." In T. H. Clutton-Brock, ed., *Primate Feeding Behavior.*

Linsdale, J. M. and P. Quentin Tomich 1953. *A Herd of Mule Deer.* Berkeley: University of California Press.

Loizos, C. 1966. "Play in Mammals." In P. A. Jewell and C. Loizos, eds., *Play, Exploration and Territory in Mammals,* pp. 1–9. New York: Academic Press.

—— 1967. "Play Behaviour in Higher Primates: A Review." In D. Morris, ed., *Primate Ethology,* pp. 176–218. London: Weidenfeld and Nicolson.

—— 1969. "An Ethological Study of Chimpanzee Play." *Proc. 2nd. Int. Congr. Primat.* 1:87–93. Basel: S. Karger.

Longford, E. 1969. *Wellington: The Years of the Sword.* New York: Harper and Row.

Lorenz, K. 1956. "Plays and Vacuum Activities." In Autuori et al., eds., *L'Instinct dans le Comportement des Animaux et de L'Homme,* pp. 633–37. Paris: Fondation Singer-Polignac, Masson et Cie.

Loy, J. 1970. "Behavioral Responses of Free-Ranging Rhesus Monkeys to Food Shortage." *Am. J. Phys. Anthrop.* 33:263–72.

—— 1971. "Estrous Behavior of Free-Ranging Rhesus Monkeys." *Primates* 12:1–31.

Manning, A. 1975. "Behaviour Genetics and the Study of Behavioural Evolution." In G. Baerends, C. Beer, and A. Manning, eds., *Function and Evolution in Behaviour,* pp. 71–91. Oxford: Clarendon Press.

Marler, P. and W. J. Hamilton 1966. *Mechanisms of Animal Behavior.* New York: John Wiley.

Marsden, H. M. 1968a. "Behavior Between Two Social Groups of Rhesus Monkeys within Two Tunnel-Connected Enclosures." *Folia primat.* 8:240–46.

—— 1968b. "Agonistic Behavior of Young Rhesus Monkeys after Changes Induced in Social Rank of Their Mothers." *Anim. Behav.* 16:38–44.

—— 1972. "The Effect of Food Deprivation on Intergroup Relations in Rhesus Monkeys." *Behavioral Biology* 7:369–74.

Mason, W. A. 1965. "The Social Development of Monkeys and Apes." In I. DeVore, ed., *Primate Behavior,* pp. 514–43. Holt, Rinehart and Winston.

Maynard Smith, J. 1972. "Game Theory and the Evolution of Fighting." In J. Maynard Smith, *On Evolution,* pp. 8–28. Edinburgh: Edinburgh University Press.

Maynard Smith, J. and G. R. Price 1973. "The Logic of Animal Conflict." *Nature* 246:15–18.

McGrew, W. C. 1972. *An Ethological Study of Children's Behavior.* New York: Academic Press.

Mears, C. E. and H. F. Harlow 1975. "Play: Early and Eternal." *Proc. Nat. Acad. Sci. USA* 72:1878–82.

Meier, G. W. and V. D. Devanney 1974. "The Ontogeny of Play within a Society: Preliminary Analysis." *American Zoologist* 14:289–94.

Menzel, E. W., Jr. 1972. "Spontaneous Invention of Ladders in a Group of Young Chimpanzees." *Folia primat.* 17:87–106.

—— 1973a. "Further Observations on the Use of Ladders in a Group of Young Chimpanzees." *Folia primat.* 19:450–57.

——, ed., 1973b. *Precultural Primate Behavior.* New York: S. Karger.

Menzel, E. W., Jr., R. K. Davenport and C. M. Rogers 1970. "The Development of Tool Using in Wild-Born and Restriction-Reared Chimpanzees." *Folia primat.* 12:273–83.

—— 1972. "Protocultural Aspects of Chimpanzees' Responsiveness to Novel Objects." *Folia primat.* 17:161–70.

Meyer-Holzapfel, M. 1956. "Uber die Bereitschaft zu Spiel- und Instinkthandlungen." *Z. Tierpsychol.* 13:442–62.

Michael, R. P. and M. Wilson 1973. "Changes in the Sexual Behaviour of Male Rhesus Monkeys (*M. mulatta*) at Puberty." *Folia primat.* 19:384–403.

Millar, S. 1968. *The Psychology of Play.* Baltimore: Penguin Books.

Miller, S. 1973. "Ends, Means, and Galumphing: Some Leitmotifs of Play." *Amer. Anthrop.* 75:87–98.

Missakian, E. A. 1972. "Genealogical and Cross-Genealogical Dominance Relations in a Group of Free-Ranging Rhesus Monkeys (*Macaca mulatta*) on Cayo Santiago." *Primates* 13:169–80.

Mitchell, G. 1970. "Abnormal Behavior in Primates." In L. A. Rosenblum, ed., *Primate Behavior, Developments in Field and Laboratory Research* 1:195–249. New York: Academic Press.

Morris, D. 1964. "The Response of Animals to a Restricted Environment." *Symp. Zool. Soc. Lond.* 13:99–118.

Moynihan, M. 1970. "Control, Suppression, Decay, Disappearance and Replacement of Displays." *J. theor. Biol.* 29:85–112.

Müller-Schwarze, D. 1968. "Play Deprivation in Deer." *Behaviour* 31:144–62.

—— 1971. "Ludic Behavior in Young Mammals." In M. B. Sterman, D. J. McGinty and A. M. Adinolfi, eds., *Brain Development and Behavior,* pp. 229–49. New York: Academic Press.

Müller-Schwarze, D. and C. Müller-Schwarze 1969. "Spielverhalten und Allgemeine Aktivitat bei Schwarzwedelhirschen." *Bonner Zoologische Beitrage* 1:282–89.

Nash, L. T. 1974. "Parturition in a Feral Baboon (*Papio anubis*)." *Primates* 15:279–85.

Neville, M. K. 1968a. "Ecology and Activity of Himalayan Foothill Rhesus Monkeys (*Macaca mulatta*)." *Ecology* 49:110–23.

—— 1968b. "Male Leadership Change in a Free-Ranging Troop of Indian Rhesus Monkeys." *Primates* 9:13–27.

Nottebohm, F. 1972. "The Origins of Vocal Learning." *Amer. Nat.* 106:116–40.

Oakley, F. B. and P. C. Reynolds 1976. "Differing Responses to Social Play Deprivation in Two Species of Macaque." In D. F. Lancy and B. A. Tindall, eds., *The Anthropological Study of Play: Problems and Prospects,* pp. 179–88. Cornwall, N.Y.: Leisure Press.

Otte, D. 1974. "Effects and Functions in the Evolution of Signaling Systems." *Annual Review of Ecology and Systematics* 5:385–417.

Owens, N. W. 1975a. "Social Play Behaviour in Free-Living Baboons, *Papio anubis.*" *Anim. Behav.* 23:387–408.

—— 1975b. "A Comparison of Aggressive Play and Aggression in Free-Living Baboons, *Papio anubis.*" *Anim. Behav.* 23:757–65.

Phoenix, C. H. 1974. "The Role of Androgens in the Sexual Behavior of Adult Male Rhesus Monkeys." In W. Montagna and W. A. Sadler, eds., *Reproductive Behavior,* pp. 249–58. New York: Plenum.

Poirier, F. E. 1970. "The Nilgiri Langur of South India." In L. A. Rosenblum, ed., *Primate Behavior* 1:254–383. New York: Academic Press.

—— 1972. Introduction. In F. E. Poirier, ed., *Primate Socialization,* pp. 3–28 New York: Random House.

Poirier, F. E. and E. O. Smith 1974. "Socializing Functions of Primate Play." *American Zoologist* 14:275–87.

Poole, T. B. 1966. "Aggressive Play in Polecats." *Symp. Zool. Soc. Lond.* 18:23–44.

—— 1967. "Aspects of Aggressive Behaviour in Polecats." *Z. Tierpsychol.* 24:351–69.

—— 1973. "The Aggressive Behaviour of Individual Male Polecats (*Mustela Putorius, M. furo* and hybrids) towards Familiar and Unfamiliar Opponents." *Journal of Zoology* 170:395–414.

Poole, T. B. and J. Fish 1975. "An Investigation of Playful Behaviour in *Rattus norvegicus* and *Mus musculus* (Mammalia)." *J. Zool. Lond.* 175:61–71.

—— 1976. "An Investigation of Individual, Age and Sexual Differences in the Play of *Rattus norvegicus* (Mammalia: Rodentia)." *J. Zool. Lond.* 179:249–60.

Rasa, O. A. E. 1971. "Social Interaction and Object Manipulation in Weaned Pups of the Northern Elephant Seal *Mirounga angustirostris.*" *Z. Tierpsychol.* 29:82–102.

Redican, W. K. 1975. "Facial Expression in Nonhuman Primates." In L. A. Rosenblum, ed., *Primate Behavior: Developments in Field and Laboratory Research* 4:104–94. New York: Academic Press.

Redican, W. K. and G. Mitchell 1974. "Play between Adult Male and Infant Rhesus Monkeys." *American Zoologist* 14:295–302.

Resko, J. A. 1970. "Androgen Secretion by the Fetal and Neonatal Rhesus Monkey." *Endocrinology* 87:680–87.

—— 1974. "The Relationship between Fetal Hormones and the Differentiation of the Central Nervous System in Primates." In W. Montagna and W. A. Sadler, eds., *Reproductive Behavior,* pp. 211–22. New York: Plenum.

Richard, A. 1970. "A Comparative Study of the Activity Patterns and Behavior of *Alouatta villosa* and *Ateles Geoffroyi.*" *Folia primat.* 12:241–63.

Richards, S. M. 1974. "The Concept of Dominance and Methods of Assessment." *Anim. Behav.* 22:914–30.

Ripley, S. 1967. "The Leaping of Langurs: A Problem in the Study of Locomotor Adaptation." *Am. J. Phys. Anthrop.* 26:149–70.

Rogers, C. M. 1973. "Implications of a Primate Early Rearing Experiment for the Concept of Culture." In E. W. Menzel, Jr., ed., *Precultural Primate Behavior,* pp. 185–91. New York: S. Karger.

Rose, R. M., I. S. Bernstein, and T. P. Gordon 1975. "Consequences of Social Conflict on Plasma Testosterone Levels in Rhesus Monkeys." *Psychosomatic Medicine* 37:50–61.

Rose, R. M., T. P. Gordon and I. S. Bernstein 1972. "Plasma Testosterone Levels in the Male Rhesus: Influences of Sexual and Social Stimuli." *Science* 178:643–54.

Rose, R. M., J. W. Holaday and I. S. Bernstein 1971. "Plasma Testosterone, Dominance Rank and Aggressive Behaviour in Male Rhesus Monkeys." *Nature* 231:366–68.

Rosenblum, L. A. 1961. *The Development of Social Behavior in the Rhesus Monkey.* Ph.D. thesis, University of Wisconsin.

Rowell, T. E. 1966. "Hierarchy in the Organization of a Captive Baboon Group." *Anim. Behav.* 14:430–43.

—— 1972. *The Social Behaviour of Monkeys.* Baltimore: Penguin Books.

—— 1974. "The Concept of Social Dominance." *Behavioral Biology* 11:131–54.

Rowell, T. E. and R. A. Hinde 1962. "Vocal Communication by the Rhesus Monkey (*Macaca mulatta.*)." *Proc. Zool. Soc. Lond.* 138:279–94.

Saayman, G. S. 1971. "Baboons' Responses to Predators." *African Wildlife* 25:46–49.

Sade, D. W. 1966. *Ontogeny of Social Relations in a Free-ranging Group of Rhesus Monkeys.* Ph.D. thesis, University of California, Berkeley.

—— 1967. "Determinants of Dominance in a Group of Free-Ranging Rhesus Monkeys." In S. A. Altmann, ed., *Social Communication among Primates,* pp. 99–114. Chicago: University of Chicago Press.

—— 1972. "A Longitudinal Study of Social Behavior of Rhesus Monkeys." In R. Tuttle, ed., *The Functional and Evolutionary Biology of Primates,* pp. 378–98. Chicago: Aldine.

—— 1973. "An Ethogram for Rhesus Monkeys." *Am. J. Phys. Anthrop.* 38:537–42.

Sahlins, M. 1972. *Stone Age Economics.* Chicago: Aldine.

Sbrzesny, Heide 1976. *Die Spiele der !Ko-Buschleute.* Munchen/Zurich: R. Piper & Co. Verlag.

Schaller, G. B. 1963. *The Mountain Gorilla.* Chicago: University of Chicago Press.

—— 1972. *The Serengeti Lion.* Chicago: University of Chicago Press.

Schenkel, R. 1966. "Play, Exploration and Territoriality in the Wild Lion." *Symp. Zool. Soc. Lond.* 18:11–22.

Seay, B. and N. W. Gottfried 1975. "A Phylogenetic Perspective for Social Behavior in Primates." *The Journal of General Psychology* 92:5–17.

Sharp, R. L. 1958. "People without Politics." *Proceedings of the 1958 Annual Spring Meeting of the American Ethnological Society*:1–8.

Silberbauer, G. B. 1972. "The G/wi Bushmen." In M. G. Bicchieri, ed., *Hunters and Gatherers Today,* pp. 271–326. New York: Holt, Rinehart and Winston.

Simonds, P. E. 1965. "The Bonnet Macaque in South India." In I. DeVore, ed., *Primate Behavior,* pp. 175–96. New York: Holt, Rinehart and Winston.

Sipes, R. G. 1973. "War, Sports and Aggression: An Empirical Test of Two Rival Theories." *Amer. Anthrop.* 75:64–86.

Southwick, C. H. 1967. "An Experimental Study of Intragroup Agonistic Behavior in Rhesus Monkeys." *Behaviour* 28:182–09.

—— 1972. "Aggression among Nonhuman Primates." An Addison-Wesley Module in Anthropology, Reading, Mass.: Addison-Wesley.

Southwick, C. H., M. A. Beg and M. R. Siddiqi 1965. "Rhesus Monkeys in North India." In I. DeVore, ed., *Primate Behavior,* pp. 111–59. New York: Holt, Rinehart and Winston.

Southwick, C. H. and M. R. Siddiqi 1967. "The Role of Social Traditions in the Maintenance of Dominance in a Wild Rhesus Group." *Primates* 8:341–53.

Southwick, C. H., M. R. Siddiqi, M. Y. Farooqui, and B. C. Pal 1974. "Xenophobia among Free-Ranging Rhesus Groups in India. In R. L. Holloway, ed., *Primate Aggression, Territoriality, and Xenophobia,* pp. 185–209. New York: Academic Press.

—— 1976. "Effects of Artificial Feeding on Aggressive Behaviour of Rhesus Monkeys in India." *Anim. Behav.* 24:11–15.

Steadman, L. B. 1971. *Neighbours and Killers: Residence and Dominance among the Hewa of New Guinea.* Ph.D. thesis, Australian National University.

Steiner, A. L. 1971. "Play Activity of Columbian Ground Squirrels." *Z. Tierpsychol.* 28:247–61.

Stephenson, G. R. 1973. "Biology of Communication and Population Structure." In C. R. Carpenter, ed., *Behavioral Regulators of Behavior in Primates,* pp. 34–55. Lewisburg, Pennsylvania: Bucknell University Press.

Stevenson, M. F. and T. B. Poole 1976. "An Ethogram of the Common Marmoset (*Calithrix jacchus jacchus*): General Behavioural Repertoire." *Anim. Behav.* 24:428–51.

Struhsaker, T. T. 1967a. *Behavior of Vervet Monkeys.* University of California Pub. in Zool., vol. 82.

—— 1967b. "Auditory Communication among Vervet Monkeys." In S. A. Altmann, ed., *Social Communication among Primates,* pp. 281–325. Chicago: University of Chicago Press.

Struhsaker, T. T. and J. S. Gartlan 1970. "Observations on the Behaviour and Ecology of the Patas Monkey (*Erythrocebus patas*) in the Waza Reserve, Cameroon." *J. Zool. Lond.* 161:49–63.

Sugiyama, Y. 1965. "Behavioral Development and Social Structure in Two Troops of Hanuman Langurs (*Presbytis entellus*)." *Primates* 6:213–47.

Suomi, S. J. and H. F. Harlow 1971. "Monkeys at Play." *Natural History,* Dec. 72–75.

Sutton-Smith, B. 1975. "Play as Adaptive Potentiation." *Sportswissenschaft* 5:103–18.

—— (in press). "Current Research and Theory on Play, Games and Sports."

Syme, G. J. 1974. "Competitive Orders as Measures of Social Dominance." *Anim. Behav.* 22:931–40.

Symons, D. 1973. *Aggressive Play in a Free-ranging Group of Rhesus Monkeys (Macaca mulatta).* Ph.D. thesis, Univ. of California, Berkeley.

—— 1974. "Aggressive Play and Communication in Rhesus Monkeys (*Macaca mulatta*)." *American Zoologist* 14:317–22.

Teleki, G. 1974. "Chimpanzee Subsistence Technology: Materials and Skills." *Journal of Human Evolution* 3:575–94.

Tiger, L. 1975. "Somatic Factors and Social Behaviour." In R. Fox, ed., *Biosocial Anthropology,* pp. 115–32. New York: John Wiley & Sons.

Tindale, N. B. 1972. "The Pitjandjara." In M. G. Bicchieri, ed., *Hunters and Gatherers Today,* pp. 217–68. New York: Holt, Rinehart and Winston.

Trivers. R. L. 1971. "The Evolution of Reciprocal Altruism." *Quarterly Review of Biology* 46:35–57.

—— 1972. "Parental Investment and Sexual Selection." In B. Campbell, ed., *Sexual Selection and the Descent of Man 1871–1971,* pp. 136–179. Chicago: Aldine-Atherton.

Turnbull, C. M. 1962. *The Forest People.* Garden City, New York: Doubleday.

Vandenbergh, J. G. 1965. "Hormonal Basis of Sex Skin in Male Rhesus Monkeys." *General and Comparative Endocrinology* 5:31–34.

—— 1967. "The Development of Social Structure in Free-Ranging Rhesus Monkeys." *Behaviour* 29:179–94.

—— 1969. "Endocrine Coordination in Monkeys: Male Sexual Responses to the Female." *Physiology and Behavior* 4:261–64.

Vandenbergh, J. G. and L. C. Drickamer 1974. "Reproductive Coordination among Free-Ranging Rhesus Monkeys." *Physiology and Behavior* 13:373–76.

Vandenbergh, J. G. and S. Vessey 1968. "Seasonal Breeding of Free-Ranging Rhesus Monkeys and Related Ecological Factors." *J. Reprod. Fert.* 15:71–79.

Venable, V. 1966. *Human Nature: The Marxian View.* Cleveland: The World Publishing Company.

Vessey, S. H. 1968. "Interactions between Free-Ranging Groups of Rhesus Monkeys." *Folia primat.* 8:228–39.

—— 1971. "Free-Ranging Rhesus Monkeys: Behavioural Effects of Removal, Separation and Reintroduction of Group Members." *Behaviour* 40:216–27.

—— 1973. "Night Observation of Free-Ranging Rhesus Monkeys." *Am. J. Phys. Anthrop.* 38:613–20.

Vincent, L. E. and M. Bekoff (in press). "Quantitative Analyses of the Ontogeny of Predatory Behavior in Coyotes, *Canis latrans.*"

Waddington, C. H. 1960. *The Ethical Animal.* Chicago: University of Chicago Press.

Washburn, S. L. 1966. "Conflict in Primate Society." In A. de Reuck and J. Knight, eds., *Conflict in Society: a Ciba Foundation Volume,* pp. 3–15. Boston: Little, Brown.

Washburn, S. L. and D. A. Hamburg 1965a. "The Study of Primate Behavior." In I. DeVore, ed., *Primate Behavior,* pp. 1–13. New York: Holt, Rinehart and Winston.

—— 1965b. "The Implications of Primate Research." In I. DeVore, ed., *Primate Behavior,* pp. 607–22. New York: Holt, Rinehart and Winston.

—— 1968. "Aggressive Behavior in Old World Monkeys and Apes." In P. C. Jay, ed., *Primates: Studies in Adaptation and Variability,* pp. 458–78. New York: Holt, Rinehart and Winston.

Washburn, S. L., P. C. Jay, and J. B. Lancaster 1965. "Field Studies of Old World Monkeys and Apes." *Science* 150:1541–47.

Washburn, S. L. and C. S. Lancaster 1968. "The Evolution of Hunting." In R. B. Lee and I. DeVore, eds., *Man the Hunter,* pp. 293–303. Chicago: Aldine.

Washburn, S. L. and S. C. Strum 1972. Concluding Comments. In S. L. Washburn and P. Dolhinow, eds., *Perspectives on Human Evolution* 2:469–91. New York: Holt, Rinehart and Winston.

Welker, W. I. 1971. "Ontogeny of Play and Exploratory Behaviors: A Definition of Problems and a Search for New Conceptual Solutions." In H. Moltz, ed., *The Ontogeny of Vertebrate Behavior,* pp. 171–228. New York: Academic Press.

West, M. 1974. "Social Play in the Domestic Cat." *American Zoologist* 14:427–36.

Williams, G. C. 1966. *Adaptation and Natural Selection.* Princeton: Princeton University Press.

—— 1975. *Sex and Evolution.* Princeton: Princeton University Press.

Wilson, A. P. and R. C. Boelkins 1970. "Evidence for Seasonal Variation in Aggressive Behavior by *Macaca mulatta.*" *Anim. Behav.* 18:719–24.

Wilson, A. P. and S. H. Vessey 1968. "Behavior of Free-Ranging Castrated Rhesus Monkeys." *Folia primat.* 9:1–14.

Wilson, E. O. 1975a. "The Origin of Sex." (Review of *Sex and Evolution* by

G. C. Williams. Princeton: Princeton University Press, 1975.) *Science* 188:139–40.

—— 1975b. *Sociobiology: The New Synthesis.* Cambridge, Massachusetts: The Belknap Press of Harvard University Press.

Wilson, S. C. 1974. "Juvenile Play of the Common Seal *Phoca vitulina vitulina* with Comparative Notes on the Grey Seal *Halichoerus grypus.*" *Behaviour* 48:37–60.

Wilson, S. C. and D. G. Kleiman 1974. "Eliciting Play: A Comparative Study." *American Zoologist* 14:341–70.

Winter, P. 1968. "Social Communication in the Squirrel Monkey." In L. A. Rosenblum and R. W. Cooper, eds., *The Squirrel Monkey,* pp. 235–53. New York: Academic Press.

Yamada, M. 1957. "A Case of Acculturation in a Subhuman Society of Japanese Monkeys." *Primates* 1:30–46.

Index